D0655784

THE LAW AND PRACTICE OF
SENTENCING IN SCOTLAND

THE LAW AND PRACTICE OF
SENTENCING IN SCOTLAND

C.G.B. NICHOLSON,

M.A., LL.B., Advocate,

*Sheriff of Lothian and
Borders at Edinburgh*

EDINBURGH
W. GREEN & SON LTD.
Law Publishers
1981

First published in 1981

©
1981. W. Green & Son Ltd.

ISBN 0 414 00684 4

PRINTED IN GREAT BRITAIN
BY JOHN G ECCLES PRINTERS LTD
INVERNESS

To Hazel, whose patience and forbearance made this possible.

PREFACE

From the earliest days the sentencing of convicted offenders has played a major part in our criminal justice system but, despite the increasing complexity of the law and procedural rules relating to it, despite its growing social and economic consequences, and despite the enhanced public interest that now surrounds it, there has so far been no textbook in Scotland which has treated sentencing as a subject in itself, separate from other aspects of general criminal law and procedure. This book is an attempt to repair that omission.

Much of the book is purely factual and sets out — I hope accurately — the relevant law and rules of procedure. In addition I have, from time to time, ventured an opinion on certain problems of interpretation and practice which have, I know, been encountered not only by myself but also by others. In particular, I have attempted, in Chapter 10, to analyse and describe the sentencing process itself. I do not expect everyone to agree with all of the opinions that I have expressed throughout the book, and especially in Chapter 10. I hope, however, that, by drawing attention to some of the problems that arise, and by offering a view as to their possible solution, I may at least slightly ease the task of all who have to deal with such problems in practice.

I have drafted the book as if the whole of the Criminal Justice (Scotland) Act 1980 has been brought into effect, though I understand that section 45 (detention of young offenders), and the related Schedule 5, are unlikely to be introduced before the spring of 1982. I have also attempted to take note of the far-reaching changes relating to "totting-up" disqualifications introduced by the Transport Act 1981. That Act was passed just as the book was about to go to press, and consequently the relevant provisions, together with a tentative commentary, have been incorporated as an Appendix to Chapter 6.

In the preparation of this book I have received invaluable assistance and advice from a great many people including, in particular, the Crown Agent, Mr W.G. Chalmers (and through him the regional procurators fiscal), Mr R.C. Allan of Prisons Division, Scottish Home and Health Department, Mr C.J. Wood and Miss Susan Morris of Lothian Region Social Work Department, and, above all, my colleague, Sheriff Caplan, who read the whole book in draft form and who offered many helpful and provocative comments on a wide range of topics. Assistance in the typing of some of my manuscript was undertaken in their spare time by Miss Helen Dignan and especially by Miss Veronica Heaney, to both of whom I am most grateful. Finally, but by no means least, I acknowledge with gratitude the courtesy extended to me by the Lord Justice-General, Lord Emslie, in permitting me to reproduce in full, as an appendix to Chapter 7, the memorandum on contempt of court which he circulated to judges in 1975.

Despite all the assistance I have received, the errors and omissions that remain in the book, together with any opinions expressed therein, are of course entirely my own responsibility.

I have attempted to state the law as at 30 September, 1981.

C.G.B.N.
Edinburgh, 1981

CONTENTS

CHAPTER 1—INTRODUCTION

CHAPTER 2—NON-CUSTODIAL DISPOSALS

CHAPTER 3—CUSTODIAL DISPOSALS

CHAPTER 4—MENTALLY DISORDERED OFFENDERS

Chapter 8—Procedure

Chapter 10—The Sentencing Process

Chapter 11—The Services Responsible for Carrying Sentences into Effect

TABLE OF CASES

para.

xvii

TABLE OF STATUTES

para.

ACTS OF ADJOURNAL

LIST OF ABBREVIATIONS
(excluding standard law reports)

Textbooks

Alison	*Principles and Practice of the Criminal Law of Scotland*, by A.J. Alison, 1832 and 1833.
Gordon	*The Criminal Law of Scotland*, by G.H. Gordon, 2nd edition, 1978.
Hume	*Commentaries on the Law of Scotland Respecting Crimes*, by Baron Hume, 4th edition by B.R. Bell, 1844.
Macdonald	*A Practical Treatise on the Criminal Law of Scotland*, by J.H.A. Macdonald (Lord Kingsburgh), 5th edition by J. Walker (later Lord Walker) and D.J. Stevenson, 1948.
Renton and Brown	*Criminal Procedure according to the Law of Scotland*, by J.W. Renton and H.H. Brown, 4th edition by G.H. Gordon, 1972.

Statutes (except where the context requires otherwise)

1907 Act	Probation of Offenders Act.
1926 Act	Criminal Appeal (Scotland) Act.
1949 Act	Criminal Justice (Scotland) Act.
1954 Act	Summary Jurisdiction (Scotland) Act.
1960 Act	Mental Health (Scotland) Act.
1967 Act	Criminal Justice Act.
1968 Act	Social Work (Scotland) Act.
1972 Act	Road Traffic Act.
1975 Act	Criminal Procedure (Scotland) Act.
1978 Act	Community Service by Offenders (Scotland) Act.
1980 Act	Criminal Justice (Scotland) Act.
1981 Act	Transport Act.

BIBLIOGRAPHY

Annual reports and statistics
Criminal Statistics, Scotland.
Prisons in Scotland.
Report of the Parole Board for Scotland.

Textbooks and other books
Lord Cockburn, *Circuit Journeys*, 1888.
Nigel Walker, *Crime and Punishment in Britain*, 1965.
Nigel Walker, *Sentencing in a Rational Society*, 1969.
D.A. Thomas, *Principles of Sentencing*, 1970.
Roger Hood and Richard Sparks, *Key Issues in Criminology*, 1970.
Sir Rupert Cross, *The English Sentencing System*, 1975.
J. Baldwin and M. McConville, *Negotiated Justice: Pressures to Plead Guilty*, 1977.

Reports of government and departmental committees (all published by HMSO)
Report of Inter-departmental Committee on the Business of the Criminal Courts (the Streatfeild Committee), 1961.
Report of Departmental Committee on the Probation Service (the Morison Committee), 1962.
Crime and the Prevention of Crime, Scottish Council on Crime, 1975.
Second Report on Criminal Procedure in Scotland (the Thomson Committee), 1975.
Report on Reparation by the Offender to the Victim in Scotland (the Dunpark Committee), 1977.
Third Report on Criminal Appeals in Scotland (the Thomson Committee), 1977.
Fifteenth Report from the Expenditure Committee of the House of Commons: The Reduction of Pressure on the Prison System, 1978.
Report of Committee of Inquiry into the United Kingdom Prison Services (the May Committee), 1979.
Reports of Advisory Council on the Penal System:
Non-Custodial and Semi-Custodial Penalties (the Wootton Committee), 1970.
Reparation by the Offender, 1970.
Young Adult Offenders, 1974.
Interim Report, The Length of Prison Sentences, 1977.
Final Report, A Review of Maximum Penalties, 1978.

Home Office Research Studies (all published by HMSO)
No. 2   *Probationers in their Social Environment*, by Martin Davies, 1969.
No. 29   *Community Service Orders*, by K. Pease and others, 1975.
No. 35   *The Effectiveness of Sentencing*, by S.R. Brody, 1976.
No. 36   IMPACT. *Intensive Matched Probation and After-care Treatment*, Vol. II, by M.S. Folkard and others, 1976.
No. 48   *Social Inquiry Reports: a survey*, by Jennifer Thorpe, 1979.
No. 64   *Taking Offenders out of Circulation*, by S. Brody and R. Tarling, 1980.

Articles
A.D. Smith, "Deferred Sentences in Scotland", 1968 S.L.T. (News) 153.
R. Baxter and C. Nuttall, "Severe Sentences: No Deterrent to Crime", New Society, 1975, reprinted in J. Baldwin and A.K. Bottomley, *Criminal Justice: Selected Readings*, 1978.

A.J. Ashworth, "Justifying the First Prison Sentence", [1977] Crim. L.R. 661.
A.E. Bottoms and W. McWilliams, "A Non-Treatment Paradigm for Probation Practice", British Journal of Social Work, 1979.
Wilkins, Sentencing Guidlines to Reduce Disparity?" [1980] Crim. L.R. 201.
D.J. Galligan, "Guidelines and Just Deserts: A Critique of Recent Trends in Sentencing Reform" [1981] Crim. L.R. 297.

CHAPTER 1

INTRODUCTION

-01 For judges in the 19th century, and probably for at least some in the present century as well, the sentencing of convicted offenders was a reasonably straightforward matter. Although, in a few cases, training and education, particularly of a moral kind, might be expected to have a rehabilitative effect, the general view was that the task of the judge was to impose a punishment to fit the crime. Furthermore, if in so doing the miscreant could be got rid of altogether, so much the better. Thus, writing about regular, professional criminals in 1842, Lord Cockburn was able to say: "I fear that [they] must be given over, and that, after all, there is nothing for it but to get rid of them by exportation".[1] Although this approach, for all its harshness, does not appear to have been notably successful in deterring others from turning to a life of crime, it was effective in preventing recidivism, at least in this country, among those who were the recipients of such sentences. Moreover, it was an approach which offered limited choices, and therefore presented few problems, to the judges themselves.

-02 Gradually, however, during the last hundred years or so society in this country (or at least those parts of it which dictate penal policy) has moved away from purely retributive aims to a point where it is difficult, if not impossible, to discern any comprehensive or clearly intelligible policy for dealing with those who break the law. In its earlier stages the reasons for this change are fairly plain to see. During the 19th century itself the views of prison reformers like John Howard and Elizabeth Fry, and more generally a growing humanitarianism and interest in the rights of the individual, began to make themselves felt. A little later, modern psychology and sociology, influenced by Freud and Durkheim and others, began to develop so that judges and penal theorists alike came increasingly to conclude that criminal behaviour could be modified, not by punishment, but by training and treatment. Thus, the early 20th century saw the introduction of probation and borstal training, and the gradual implementation in the prison service of the principle enunciated by the Gladstone Committee in 1895 that "prison treatment should have as its primary and concurrent objects

---

[1] *Circuit Journeys*, Spring 1842.

1

deterrence and reformation". It may be thought that these two objectives are not obviously compatible, and subsequent experience within the prison system has tended to confirm that this is so. Nonetheless, belief in the treatment approach to criminality has continued to flourish during this century, and has shown itself in the growing statutory insistence on what may be termed the diagnostic approach to sentencing whereby courts are encouraged, and frequently compelled, to obtain a battery of "expert" reports before a sentencing decision can be made.

1–03   More recently a further factor has begun increasingly to intrude into consideration of penal policy and, to an extent, sentencing decisions. This is the cost and space factor whereby alternatives to imprisonment are thought to be desirable simply because prisons are expensive and overcrowded. Attention has in recent years been drawn to this by, among others, the Expenditure Committee of the House of Commons[2] and the May Committee of Inquiry into the UK Prison Services.[3] Neither of these committees went so far as to suggest that sentences should be determined solely by reference to such practical considerations, and of course non-custodial disposals can frequently, if not always, be justified on treatment or other similar grounds. Nonetheless, judges must be aware of such factors and will, it is suggested, often give them some weight when making their decisions.

1–04   Thus, the stage has been reached when judges must take into account, when passing sentence, many, often competing, considerations which make the sentencing process an altogether more complex business than it was a century ago. As if that was not enough, the former Cinderella of the social sciences, criminology, has now attained a respectability and an authority where its findings must be taken note of: and, at the risk of some over-generalisation, they seem to suggest that, however measured, no form of sentence is any more or less successful than another in preventing recidivism.[4] So, at least one of the possible aims of sentencing has been thrown open to question and, at least in the United States, there are some signs of a reversion, under the banner of "just deserts", to earlier and simpler aims and objectives. Thus, in one

---

[2] Fifteenth Report from the Expenditure Committee, 27 July 1978.
[3] 1979, Cmnd. 7673.
[4] See, for example, *The Effectiveness of Sentencing*, Home Office Research Study No. 35, by S.R. Brody, HMSO.

state it is now expressly provided that "the Legislature finds and declares that the purpose of imprisonment for crime is punishment".[5]

-05 There are three other factors which contribute to the growing complexity of the sentencing process in this country in the latter part of the 20th century. One is the increase in crime itself, which can be seen by looking at a recent ten year period. In 1968 there were 396,393 crimes and offences made known to the police in Scotland, whereas by 1978 that figure had risen to 643,922.[6] This not only imposes much greater pressure on the courts than was formerly the case, but also is thought by some to demonstrate the lack of success of sentencing decisions. The second factor, which to an extent goes hand in hand with the rise in crime itself, is public opinion which is sharply divided between those, possibly the majority, who are openly retributive and who call out for harsher penalties and longer prison sentences in the belief that only in that way can the rise in crime be deterred, and on the other hand those who, for practical or humanitarian reasons (or both), argue for shorter prison sentences and greater use of non-custodial disposals. The third factor is the wide range of available disposals themselves, and the proliferation of procedural rules which must be observed before any particular disposal is ordered. The last ten years or so alone have seen enormous developments here with the introduction of a completely new system for dealing with children, the development of community service, and, most recently, in the Criminal Justice (Scotland) Act 1980, the abolition of the borstal sentence, and the introduction of the power to make compensation orders.

-06 Today, then, sentencing is totally different from what it was for our Victorian forefathers, and poses problems which were quite unknown even 20 or 30 years ago. It requires, on the part not only of judges but also of all who have business in the criminal courts, a detailed knowledge of all available disposals and of the procedures that govern their use. In addition, it is suggested, it requires an understanding of what these disposals involve in practice, of what they may be expected to achieve, and of what are their limitations. Lastly, it requires some appreciation of sentencing aims and objectives, of what judges can, and perhaps should, be trying to

---

[5] Uniform Determinate Sentencing Act 1976 (California), s.1170.
[6] Criminal Statistics, Scotland 1978, HMSO.

achieve when they select a particular disposal in a particular case; and, along with that, what factors they ought to take into account, and what relative weight they ought to give to these factors when making sentencing decisions. This book is an attempt to deal with all of these matters.

CHAPTER 2

NON-CUSTODIAL DISPOSALS

ABSOLUTE DISCHARGE

–01 Where a person is, under solemn jurisdiction, convicted of an offence, or is charged before a court of summary jurisdiction with an offence and the court is satisfied that he committed the offence, the court, if it is of opinion, having regard to the circumstances, including the nature of the offence and the character of the offender, that it is inexpedient to inflict punishment and that a probation order is not appropriate may, instead of sentencing him (under solemn jurisdiction) or without proceeding to conviction (under summary jurisdiction), make an order discharging him absolutely.[1] This disposal is available to all courts, both solemn and summary, and may be used in respect of all offenders regardless of their age.

–02 Generally, a conviction on indictment of an offence for which an order is made under Part I of the 1975 Act discharging the offender absolutely is to be deemed not to be a conviction for any purpose other than the purposes of the proceedings in which the order is made and of laying it before a court as a previous conviction in subsequent proceedings for another offence.[2] Furthermore, and without prejudice to the foregoing, the conviction of an offender who is discharged absolutely is generally to be disregarded for the purposes of any enactment which imposes any disqualification or disability upon convicted persons, or authorises or requires the imposition of any such disqualification or disability.[3] An exception to this general rule has, however, been made by section 55 of the 1980 Act which provides that a person granted an absolute discharge is to be treated as if he had been convicted for the purpose of ordering endorsement of his driving licence, or disqualification for driving, under sections 101 and 93 respectively of the Road Traffic Act 1972. A further exception is provided by the Licensed Premises (Exclusion of Certain Persons) Act 1980 (see para. 7-26 *et seq.*). Although, arguably, an order for forfeiture of property used in the

---

[1] 1975 Act, ss. 182, 383.
[2] *Ibid.* s. 191 (1), but see National Insurance (Industrial Injuries) Act 1965, s. 69, Civil Evidence Act 1968, s. 11, and Law Reform (Miscellaneous Provisions) (Scotland) Act 1968, s. 10, under which this provision is excluded.
[3] *Ibid.* s. 191 (2).

commission of an offence is not a "disqualification or disability" within the meaning of section 191 (2) of the 1975 Act it would also appear to be incompetent where an order is made for absolute discharge since it can proceed only upon a conviction,[4] and would thus be excluded by the general provisions of s.191 (1). *A fortiori* an order for forfeiture in summary proceedings[5] would also be incompetent since an order for absolute discharge is made without proceeding to conviction.[6] Under section 58 (1) of the 1980 Act a compensation order is not competent against a person who has been granted an absolute discharge.

2–03   The provisions mentioned in para. 2-02 above do not affect:

    (a)   any right of such offender to appeal against his conviction; or

    (b)   the operation, in relation to any such offender, of any enactment which was in force as at the commencement of section 9 (3) (*b*) of the Criminal Justice (Scotland) Act 1949 and is expressed to extend to persons dealt with under section 1 (1) of the Probation of Offenders Act 1907 as well as to convicted persons.[7]

The whole of the Probation of Offenders Act 1907 was repealed by the 1949 Act, and it is thought that the provision in (b) above is now of only historical interest.

2–04   Where an offender is discharged absolutely by a court of summary jurisdiction he is, as already noted, not convicted, but he has the like right of appeal against the finding that he committed the offence as if that finding were a conviction.[8] Where a person charged with an offence has at any time previously been discharged absolutely in respect of the commission by him of an offence, it is competent, in the proceedings for the current offence, to bring before the court the order of absolute discharge in like manner as if the order were a conviction.[9] Formerly, an absolute discharge ordered by a court of summary jurisdiction in respect of an offender of or over the age of 17 was to be regarded as a conviction for the purpose of determining whether that person subsequently fell to be

---

[4] 1975 Act, s. 223 (1).
[5] *Ibid*. s. 436, as amended by 1980 Act, Sched. 7, para. 71.
[6] *Ibid*. s. 383.
[7] *Ibid*. s. 191 (3).
[8] *Ibid*. s. 392 (4).
[9] *Ibid*. ss. 191 (4), 392 (5).

regarded as a first offender. That provision has now been repealed by the 1980 Act.[10]

-05   The provisions of sections 191 and 392 of the 1975 Act apply equally, with the addition of one proviso, to offenders who are placed on probation (see *infra*, para. 2–52). It was held in one case[11] that the corresponding provisions in section 9 of the 1949 Act did not, in a question whether an accused person had the character of a known thief, prevent regard being had to previous convictions which had resulted in the offender being placed on probation. It is submitted that previous convictions resulting in an absolute discharge could be regarded in the same way.

ADMONITION

-06   Any court may, if it appears to meet the justice of the case, dismiss with an admonition any person found guilty by the court of any offence.[12] This disposal may be used in respect of all offenders regardless of their age. Under both solemn and summary jurisdiction an admonition follows upon a conviction and, unlike an order for absolute discharge, is not subject to any statutory limitation as to its effects. Consequently it may, in appropriate cases, be used in conjunction with an order for forfeiture, or an order imposing a disqualification or disability. While an admonition may simply be ordered by a court without any further comment it is common and, it is submitted, perfectly proper for a court to elaborate on the order by a suitable verbal warning.

DEFERRED SENTENCE

-07   It is competent for a court to defer sentence after conviction for a period and on such conditions as the court may determine.[13] Statutory authority for what had long been a well-established practice in Scottish courts was first provided by section 47 of the Criminal Justice (Scotland) Act 1963. There is no restriction on the length of time for which sentence may be deferred, and it may be — and commonly is — deferred more than once in respect of a single indictment or complaint. Formerly, when sentence had been deferred in a summary case, no appeal by stated case was competent until

---

[10] 1975 Act, s. 417, repealed by 1980 Act, Sched. 8.
[11] *Johnston* v. *Heatly*, 1960 J.C. 26.
[12] 1975 Act, ss. 181, 382.
[13] *Ibid.* ss. 219, 432.

the cause had been finally determined and sentence pronounced.[14] This rule has been altered by the amendments to sections 442 and 451 of the 1975 Act contained in Schedule 3 to the 1980 Act. These amendments give a right of appeal to "any person convicted", and an appeal is accordingly now competent notwithstanding that sentence has been deferred. The statutory provisions relating to appeals under solemn procedure[15] also refer to "a person convicted" and consequently the position is the same in that case. In summary cases it is now competent to make a probation order after a period of deferred sentence notwithstanding that in such a case the offender has been convicted.[16]

2–08   Sometimes a sentence is deferred as a matter of convenience as, for example, when a court is informed that an offender is to answer other charges at a later date and it is considered appropriate that all outstanding matters should be dealt with at the same time. More frequently some sort of condition is attached to a deferred sentence. This may simply be that the offender should be of good behaviour, but it may be more specific, for example that the offender should pay compensation to a victim, or that he should pay for the cost of repairing something damaged by him. There is, however, no limitation on the nature of any condition that may be imposed. The court cannot in a strict sense enforce compliance with a condition attached to a deferred sentence but, since at the deferred diet the court has the same power of sentence as at the time of conviction, there are compelling reasons why an offender should comply with the condition that has been imposed. If he does comply, the court will generally be more lenient than would otherwise be the case. Where an offender is convicted of more than one charge it has been held inappropriate to sentence him in respect of one of these charges and to defer sentence on another,[17] though the same principle may not apply where two or more complaints are dealt with simultaneously on the same day. When sentence has been deferred, and particularly where there has been a condition of good behaviour, it is common, and frequently helpful, to have a sup-

---

[14] *Walker* v. *Gibb*, 1965 S.L.T. 2; *Lee* v. *Lasswade Local Authority* (1883) 5 Couper 329; *Torrance* v. *Miller* (1892) 3 White 254.

[15] 1975 Act, s. 228.

[16] *Ibid.* ss. 384 (1), 432, each as amended by 1980 Act, s. 53.

[17] *Lennon* v. *Copeland*, 1972 S.L.T. (Notes) 68; *cf. Downie* v. *Irvine*, 1964 J.C. 52.

plementary social inquiry report available at the deferred diet.[18] It is to be noted that, where a person is convicted during a period of deferment of an offence committed during that period, procedure now exists, under section 54 of the 1980 Act, to deal with the deferred sentence in advance of the date originally fixed for its disposal (see para. 8–50).

PROBATION

–09   A probation order is an order requiring an offender to be under supervision for a period to be specified in the order of not less than one nor more than three years. Such an order may be made by any court of solemn or summary jurisdiction in relation to any offence other than one the sentence for which is fixed by law. If the order is made by a court of solemn jurisdiction it may be made after conviction: if by a court of summary jurisdiction it may be made where the court is satisfied that the person charged committed the offence in question. In that event the order is made without proceeding to conviction except where sentence has previously been deferred following upon a conviction (see *supra*, para. 2–07). In both cases the court should be of opinion, having regard to the circumstances, including the nature of the offence and the character of the offender, that it is expedient to make such an order.[19]

Background inquiry

–10   Although there is no statutory obligation to do so, it is customary and desirable for a court to obtain and consider a social inquiry report before making a probation order.[20] A case may be adjourned to enable this to be done but that should not be for any single period exceeding three weeks.[21] When a social inquiry report has been obtained a copy of it must be given by the clerk of court to the offender or his solicitor or, in the case of an offender under 16 years of age, who is not represented by counsel or a solicitor, to his parent or guardian if present in court.[22] A first offender, whose case is adjourned for the preparation of reports, should generally not be

---

[18] Generally, on deferred sentences and their use, see A.D. Smith, "Deferred Sentences in Scotland", 1968 S.L.T. (News) 153; and see *infra*, para. 10–40.

[19] 1975 Act, ss. 183 (1), 384 (1).

[20] *Jamieson* v. *Heatly*, 1959 J.C. 22.

[21] 1975 Act, ss. 179, 380, as amended by Bail etc. (Scotland) Act 1980, s. 5, and as further amended by 1980 Act, Sched. 7, paras. 36 and 59.

[22] *Ibid.* ss. 192, 393.

remanded in custody unless there are special circumstances which make such a course necessary.[23] The likelihood of a custodial sentence, or the fact that the offender has previously been remanded in custody prior to conviction may be such a special circumstance. If not being remanded in custody, such an offender should be granted bail or be ordained to attend at the next diet of the case. Sometimes a social inquiry report may disclose previous convictions which have not been libelled by the prosecutor. The court may competently take these into account when considering sentence, but should first give the offender an opportunity to admit or deny them.[24]

Restrictions on use of probation

2–11   Probation and imprisonment are quite inconsistent. Thus, where a person is found guilty of two or more charges on the same complaint or indictment, he should not be imprisoned in respect of one charge and placed on probation in respect of another.[25] Formerly, probation was in the same position as absolute discharge in relation to orders for endorsement of a driving licence or disqualification for driving.[26] However, the amendment made to sections 93 and 101 of the Road Traffic Act 1972 by section 55 of the 1980 Act applies also to cases where a probation order is made, and consequently such an order may now be coupled with endorsement or disqualification under the Road Traffic Act. Under section 58 (1) of the 1980 Act a compensation order may not be made along with a probation order. In relation to forfeiture of implements express statutory provision no longer exists to enable this to be ordered where a probation order has been made by a court of summary jurisdiction.[27] The provisions of the Licensed Premises (Exclusion of Certain Persons) Act 1980 apply to probation orders as they do to absolute discharge (see para. 7–26 et seq.).

Contents of probation orders

2–12   A probation order must be as nearly as possible in the form prescribed by Act of Adjournal.[28] There are certain provisions

---

[23] *Morrison* v. *Clark*, 1962 S.L.T. 113.
[24] *Sillars* v. *Copeland*, 1966 S.L.T. 89.
[25] *Downie* v. *Irvine*, 1964 J.C. 52.
[26] *Herron* v. *Kent*, High Court, 14 July 1976.
[27] 1975 Act, s. 436, and see para 7–01 et seq.
[28] *Ibid*. ss. 183 (2), 384 (2); Act of Adjournal (Probation Orders) 1969.

which the order must contain, and others which it may contain.
Those in the first category are as follows:

(1)   The order must name the local authority area in which
the offender resides or is to reside, and must make
provision for the offender to be under the supervision
of an officer of the local authority of that area.[29]

(2)   Where the offender resides or is to reside in a local
authority area in which the court has no jurisdiction
(except where that area is in England, see *infra*, para.
2–40 *et seq.*) the court must name the appropriate
court[30] in the area of residence or intended residence,
and that court must require the local authority for that
area to arrange for the offender to be under the supervision of an officer of that authority.[29]

(3)   In either of the foregoing cases the offender must be
required to be under the supervision of an officer of the
appropriate local authority.[31]

(4)   The offender must be ordered to be of good behaviour,
to conform to the directions of an officer of the local
authority, and to inform that officer of any change of
address or employment.[32]

The provisions which a probation order may contain are as
follows:

(1)   The order may require the offender to comply during
the whole or any part of the probation period with such
requirements as the court, having regard to the circumstances of the case, considers necessary for securing the good conduct of the offender or for preventing a
repetition by him of the offence or the commission of
other offences.[33] In particular, any court may, if it
thinks that such a course is expedient for the purpose of
the order, require the offender to give security for his

---

[29] 1975 Act, ss. 183 (2), 384 (2).

[30] The "appropriate court" is to be a sheriff or district court exercising jurisdiction in the place where the probationer is to reside according to whether the
probation order is made by a sheriff or district court, provided that, if there is no
district court exercising jurisdiction in that place, the appropriate court will be the
sheriff court: 1975 Act, 5th Sched., para. 2.

[31] 1975 Act, ss. 183 (3), 384 (3).

[32] Act of Adjournal, *supra.*

[33] 1975 Act, ss. 183 (4), 384 (4).

good behaviour.[34] Such security may be given by consignation with the clerk of the court or by entering into
an undertaking to pay the amount, but not otherwise,
and such security may be forfeited and recovered in the
same manner as caution.[35] Although there is no statutory provision for the payment of caution by instalments, it is submitted, since the reference to caution is
only to forfeiture and recovery, that security under a
probation order may be paid by instalments if the court
considers that to be appropriate.

(2)   The order may also include requirements relating to the
residence of the offender, provided that

(a)   before making an order containing any such requirements, the court must consider the home
surroundings of the offender,[36] and

(b)   where the order requires the offender to reside in
any institution or place, the name of the institution
or place and the period for which he is so required
to reside must be specified in the order, and that
period must not extend beyond 12 months from
the date of the requirement or beyond the date
when the order expires.[37]

It is submitted that the last part of the above proviso would apply
when a requirement as to residence was added to a probation order
by amendment less than 12 months before the expiry of the order.

(3)   A probation order may include requirements as to
treatment of an offender's mental condition. This is
dealt with in detail in paras. 2–14 to 2–19.

(4)   A probation order may also include requirements as to
the performance by the offender of unpaid work. This
is dealt with in detail in paras. 2–20 to 2–22.

The making of probation orders

2–13   Before making a probation order, the court must explain to the
offender in ordinary language the effect of the order (including any
additional requirements proposed to be inserted) and that if he fails
to comply therewith or commits another offence during the

---

[34] 1975 Act, ss. 190 (1), 391 (1).
[35] *Ibid*. ss. 190 (2), 391 (2); see *infra*, para. 2–113.
[36] *Ibid*. ss. 183 (5) (*a*), 384 (5) (*a*).
[37] *Ibid*. ss. 183 (5) (*b*), 384 (5) (*b*).

probation period he will, under summary jurisdiction, be liable to be convicted of the original offence and in that case, and under solemn jurisdiction also, sentenced for it.[38] The court must ask the offender if he is willing to comply with the requirements of the order, and must not make the order unless he expresses such willingness.[38] When an order has been made the clerk of the court by which the order was made, or of the appropriate court, as the case may be, must have copies given to the officer of the local authority who is to supervise the probationer, to the probationer himself, and to the person in charge of any institution or place in which the probationer is required to reside under the order.[39]

Probation orders requiring treatment for mental condition

–14   Where the court is satisfied, on the evidence[40] of a registered medical practitioner approved for the purposes of section 27 of the Mental Health (Scotland) Act 1960, that the mental condition of an offender is such as requires and may be susceptible to treatment, but is not such as to warrant his detention in pursuance of a hospital order under Part V of that Act, or under the 1975 Act, the court may, if it makes a probation order, include therein a requirement that the offender shall submit, for such period not extending beyond 12 months from the date of the requirement as may be specified therein, to treatment by or under the direction of a registered medical practitioner with a view to the improvement of the offender's mental condition.[41] The corresponding provision in section 3 of the Criminal Justice (Scotland) Act 1949 (as amended by the Mental Health (Scotland) Act 1960) was considered in the case of *Isaacs* v. *H.M.A.*[42] when the Lord Justice-General (Clyde) observed: "the section does not mean that the determination of sentence is taken out of the hands of the court and left to the decision of either a probation officer or a psychiatrist. Their views are only facets of the problem which the court has to determine".

–15   The rules governing the giving of medical evidence for the purposes of a probation order are the same as those that apply

---

[38] 1975 Act, ss. 183 (6), 384 (6).
[39] *Ibid.* ss. 183 (7), 384 (7).
[40] As to the nature of such evidence, and the procedures to be followed, see *infra*, para. 2–15.
[41] 1975 Act, ss. 184 (1), 385 (1).
[42] 1963 J.C. 71.

where a hospital order is being made.[43] These rules are:

(a) a report in writing purporting to be signed by a medical practitioner may be received in evidence without proof of the signature or qualifications of the practitioner;

(b) the court may, however, in any case require that the practitioner by whom such a report was signed be called to give oral evidence;

(c) in any case, the accused may require that the practitioner be called to give oral evidence;

(d) where any such report is tendered in evidence otherwise than by or on behalf of the accused, and the accused is represented by counsel or solicitor, a copy of the report must be given to his counsel or solicitor. If he is not so represented, the substance of the report must be disclosed to the accused or, where he is under 16 years of age, to his parent or guardian if present in court;

(e) evidence to rebut the evidence contained in the report may be called by or on behalf of the accused;

(f) if the court is of opinion that further time is necessary in the interests of the accused for consideration of the report, or the substance of any such report, it must adjourn the case;

(g) for the purpose of calling evidence to rebut the evidence contained in any such report, arrangements may be made by or on behalf of an accused person detained in a hospital for his examination by any medical practitioner, and any such examination may be made in private.

2–16 The treatment which may be required by a probation order must be specified in the order and must be one of the following kinds:

(a) treatment as a resident patient in a hospital within the meaning of the Mental Health (Scotland) Act 1960, not being a state hospital within the meaning of that Act;

(b) treatment as a non-resident patient at such institution or place as may be specified in the order; or

(c) treatment by or under the direction of such registered

---

[43] 1975 Act, ss. 176, 377, applied by ss. 184 (7), 385 (7); for hospital orders see *infra*, Chap. 4.

medical practitioner as may be specified in the order. Apart from the foregoing the nature of the treatment is not to be specified in the order.[44]

2–17   A court must not make an order containing a requirement of treatment for a mental condition unless it is satisfied that arrangements have been made for the treatment intended to be specified in the order, and, if the offender is to be treated as a resident patient, for his reception.[45] While a probationer is under treatment as a resident patient in pursuance of a requirement of the probation order, any officer responsible for his supervision may not carry out the supervision except to such extent as is necessary for the purpose of the discharge or amendment of the order.[46]

2–18   Where the medical practitioner by whom or under whose direction a probationer is being treated for his mental condition in pursuance of a probation order is of opinion that part of the treatment can be better or more conveniently given in or at an institution or place not specified in the order, being an institution or place in or at which the treatment of the probationer will be given by or under the direction of a registered medical practitioner, he may, with the consent of the probationer, make arrangements for him to be treated accordingly. Such arrangements may provide for the probationer to receive part of his treatment as a resident patient in an institution or place notwithstanding that the institution or place is not one which could have been specified in that behalf in the probation order.[47] Where any such arrangements are made the medical practitioner by whom they are made must give notice in writing to any officer responsible for the supervision of the probationer, specifying the institution or place in or at which the treatment is to be carried out.[48] Any such treatment is to be deemed to be treatment to which the probationer is required to submit in pursuance of the probation order.[49]

2–19   Except as provided by sections 184 and 385 of the 1975 Act, a court must not make a probation order requiring a probationer to submit to treatment for his mental condition.[50]

---

[44] 1975 Act, ss. 184 (2), 385 (2).
[45] *Ibid*. ss. 184 (3), 385 (3).
[46] *Ibid*. ss. 184 (4), 385 (4).
[47] *Ibid*. ss. 184 (5), 385 (5).
[48] *Ibid*. ss. 184 (6) (*a*), 385 (6) (*a*).
[49] *Ibid*. ss. 184 (6) (*b*), 385 (6) (*b*).
[50] *Ibid*. ss. 184 (8), 385 (8), but see *infra*, para. 2–42.

Probation orders requiring performance of unpaid work

2–20   After an experimental period when, in four selected areas in Scotland, arrangements were made enabling a requirement for the performance of community service by offenders to be included in probation orders, the Community Service by Offenders (Scotland) Act 1978 gave statutory authority to the experiment, as well as providing for the making of community service orders which are independent of probation orders.[51] Where the requirement is contained in a probation order the community service is referred to as "unpaid work".

2–21   A court which is considering making a probation order may include in the order, in addition to any other requirement, a requirement that the offender shall perform unpaid work where the court:

(a)   is satisfied that the offender is of or over 16 years of age and has committed an offence punishable with imprisonment and that the conditions for the making of a community service order under the 1978 Act have been met;[52]

(b)   has been notified by the Secretary of State that arrangements exist for persons who reside in the locality where the offender resides, or will be residing when the probation order comes into force, to perform unpaid work as a requirement of a probation order; and

(c)   is satisfied that provision can be made under the arrangements mentioned in (b) above for the offender to perform unpaid work under the probation order.[53]

2–22   The number of hours of unpaid work which may be required in a probation order is in total not less than 40 or more than 240. The precise number must be specified in the order.[53] The Secretary of State may by order amend the maximum and minimum number of hours that may be required.[54]

Discharge and amendment of probation orders

2–23   The discharge and amendment of probation orders are governed by the provisions contained in Schedule 5 to the 1975

---

[51] See *infra*, para. 2–53.
[52] For conditions see *infra*, para. 2–54.
[53] 1975 Act, ss. 183 (5A), 384 (5A), added by 1978 Act, s. 7.
[54] 1978 Act, ss. 1 (5), 7.

Act.[55] Where, under either section 186 or 387 of that Act, a probationer is sentenced for the offence for which he was placed on probation, the probation order shall cease to have effect.[56]

-24 A probation order may, on the application of the officer supervising the probationer, or of the probationer himself, be discharged:

(a) by the appropriate court, or

(b) if no appropriate court has been named in the original or in any amending order, by the court which made the order.[57]

-25 If the court by which a probation order was made, or the appropriate court, is satisfied that the probationer proposes to change or has changed his residence from the area of a local authority named in the order to another area of a local authority, the court may, and if application is made in that behalf by the officer supervising the probationer must, by order, amend the probation order by:

(a) substituting for the area named therein that other area, and

(b) naming the appropriate court to which all the powers of the court by which the order was made are to be transferred, and must require the local authority for that other area to arrange for the probationer to be under the supervision of an officer of that authority.[58]

If the probation order contains requirements which in the opinion of the court cannot be complied with unless the probationer continues to reside in the local authority area named in the order, the court must not amend the order as above unless it cancels those requirements or substitutes therefor other requirements which can be so complied with.[59]

-26 When a probation order is so amended as to local authority area the clerk of the court amending it must send to the clerk of the appropriate court four copies of the order together with such documents and information relating to the case as the court amending the order considers likely to be of assistance to the appropriate court. The clerk of the appropriate court must send one

---

[55] 1975 Act, ss. 185 (1), 386 (1).

[56] *Ibid.* ss. 185 (2), 386 (2).

[57] *Ibid.* 5th Sched., para. 1. For definition of "appropriate court" see n. 30.

[58] *Ibid.* 5th Sched., para. 2 (1).

[59] *Ibid.* 5th Sched., para. 2 (2) (ii).

copy of the probation order to the local authority of the substituted local authority area and two copies to the officer supervising the probationer. That officer must give one of these copies to the probationer.[60]

2–27   Special provisions apply where a probation order has been made by the High Court and is to be amended as to local authority area. In that event:

(a)   the court does not name an appropriate court, but may substitute for the local authority named in the order the local authority for the area in which the probationer is to reside; and

(b)   the Clerk of Justiciary must send to the director of social work of that area in which the probationer is to reside three copies of the amending order together with such documents and information relating to the case as are likely to be of assistance to the director. The director must send two copies of the amending order to the officer supervising the probationer, and that officer must give one of these copies to the probationer.[61]

2–28   The court by which a probation order was made or the appropriate court may, upon application made by the officer supervising the probationer or by the probationer himself, by order amend a probation order by cancelling any of the requirements thereof or by inserting therein (either in addition to or in substitution for any such requirement) any requirement which could be included in the order if it were then being made by that court in accordance with the provisions of sections 183, 184, 384 and 385 of the 1975 Act.[62] This may include a requirement as to the performance of unpaid work. The power to amend an order in this way is subject to three limitations:

(a)   the court must not amend a probation order by reducing the probation period, or by extending that period beyond the end of three years from the date of the original order;

(b)   the court must not so amend a probation order that the probationer is thereby required to reside in any institution or place, or to submit to treatment for his

---

[60] 1975 Act, 5th Sched., para. 2 (3).
[61] *Ibid*. 5th Sched., para. 2 (4).
[62] *Ibid*. 5th Sched., para. 3.

mental condition, for any period or periods exceeding
12 months in all;

(c)   the court must not amend a probation order by
        inserting therein a requirement that the probationer is
        to submit to treatment for his mental condition unless
        the amending order is made within three months after
        the date of the original order.[62]

2–29   Where the medical practitioner by whom or under whose
direction a probationer is being treated for his mental condition in
pursuance of any requirement of the probation order is of opinion:

(a)   that the treatment of the probationer should be
        continued beyond the period specified in that behalf in
        the order; or

(b)   that the probationer needs different treatment, being
        treatment of a kind to which he could be required to
        submit in pursuance of a probation order; or

(c)   that the probationer is not susceptible to treatment; or

(d)   that the probationer does not require further treat-
        ment,

or where the practitioner is for any reason unwilling to continue to
treat or direct the treatment of the probationer, he must make a
report in writing to the officer supervising the probationer. That
officer must then apply to the court which made the order or the
appropriate court for the variation or cancellation of the
requirement.[63] In practice these provisions are rarely required since
courts frequently insert in a probation order an open-ended and
unspecific requirement such as "to submit, for a period not
exceeding 12 months, to such treatment for his mental condition as
may be prescribed by Dr. X". It may, however, be argued with some
force that, in taking such a course, courts are yielding to doctors a
power of decision which ought properly to remain in the hands of
the court.

2–30   Where the court which made the order or the appropriate court
proposes to amend a probation order, otherwise than on the
application of the probationer, it must cite him to appear before the
court, and the order must not be amended unless the probationer
expresses his willingness to comply with the requirements of the
order as amended. This provision does not, however, apply to an

---

[62] 1975 Act, 5th Sched., para. 3.
[63] *Ibid.* 5th Sched., para. 4.

order cancelling a requirement of the probation order or reducing the period of any requirement, or substituting a new area of a local authority for the area named in the probation order.[64]

2–31   On the making of an order discharging or amending a probation order, the clerk of the court must forthwith give copies of the discharging or amending order to the officer supervising the probationer. The officer must then give a copy to the probationer and to the person in charge of any institution in which the probationer is or was required by the order to reside.[65]

Failure to comply with requirements

2–32   If, on information on oath from the officer supervising the probationer, it appears to the court by which the order was made or to the appropriate court that the probationer has failed to comply with any of the requirements of the order, that court may issue a warrant for the arrest of the probationer, or may, if it thinks fit, instead of issuing such a warrant in the first instance, issue a citation requiring the probationer to appear before the court at such time as may be specified in the citation.[66] It is to be noted that the definition of "probationer" in section 462(1) of the 1975 Act has been amended by section 25(*b*) of the 1980 Act so as to make breach of probation proceedings competent even after a probation order has expired, provided of course that the breach itself occurred during the currency of the order.

2–33   If it is proved to the satisfaction of the court before which a probationer appears or is brought in pursuance of the foregoing provisions that he has failed to comply with any of the requirements of the probation order, the court may:

    (a)   without prejudice to the continuance in force of the probation order, impose a fine not exceeding £50; or

    (b)   (i)   where the probationer has been convicted for the offence for which the order was made, sentence him for that offence;

            (ii)   where the probationer has not been so convicted, convict him and sentence him as aforesaid; or

    (c)   vary any of the requirements of the probation order, so

---

[64] 1975 Act, 5th Sched., para. 5.
[65] *Ibid*. 5th Sched., para. 6.
[66] *Ibid*. ss. 186 (1), 387 (1).

however that any extension of the probation period
shall terminate not later than three years from the date
of the probation order; or

(d)   without prejudice to the continuance in force of the
probation order, in a case where the conditions
required by the Community Service by Offenders
(Scotland) Act 1978 are satisfied, make a community
service order. The provisions of that Act are to apply to
such an order as if the failure to comply with the
requirement of the probation order were the offence in
respect of which the order had been made.[67]

2–34   The 1975 Act is silent as to how, and by whom, any failure by a
probationer to comply with a requirement of the order is to be
proved. By local arrangement this task is often in practice
undertaken by the procurator fiscal. It is submitted that the
standard of proof in such a case should be the same as applies in
criminal trials. It is imperative that the correct procedure should be
followed.[68]

2–35   A fine imposed under the above provisions in respect of a
failure to comply with the requirements of a probation order shall
be deemed for the purposes of any enactment to be a sum adjudged
to be paid by or in respect of a conviction or a penalty imposed on a
person summarily convicted.[69]

2–36   A probationer who is required by a probation order to submit
to treatment for his mental condition is not to be deemed for the
purpose of these provisions to have failed to comply with that
requirement on the ground only that he has refused to undergo any
surgical, electrical or other treatment if, in the opinion of the court,
his refusal was reasonable having regard to all the circumstances.[70]

2–37   Without prejudice to the provisions of sections 187 and 388 of
the 1975 Act (see *infra*, paras. 2–38 and 2–39), a probationer who is
convicted of an offence committed during the probation period is
not on that account to be liable to be dealt with under sections 186
and 387 for failing to comply with any requirement of the probation
order.[71] It has been observed that, where circumstances permit, it is

---

[67] 1975 Act, ss. 186 (2), 387 (2), as amended by 1978 Act, s. 8, and 1980 Act, s. 46
(1).
[68] *Roy* v. *Cruickshank*, 1954 S.L.T. 217.
[69] 1975 Act, ss. 186 (3), 387 (3).
[70] *Ibid.* ss. 186 (4), 387 (4).
[71] *Ibid.* ss. 186 (5), 387 (5).

preferable to proceed under what are now sections 187 and 388 rather than under sections 186 and 387.[72]

Commission of further offence

2–38   If it appears to the court by which a probation order has been made, or to the appropriate court, that the probationer to whom the order relates has been convicted by a court in any part of Great Britain of an offence committed during the probation period and has been dealt with for that offence, the first-mentioned court, or the appropriate court, may issue a warrant for the arrest of the probationer, or may, if it thinks fit, instead of issuing such a warrant in the first instance issue a citation requiring the probationer to appear before that court at such time as may be specified in the citation. On his appearance or on his being brought before the court, the court may, if it thinks fit, deal with him under section 186 (2) (*b*) or 387 (2) (*b*) of the 1975 Act, as the case may be.[73]

2–39   Where a probationer is convicted by the court which made the probation order, or by the appropriate court, of an offence committed during the probation period, that court may, if it thinks fit, deal with him under section 186 (2) (*b*) or 387 (2) (*b*) for the offence for which the order was made as well as for the offence committed during the period of probation. Questions may arise in such a case as to whether consecutive or cumulative sentences may competently be imposed where the effect would be to exceed the particular court's maximum powers in respect of any one complaint or indictment. This is dealt with in para. 8–45.

Probation orders relating to persons residing in England
(a) Persons aged 17 and over

2–40   Where the court by which a probation order is made under the 1975 Act is satisfied that the offender has attained the age of 17 years and resides or will reside in England, subsection (2) of sections 183 and 304 does not apply, that is there is no nomination of a local authority area or an appropriate court, and no provision for the offender to be under the supervision of an officer of the local authority. Instead the order should contain a requirement that the offender is to be under the supervision of a probation officer appointed for or assigned to the petty sessions area in which the

---

[72] *Roy* v. *Cruickshank, supra.*
[73] 1975 Act, ss. 187 (1), 388 (1); see *supra*, para. 2–33.

offender resides or will reside. That area must be named in the order.[74]

41 Where a probation order has been made under the 1975 Act and the court in Scotland by which the order was made, or the appropriate court, is satisfied that the probationer has attained the age of 17 years and proposes to reside or is residing in England, the power of that court to amend the order under the 5th Schedule to the Act is to include power to insert the provisions set out in para. 2–40 *supra.* Such an amendment may be made without summoning the probationer and without his consent.[75] (But, see *infra*, para. 2–51.)

42 A probation order made or amended by virtue of the foregoing provisions may include a requirement that the probationer shall submit to treatment for his mental condition. In that event the provisions of sections 184 and 385 of the 1975 Act and section 3 of the Powers of Criminal Courts Act 1973 (which governs the making in England of a probation order containing such a requirement) are in effect assimilated in relation to the making of such orders and the functions of supervising officers and medical practitioners.[76]

43 The provisions of the 1975 Act relating to the discharge and amendment of probation orders, and to the procedure where it appears that a probationer has failed to comply with a requirement of the order,[77] do not apply to an order made or amended as above. Subject to certain exceptions the provisions of the Powers of Criminal Courts Act 1973 apply instead.[78]

44 If it appears on information to a justice acting for the petty sessions area for which the supervising court within the meaning of the Powers of Criminal Courts Act 1973 acts that a person in whose case a probation order has been made or amended as above has been convicted by a court in any part of Great Britain of an offence committed during the period specified in the order, he may issue a summons requiring that person to appear, at the place and time specified therein, before the court in Scotland by which the probation order was made or, if the information is in writing and on oath, may issue a warrant for his arrest, directing that person to be brought before the last-mentioned court.[79]

---

[74] 1975 Act, ss. 188 (1), 389 (1).
[75] *Ibid.* ss. 188 (2), 389 (2).
[76] *Ibid.* ss. 188 (3), 389 (3).
[77] *Ibid.* ss. 185 (1), 186 (1), 386 (1), 387 (1).
[78] *Ibid.* ss. 188 (4), 389 (4).
[79] *Ibid.* ss. 188 (5), 389 (5).

2–45   If a warrant for the arrest of a probationer issued under section 187 or 388 of the 1975 Act (*i.e.* on commission of a further offence) is executed in England, and the probationer cannot forthwith be brought before the court which issued the warrant, the warrant has effect as if it directed him to be brought before a magistrates' court for the place where he is arrested. The magistrates' court must commit him to custody or release him on bail (with or without sureties) until he can be brought or appear before the court in Scotland.[80]

2–46   The court by which a probation order is made or amended in accordance with the foregoing provisions must send three copies of the order to the clerk to the justices for the petty sessions area named therein, together with such documents and information relating to the case as it considers likely to be of assistance to the court acting for that petty sessions area.[81]

2–47   Section 10 of the Powers of Criminal Courts Act 1973 makes provision for the transfer of English probation orders to courts in Scotland when the probationer resides there. The court to be specified is a court of summary jurisdiction but, where the order was made on indictment, the court is to be the appropriate sheriff court. Subject to certain exceptions the provisions of the 1975 Act apply to such transferred orders as though they had been made by the appropriate court in Scotland. However, where an order is so transferred and is then amended under subsection (2) of section 188 or 389 of the 1975 Act (because the offender is or is to be resident in England) the order is in that event to have effect, as from the date of the amendment, as if it were an order made by a court in England in the case of a person residing there.[82]

2–48   Where the appropriate court in Scotland, dealing with an order transferred from England, is satisfied that the probationer has failed to comply with a requirement of the order it may, instead of dealing with him under the 1975 Act, commit him to custody or release him on bail until he can appear before the English court which made the order. A certificate by the clerk of the Scottish court is evidence of the failure to comply with the requirement of the order which is specified in the certificate.[83]

---

[80] 1975 Act, ss. 188 (6), 389 (6).
[81] *Ibid*. ss. 188 (7), 389 (7).
[82] *Ibid*. ss. 188 (8), 389 (8).
[83] Powers of Criminal Courts Act 1973, s. 10 (5).

(b) Persons under the age of 17

49 Where the court by which a probation order is made is satisfied that the person to whom the order relates is under the age of 17 and resides or will reside in England, similar provisions apply as in the case of probation orders relating to persons above that age so far as the making and amendment of such orders is concerned.[84] It is the duty of the clerk to the justices for the area where the probationer resides, upon receiving notification of the order, to refer the notification to a juvenile court acting for the petty sessions area named in the order, and on such a reference the court:

(a)   may make a supervision order under the Children and Young Persons Act 1969 in respect of a person to whom the notification relates; and

(b)   if it does not make such an order, must dismiss the case.[85]

When a juvenile court disposes of a case referred to it in either of the above ways the probation order in consequence of which the reference was made ceases to have effect.[86]

50 When a person who is subject to a supervision order made in England moves to Scotland, and his case is referred to a Scottish court under section 73 (1) of the Social Work (Scotland) Act 1968, that court:

(a)   may, if it is of opinion that the person to whom the notification relates should continue to be under supervision, make a probation order in respect of him for a period specified in the order; and

(b)   if it does not make such an order, must dismiss the case.

When the court disposes of a case in either of the above ways the supervision order ceases to have effect.[87] Provided that the probation order includes only requirements having the like effect as any requirement or provision of the supervision order, it may be made without summoning the person concerned and without his consent.[88]

(c) Orders with a requirement to perform unpaid work

51 No facilities exist in England for the carrying into effect of

---

[84] 1975 Act, ss. 189 (1) to (3), 390 (1) to (3); see *supra*, paras. 2–40, 2–41 and 2–46.

[85] *Ibid.* ss. 189 (4), 390 (4).

[86] *Ibid.* ss. 189 (5), 390 (5).

[87] *Ibid.* ss. 189 (6), 390 (6).

[88] *Ibid.* ss. 189 (7), 390 (7).

probation orders made in Scotland which contain a requirement that the probationer should perform a number of hours of unpaid work, and they are expressly excluded from the provisions of sections 188 (1) and 389 (1) of the 1975 Act by paras. 2 and 3 of the 2nd Schedule to the 1978 Act. Consequently no such requirement should be included in an order being made under either section 188 (1) or 389 (1); and, where an existing order containing such a requirement is to be transferred to England under subsection (2) of these sections, it should first be amended so as to remove that requirement.

Effects of probation

2–52   A probation order has the same effect as an absolute discharge in so far as it does or does not fall to be treated as a conviction for the purposes of an appeal or other proceedings (see *supra*, paras. 2–04 to 2–05).[89] There is, however, one provision which applies only in relation to probation orders. Where an offender, being not less than 16 years of age at the time of his conviction of an offence for which he is placed on probation, is subsequently sentenced under the 1975 Act for that offence, the provisions of subsection (1) of sections 191 and 392 do not apply, that is to say that the effect of a conviction on indictment is not then restricted in any way.[90]

COMMUNITY SERVICE ORDERS

2–53   In addition to empowering courts, when making a probation order, to include a condition that the offender should perform a number of hours of unpaid work,[91] the Community Service by Offenders (Scotland) Act 1978 also gave power in certain circumstances to make community service orders which stand on their own and do not form part of a probation order.

2–54   In general, where a person of or over 16 years of age is convicted of an offence punishable by imprisonment, other than an offence the sentence for which is fixed by law, the court may, instead of dealing with him in any other way, make an order, referred to as "a community service order", requiring him to perform unpaid work for such number of hours (being in total not less than 40 nor more than 240) as may be specified in the order.[92] A

---

[89] 1975 Act, ss. 191, 392.
[90] *Ibid.* ss. 191 (1), 392 (1).
[91] *Supra*, paras. 2–20 to 2–22.
[92] 1978 Act, s. 1 (1).

court must not make a community service order in respect of any offender unless:

(a)   the offender consents;

(b)   the court has been notified by the Secretary of State that arrangements exist for persons who reside in the locality in which the offender resides, or will be residing when the order comes into force, to perform work under such an order;

(c)   the court is satisfied, after considering a report by an officer of a local authority about the offender and his circumstances, and, if the court thinks it necessary, hearing that officer, that the offender is a suitable person to perform work under such an order; and

(d)   the court is satisfied that provision can be made under the arrangements mentioned in (b) above for the offender to perform work under such an order.[93]

A copy of the report mentioned in (c) above must be supplied to the offender or his solicitor.[94]

Before making a community service order the court must explain to the offender in ordinary language:

(a)   the purpose and effect of the order and in particular the obligations on the offender as specified in section 3 of the Act;[95]

(b)   the consequences which may follow under section 4 of the Act if he fails to comply with any of those requirements;[96]

(c)   that the court has under section 5 of the Act[97] the power to review the order on the application either of the offender or of an officer of the local authority in whose area the offender for the time being resides.[98]

The Secretary of State may by order amend the minimum and maximum number of hours specified in para. 2–54 above, and may specify a different maximum or minimum number of hours for different classes of case.[99] Any such order is subject to positive resolution by both Houses of Parliament.[100]

---

[93] 1978 Act, s. 1 (2).
[94] *Ibid.* s. 1 (3).
[95] See *infra*, paras. 2–61 to 2–62.
[96] See *infra*, paras. 2–63 to 2–64.
[97] See *infra*, paras. 2–65 to 2–66.
[98] 1978 Act, s. 1 (4).
[99] *Ibid.* s. 1 (5).
[100] *Ibid.* s. 1 (6).

2–57   The making of a community service order does not affect the court's power, at the same time:

(a)   to impose any disqualification on an offender;

(b)   to make an order for forfeiture in respect of the offence; and

(c)   to order the offender to find caution for good behaviour.[1]

2–58   A community service order must:

(a)   specify the locality in which the offender resides or will be residing when the order comes into force;

(b)   require the local authority in whose area the locality specified is situated to appoint or assign an officer (referred to in the Act as "the local authority officer") who will discharge the functions assigned to him by the Act; and

(c)   state the number of hours of work which the offender is required to perform.[2]

2–59   Where, whether on the same occasion or on separate occasions, an offender is made subject to more than one community service order, or to both a community service order and a probation order which includes a requirement that the offender is to perform unpaid work, the court may direct that the hours of work specified in any of those orders shall be concurrent with or additional to those specified in any other of those orders. At no time, however, must the offender have an outstanding number of hours of work to perform in excess of the maximum provided for in section 1(1) of the Act.[3]

2–60   Upon making a community service order the court must:

(a)   give a copy of the order to the offender;

(b)   send a copy of the order to the director of social work of the local authority in whose area the offender resides or will be residing when the order comes into force; and

(c)   where it is not the appropriate court,[4] send a copy of the order (together with such documents and informa-

---

[1] 1978 Act, s. 1 (7).

[2] *Ibid*. s. 2 (1).

[3] *Ibid*. s. 2 (2).

[4] The "appropriate court" means (a) where the relevant community service order has been made by the High Court, the High Court; (b) in any other case the sheriff or district court having jurisdiction in the relevant locality according to whether the order was made by the sheriff or district court but, where there is no district court in the locality, the sheriff court: 1978 Act, s.12 (1).

tion relating to the case as are considered useful) to the clerk of the appropriate court.[5]

Obligations on the offender

–61 An offender in respect of whom a community service order is in force must:

(a) report to the local authority officer and notify him without delay of any change of address or in the times, if any, at which he usually works; and

(b) perform for the number of hours specified in the order such work at such times as the local authority officer may instruct.[6]

–62 Subject to section 5 (1) of the Act (see *infra*, para. 2–65), the work required to be performed under a community service order must be performed during the period of 12 months beginning with the date of the order. Unless revoked, however, the order will remain in force until the offender has worked under it for the number of hours specified in it.[7] The instructions given by the local authority officer in relation to the work must, so far as practicable, be such as to avoid any conflict with the offender's religious beliefs and any interference with the times, if any, at which he normally works or attends a school or other educational establishment.[8]

Failure to comply with requirements of order

–63 If at any time while a community service order is in force it appears to the appropriate court, on evidence on oath from the local authority officer, that the offender has failed to comply with any of the requirements set out in paras. 2–61 and 2–62 above (including any failure satisfactorily to perform the work which he has been instructed to do), that court may issue a warrant for the arrest of that offender, or may, if it thinks fit, instead of issuing a warrant in the first instance issue a citation requiring that offender to appear before that court at such time as may be specified in the citation.[9]

–64 If it is proved[10] to the satisfaction of the court before which an

---

[5] 1978 Act, s. 2 (3).
[6] *Ibid.* s. 3 (1).
[7] *Ibid.* s. 3 (2).
[8] *Ibid.* s. 3 (3).
[9] *Ibid.* s. 4 (1).
[10] As in the 1975 Act in relation to failure to comply with requirements under a probation order, this Act is also silent about how and by whom a failure is to be proved. Once again procurators fiscal will no doubt come to the rescue. See *supra*, para. 2–34.

offender appears or is brought that he has failed without reasonable excuse to comply with any of the requirements of section 3 of the Act, that court may:

(a) without prejudice to the continuance in force of the order, impose on him a fine not exceeding £50;

(b) revoke the order and deal with the offender in any manner in which he could have been dealt with for the original offence by the court which made the order if the order had not been made; or

(c) subject to the restrictions on the minimum and maximum number of hours that may be ordered, vary the number of hours specified in the order.[11]

Amendment and revocation of orders

2–65   Where a community service order is in force in respect of any offender and, on the application of that offender or of the local authority officer, it appears to the appropriate court that it would be in the interests of justice to do so having regard to circumstances which have arisen since the order was made, that court may:

(a) extend, in relation to the order, the period of twelve months specified in para. 2–62 above;

(b) subject to the restrictions on the minimum and maximum number of hours that may be ordered, vary the number of hours specified in the order;

(c) revoke the order; or

(d) revoke the order and deal with the offender for the original offence in any manner in which he could have been dealt with for that offence by the court which made the order if the order had not been made.[12]

Where the court proposes to exercise its powers under head (a), (b) or (d) of the above provisions otherwise than on the application of the offender, it must issue a citation requiring him to appear before the court and, if he fails to appear, may issue a warrant for his arrest.[13]

2–66   If the appropriate court is satisfied that the offender proposes to change, or has changed, his residence from the locality for the time being specified in the order to another locality and:

---

[11] 1978 Act, s. 4 (2).
[12] *Ibid*. s. 5 (1)
[13] *Ibid*. s. 5 (3).

(a)   that court has been notified by the Secretary of State that arrangements exist for persons who reside in that other locality to perform work under community service orders; and

(b)   it appears to that court that provision can be made under those arrangements for him to perform work under the order;

that court may, and on the application of the local authority officer must, amend the order by substituting that other locality for the locality for the time being specified in the order.[14]

Persons resident in England or Wales

-67   Where a court is considering the making of a community service order, and the offender resides, or will be residing when the order comes into force, in England or Wales, a community service order may be made provided the court is satisfied that the offender has attained the age of 17 years. Before making such an order the court must have been notified by the Secretary of State that suitable arrangements exist in the petty sessions area in question, and it must appear to the court that provision can be made under those arrangements for the offender to perform work under the order.[15] The order must specify that the unpaid work is to be performed under the arrangements mentioned above.[16]

-68   Where a community service order has been made in Scotland, and the appropriate court is satisfied that the offender has attained the age of 17 years and proposes to reside or is residing in England or Wales, it may amend the order to the same effect, and subject to the same conditions, as an order made in the manner described in para. 2–67 above.[17]

-69   Where a community service order is made or amended as described above the court must send three copies of the order to the clerk to the justices for the petty sessions area specified therein, together with such documents and information relating to the case as it considers likely to be of assistance to the court acting for that petty sessions area.[18]

---

[14] 1978 Act, s. 5 (2).
[15] *Ibid.* s. 6 (1)(*a*).
[16] *Ibid.* s. 6 (1)(*b*).
[17] *Ibid.* s. 6 (2).
[18] *Ibid.* 1st Sched., para. 8.

2–70   When a community service order is made in relation to an offender residing or proposing to reside in England or Wales the court must, when giving the offender the explanations required by section 1 (4) of the 1978 Act, substitute an explanation of the appropriate provisions of sections 15, 16 and 17 of the Powers of Criminal Courts Act 1973.[19] Section 2 (1) (*a*) and (*b*), section 2 (3) (*b*) and (*c*), and sections 3 to 5 of the 1978 Act do not apply to an order made or amended under section 6. Instead, and subject to certain amendments, such an order is to be governed by section 14 (4) and sections 15 to 17 of the English Act as if the order had been made under section 14 of that Act.[20]

2–71   Where it is proved to the satisfaction of a magistrates' court that an offender, who is subject to an order made or amended under section 6 of the 1978 Act, has failed without reasonable excuse to comply with any of the requirements of section 15 of the English Act, that court may, without prejudice to the continuance of the order, impose on him a fine not exceeding £50 or issue a summons requiring him to appear before the court in Scotland by which the order was made.[21] In that latter event the court in Scotland may, if he fails to appear, issue a warrant for his arrest and, in relation to the community service order, exercise the powers conferred on an appropriate court by section 4 (2) of the 1978 Act (fine, revocation of the order, or variation of the number of hours specified in the order).[22]

2–72   Where, on the application of the offender or the relevant officer, it appears to the magistrates' court specified in the order that it would be in the interests of justice (having regard to circumstances which have arisen since the order was made or amended) that the order should be revoked or that the offender should be dealt with in some other manner for the offence in respect of which the order was made, the magistrates' court must refer the case to the court in Scotland by which the order was made.[23] In that event, the court in Scotland may exercise the powers conferred on an appropriate court by section 5 (1) (*b*), (*c*) or (*d*) of the 1978 Act (vary the number of hours, revoke the order, or revoke the order

---

[19] 1978 Act, 1st Sched., para. 1.
[20] *Ibid.* 1st Sched., para. 2.
[21] *Ibid.* 1st Sched., para. 3.
[22] *Ibid.* 1st Sched., para. 4.
[23] *Ibid.* 1st Sched., para. 5.

and deal with offender in another manner).[24] If the court in Scotland proposes to deal with the matter other than by varying the number of hours, it must issue a citation requiring the offender to appear before it.[24] If the offender fails to appear the court may grant a warrant for his arrest.[25]

FINES

Amounts
(a) On conviction on indictment

-73   A court of solemn jurisdiction may, subject to one exception noted below, on conviction impose a fine of any amount in respect of any crime or offence. Formerly this unlimited power extended to common law crimes only but, by the Criminal Law Act 1977, section 63 and Schedule 11, (creating a new section, 193A, in the 1975 Act), it was provided that where a person convicted on indictment of any offence (whether triable only on indictment or triable either on indictment or summarily) would, apart from that section, be liable to a fine not exceeding a specified amount, he is to be liable to a fine of any amount. The exception mentioned above arises in cases where, under section 8 (1) of the 1980 Act, an offence which is normally triable only summarily is libelled as an additional or alternative charge in an indictment: on conviction for that offence the offender is not to be liable to any higher penalty than he would have been on summary conviction.[26]

-74   Where a statute provides only for imprisonment a court of solemn jurisdiction may substitute (either with or without caution for good behaviour, not exceeding the amount of the prescribed sum for the time being and a period of 12 months) a fine of any amount.[27] Where a statute provides for a minimum penalty it has been held competent to modify the penalty still further.[28]

(b) On summary conviction

-75   The maximum fine which may at present be imposed by a district court in respect of a common law offence is £200.[29] The maximum fine which may at present be imposed by a sheriff

---

[24] 1978 Act, 1st Sched., para. 6.
[25] *Ibid.* 1st Sched., para. 7.
[26] 1980 Act, s. 8 (2).
[27] 1975 Act, s. 193 (2) as amended by 1980 Act, ss. 46 (2), 83 (3) and 8th Sched.
[28] *Lambie* v. *Mearns* (1903) 4 Adam 207.
[29] 1975 Act, s. 284 (b).

summary court, or by a district court constituted by a stipendiary magistrate,[30] is £1,000.[31] The Secretary of State has power, by order, to alter either of these sums so as to take account of a change in the value of money.[32] The figure of £1,000, or such other sum as may be substituted therefor by the Secretary of State, is referred to in the 1975 Act as "the prescribed sum".

2–76   Where a statute provides only for imprisonment the court may substitute a fine, with or without caution for good behaviour. In the case of an offence triable either summarily or on indictment the fine is not to exceed the prescribed sum: in the case of an offence triable only summarily it is not to exceed £200.[33]

Imposition and payment of fines
2–77   Prior to the passing of the 1980 Act the rules regulating the imposition and payment of fines were substantially different depending on whether the fines arose from a conviction on indictment or summarily. Section 47 of that Act, however, effectively assimilated the two procedures, and it is now possible to describe a substantially uniform system by reference, mainly, to those parts of the 1975 Act which previously related only to fines imposed under summary procedure.

Determination of amount of fine
2–78   Any court, in determining the amount of any fine to be imposed on an offender, must take into consideration, amongst other things, the means of the offender so far as known to the court.[34] The effect of this provision, it is submitted, is that it would be competent for a court, when fining two offenders in respect of the same offence, to impose fines of different amounts if the offenders' means were significantly different.[35]

Application of money in offender's possession
2–79   Where a court of summary jurisdiction imposes a fine it may order the offender to be searched, and any money found on him on apprehension or search, or when taken to prison or to a young

---

[30] District Courts (Scotland) Act 1975, s. 3 (2).
[31] 1975 Act, s. 289B (6).
[32] *Ibid.* s. 289D, as amended by 1980 Act, 7th Sched., para. 50.
[33] *Ibid.* s. 394 (*b*). See *Lambie* v. *Mearns* (*supra*); *McDonald* v. *Wood & Bruce*, 1950 J.C. 72; *Paton* v. *Neilson* (1903) 4 Adam 268.
[34] 1975 Act, s. 395 (1).
[35] For more detailed consideration of this see para. 10–51 *et seq.*

offenders' institution in default of payment of the fine, may, unless the court otherwise directs, be applied towards payment of the fine. Such money is not to be so applied if the court is satisfied that it does not belong to the person on whom it was found, or that the loss of the money will be more injurious to his family than his imprisonment or detention.[36] This power may be particularly useful in, for example, the case of overseas tourists who are convicted of thefts from shops.

-80   When a court of summary jurisdiction, which has adjudged that a sum of money is to be paid by an offender, considers that any money found on him on apprehension, or after he has been searched by order of the court, should not be applied towards payment of such sum, the court must make a direction in writing to that effect. That direction is to be written on the extract of the sentence which imposes the fine before that is issued by the clerk of the court.[37]

-81   An accused may make an application to such a court either orally or in writing, through the governor of the prison in whose custody he may be at the time, that any sum of money found on his person should not be applied in payment of the fine adjudged to be paid by him.[38] A person who alleges that any money found on the person of an offender is not the property of the offender, but belongs to such person, may apply to the court either orally or in writing for a direction that such money should not be applied in payment of the fine; and the court after inquiry may so direct.[39]

-82   A court of summary jurisdiction may order the attendance in court of the offender, if he is in prison, for the purpose of ascertaining the ownership of money found on his person.[40] In such a case a notice, of the appropriate form contained in an Act of Adjournal,[41] addressed to the governor of the relevant prison, signed by the judge of the court, is sufficient warrant to the governor for conveying the offender to the court.[42]

Remission of fine

-83   A fine may at any time be remitted in whole or in part by:

[36] 1975 Act, s. 395 (2).
[37] *Ibid.* s. 395 (3).
[38] *Ibid.* s. 395 (4).
[39] *Ibid.* s. 395 (5).
[40] *Ibid.* s. 395 (6).
[41] Act of Adjournal (Summary Procedure) 1964 No. 249, Form 7.
[42] 1975 Act, s. 395 (7).

(a)   in a case where a transfer of fine order is effective (see *infra*, para. 2–97) and the court by which payment is enforceable is, in terms of the order, a court of summary jurisdiction in Scotland, that court; or

(b)   in any other case, the court which imposed the fine (or, where that court was the High Court, an appropriate sheriff court).[43]

Where the court remits the whole or part of a fine after imprisonment has been imposed in default, it must also remit the whole period of imprisonment or reduce the period by an amount which bears the same proportion to the whole period as the amount remitted bears to the whole fine.[44] The above power to remit a fine in whole or in part may be exercised without requiring the attendance of the accused.[45] It is a new power which was introduced for the first time by the 1980 Act.

Time to pay

2–84   Unless payment of a fine is tendered at the time of its imposition a court must normally allow an offender at least seven days to pay the fine or the first instalment thereof.[46] A court may allow time for payment even where that has not been requested by an accused.[47]

Refusal of time to pay

2–85   The court may refuse to allow time for payment if:

(a)   the offender appears to possess sufficient means to enable him to pay the fine forthwith; or

(b)   on being asked whether he wishes to have time for payment he does not ask for time; or

(c)   he fails to satisfy the court that he has a fixed abode; or

(d)   the court is satisfied for any other special reason that no time should be allowed for payment.

If, in any of these events, the offender fails to pay, the court may exercise its power to impose imprisonment but, if it does so, it must state the special reason for its decision.[48] This power is now

---

[43] 1975 Act, s. 395A (1), added by 1980 Act, s. 49.

[44] *Ibid*. s. 395A (2).

[45] *Ibid*. s. 395A (3).

[46] *Ibid*. s. 396 (1).

[47] *Fraser* v. *Herron*, 1968 J.C. 1.

[48] 1975 Act, s. 396 (2); and see *Sullivan* v. *McLeod*, 1980 S.L.T. (Notes) 99.

restricted by the provisions of section 41 of the 1980 Act which provides *inter alia* that, unless certain conditions are satisfied, imprisonment is not to be imposed in such a case on an accused who is not legally represented and has not been previously sentenced to imprisonment or detention by a court in any part of the United Kingdom. This provision is examined more fully in Chapter 3. The nature of the offence is not a relevant consideration when determining whether time should be allowed for payment. Where the nature of the offence is such as to warrant a sentence of imprisonment the proper course is to impose such a sentence in the first instance.[49] In all cases where time is not allowed for payment of a fine the reasons of the court must be stated in the extract of the finding and sentence as well as in the finding and sentence itself.[50] A failure to record the reasons, provided that they were in any event valid and had been stated in the presence of the offender, would probably not invalidate the sentence.[51]

Restriction on imprisonment after fine

86 Where time is allowed for payment of a fine or payment by instalments is ordered, a court must not, on the occasion of the imposition of the fine, impose imprisonment in the event of a future default unless the offender is before it and the court determines that, having regard to the gravity of the offence or to the character of the offender, or to other special reason, it is expedient that he should be imprisoned without further inquiry in default of payment. Where a court so determines it must state the special reason for its decision.[52] If a court has imposed imprisonment in the event of future default then, if at any time the offender asks the court to commit him to prison, the court may do so.[53]

87 Where time has been allowed for payment of a fine the court may, on an application by or on behalf of the offender, and after giving the prosecutor an opportunity of being heard, allow further time for payment.[54] Such an application, which may be made orally or in writing,[55] should be made to the court which imposed the fine unless there has been a transfer of fine order in which event the

---

[49] *Barbour* v. *Robertson, Ram* v. *Robertson*, 1943 J.C. 46.
[50] 1975 Act, s. 396 (3).
[51] *Bruce* v. *Hogg*, 1966 J.C. 33, distinguishing *Winslow* v. *Farrell*, 1965 J.C. 49.
[52] 1975 Act, s. 396 (4).
[53] *Ibid*. s. 396 (5).
[54] *Ibid*. s. 396 (7).
[55] *Ibid*. s. 397 (3).

application should be made to the court specified therein.[56] A court to which such an application is made must allow further time for payment unless it is satisfied that the failure to make payment has been wilful or that the offender has no reasonable prospect of being able to pay if further time is allowed.[57] Two points arising from the foregoing may be mentioned. The first concerns the requirement that the prosecutor should be given an opportunity of being heard. This is a curious provision since, traditionally, the prosecutor is not concerned with matters relating to sentence, and moreover there is no comparable provision in relation to cases where an offender who has not paid timeously is brought to court to explain the reasons for the non-payment. (See *infra*, para. 2–88). In practice, it is thought, this provision is regularly ignored, and probably most prosecutors would be rather surprised to be offered an opportunity to be heard. The second point is that section 396 (7) of the 1975 Act does not in terms apply to a case where imprisonment has already been imposed in the event of future default. It is submitted, however, that the subsection applies in such a case also.

2–88 Where a court has imposed a fine without imposing imprisonment in default of payment, it must not impose imprisonment for failing to make payment unless, on an occasion subsequent to that sentence, the court has inquired, in the offender's presence, into the reason why the fine has not been paid. This requirement does not apply where the offender is in prison.[58]

2–89 For the purpose of enabling such an inquiry to be made a court may issue a citation requiring the offender to appear at an appointed time and place, or may issue a warrant of apprehension.[59] Such a warrant may also be issued if an offender fails to appear in response to a citation.[60] The form of warrant and the form of minute of procedure in such cases are prescribed by Act of Adjournal.[61] It is normal practice in most sheriff courts for the clerk of court to send a

---

[56] 1975 Act, s. 397 (1).

[57] *Ibid*. s. 397 (2).

[58] *Ibid*. s. 398 (1), as amended by 1980 Act, 7th Sched., para. 61; but see Re Hamilton and Anr. [1981] 3W.L.R. 79, which establishes that, under English procedure, an offender in prison must not be given a consecutive sentence without having been given the opportunity to make representations to the court.

[59] 1975 Act, s. 398 (2).

[60] *Ibid*. s. 398 (3).

[61] *Ibid*. s. 398 (4) and (5). Act of Adjournal (Summary Procedure) 1964 No. 249.

warning letter to an offender who is in default before the inquiry procedure is initiated.

Payment by instalments

–90   Without prejudice to a court's right under section 396 (2) of the 1975 Act, *supra*, to refuse time for payment of a fine, a court may, of its own accord or on the application of the offender, order payment of the fine by instalments of such amounts and at such time as it may think fit.[62] Where payment by instalments has been ordered the court, without requiring the attendance of the accused, may allow further time for payment of any instalment, or may order payment by instalments of lesser amounts or at longer intervals than those originally fixed.[63] Although this provision does not empower a court to increase the instalments originally fixed, it is submitted that it would be open to a court to take that course where the offender was in default and had been brought before the court for inquiry under section 398 of the 1975 Act.

Supervision

–91   Where an offender has been allowed time for payment of a fine the court may, either on the occasion of the imposition of the fine or on a subsequent occasion, order that he be placed under the supervision of such person as the court may from time to time appoint for the purpose of assisting and advising the offender in regard to payment of the fine.[64] This task is normally given to members of a local social work department. A supervision order remains in force so long as the offender to whom it relates remains liable to pay the fine or any part of it,[65] but the court may discharge the order within that period and, in any event, the order ceases to have effect on the making of a transfer of fine order (see *infra*, para. 2–97). In either case the court may, if it wishes, make a new order.[66]

–92   Where an offender under 21 years of age has been allowed time for payment of a fine the court must not order the form of detention appropriate to him in default of payment unless he has been placed under supervision in respect of the fine, or the court is satisfied that it is impracticable to place him under supervision.[67] In the latter

---

[62] 1975 Act, s. 399 (1), as amended by 1980 Act, 7th Sched., para. 62.
[63] *Ibid.* s. 399 (2) and (3), as amended by 1980 Act, 7th Sched., para. 62.
[64] *Ibid.* s. 400 (1).
[65] *Ibid.* s. 400 (2).
[66] *Ibid.* s. 400 (3).
[67] *Ibid.* s. 400 (4).

event the court must state the grounds on which it is satisfied that supervision is impracticable and these must be entered in the record of proceedings.[68] The general requirement in relation to offenders under 21 means in practice that, if a supervision order is not made at the time when a fine is imposed, and the offender subsequently defaults, he will have to be brought before the court for an inquiry under section 398 of the 1975 Act and will then, generally, have to be placed under a supervision order (no detention then being competent), and allowed further time to pay. To avoid this process, which some believe encourages young offenders to be dilatory in the payment of fines, it is the practice in some courts to place all such offenders under a supervision order at the time when a fine is imposed. This practice, however, places a considerable burden on the social work departments concerned and thereby reduces the likelihood of effective supervision being carried out. It is submitted that it is generally better practice to make a supervision order at the time of imposing a fine only when special features are present, *e.g.* the fine is substantial, the offender has a considerable criminal record, or there are indications that he will have difficulty in efficiently managing his finances. It is also submitted that the provision about impracticability should be used sparingly. Although there is no authority on the matter it is suggested that supervision could properly be considered impracticable where an offender was employed in a place where contact with a supervising officer would be difficult or impossible, *e.g.* at sea, or where there was evidence that, on a previous occasion, the offender had failed to co-operate with the terms of a supervision order.

2–93   Where a supervision order is in force the court must not impose imprisonment or detention in default of payment of the fine unless it has, before so doing, taken such steps as may be reasonably practicable to obtain from the person appointed for the supervision of the payment of the fine a report, which may be oral, on the offender's conduct and means. The court must also consider any such report in a case where inquiry is required under section 398 of the 1975 Act, in addition to the inquiry called for by that section.[69]

2–94   Upon the making of a supervision order the clerk of court must send a notice to the offender in, as nearly as may be, the form contained in the Act of Adjournal (Summary Procedure) 1964.[70]

---

[68] 1975 Act, ss. 400 (5), 401 (1).
[69] *Ibid.* s. 400 (6).
[70] *Ibid.* s. 400 (7).

The person appointed to supervise the offender must communicate with him with a view to assisting and advising him in regard to payment of the fine, and unless the fine or any instalment has been paid within the time allowed that person must report to the court without delay as to the conduct and means of the offender.[71]

Enforcement in other districts, and enforcement of High Court fines

–95 Any sentence or decree for any fine or expenses (see *infra*, para. 7–07) pronounced by any court may be enforced against the person or effects of any party against whom any such sentence or decree has been awarded in any other sheriff court district, as well as in the district where the sentence or decree was pronounced. However, such sentence or decree, or an extract thereof, must first be produced to and endorsed by the sheriff or justice of such other district competent to have pronounced the sentence or decree in that other district.[72]

–96 A fine imposed by the High Court is to be remitted for enforcement:

(a) where the person upon whom the fine was imposed resides in Scotland, to the sheriff for the district where the person resides;

(b) where the person resides outwith Scotland, to the sheriff before whom he was brought for examination in relation to the offence for which the fine was imposed.[73]

Transfer of fine orders

–97 Where a court has imposed a fine and it appears to the court charged with the enforcement of that fine that the offender is residing within the jurisdiction of another court of summary jurisdiction in Scotland, or in any petty sessions area in England and Wales, the court, if no term of imprisonment has been fixed in default of payment, may order that payment of the fine is to be enforceable by that other court of summary jurisdiction or in that petty sessions area.[74] Such a transfer of fine order must specify the court by which, or the petty sessions area in which, payment is to be enforceable. If a court is specified it must be a sheriff court where

---

[71] 1975 Act, s. 400 (8).
[72] *Ibid*. s. 402 (1).
[73] *Ibid*. s. 196 (2), as added by 1980 Act, s. 48.
[74] *Ibid*. s. 403 (1).

the transfer of fine order is itself made by a sheriff court.[75]

2–98   A fine imposed in England or Wales may, under the Magistrates' Courts Act 1980, be transferred for enforcement to a court of summary jurisdiction in Scotland, in which event that court has the same functions and powers as if the fine had been imposed by that court. However, in the event of imprisonment being imposed by the court in Scotland for default in payment, the period that may be imposed is to be that provided for in paragraph 1 of the 4th Schedule to the Magistrates' Courts Act, where the fine was originally imposed by a magistrates' court, and that provided for in section 31 of the Powers of Criminal Courts Act 1973, where the fine was originally imposed by a Crown Court.[76] In fact, since the passing of the 1980 Act the periods that may be imposed in Scotland are now the same as those competent under the Magistrates' Courts Act (see *infra*, para. 2–102).

2–99   Where a transfer of fine order has been made as above the clerk of the court must send to the clerk of the court specified in the order a notice in a form prescribed by Act of Adjournal[77] together with any other relevant information relative to the fine.[78] The clerk of the court where the fine was originally imposed is to be kept informed of any further transfer of fine orders, and of any enforcement of the fine otherwise than by payment. Where any payment of the fine is received the clerk of the court specified in the transfer of fine order must remit or otherwise account for it to the clerk of the court by which the fine was imposed.[79]

Default by a child in payment of a fine

2–100   Where a child would, if he were an adult, be liable to be imprisoned in default of payment of a fine, damages or expenses, the court may, if it considers that none of the other methods by which the case may legally be dealt with is suitable, order that the child be detained for a period not exceeding one month in a place chosen by the local authority in whose area the court is specified.[80] It is thought that this power is rarely used since, subsequent to the introduction of the children's hearing system, very few children are

---

[75] 1975 Act, s. 403 (2).
[76] *Ibid*. s. 403 (4) to (6).
[77] (Summary Procedure) 1964 No. 249.
[78] 1975 Act, s. 404 (1).
[79] *Ibid*. s. 404 (2) and (4).
[80] *Ibid*. s. 406.

prosecuted and, when they are, a fine is very unlikely to be a
suitable disposal.

Imprisonment for non-payment of fine

-101   Subject to sections 396 to 401 of the 1975 Act (see above):

  (a)   a court may, when imposing a fine, impose a period of
            imprisonment in default of payment; or

  (b)   where no such order has been made, and a person fails
            to pay a fine or any part or instalment of a fine by the
            time ordered, the court may impose a period of
            imprisonment for that failure,

whether or not the fine is imposed under an enactment which makes
provision for its enforcement or recovery.[81]

-102   The maximum period of imprisonment which may be imposed
for such failure is as follows:

Amount of Fine	*Maximum Period of Imprisonment*
Not exceeding £25	7 days
Exceeding £25 but not exceeding £50	14 days
Exceeding £50 but not exceeding £200	30 days
Exceeding £200 but not exceeding £500	60 days
Exceeding £500 but not exceeding £1,000	90 days
Exceeding £1,000 but not exceeding £2,500	6 months
Exceeding £2,500 but not exceeding £5,000	9 months
Exceeding £5,000	12 months[82]

-103   Where an offender is fined on the same day before the same
court for offences charged in the same complaint or in separate
complaints, the amount of the fine, for the purpose of fixing a
period of imprisonment, is to be taken to be the total of the fines
imposed.[83] This provision, introduced by the 1980 Act, substantially alters a summary court's powers of imprisonment in the event of
default. Previously, when there were separate tables of maximum
periods of imprisonment in respect of fines imposed summarily and
on indictment, it was the case that, if an offender was being dealt

---

[81] 1975 Act, s. 407 (1), as amended by 1980 Act, s. 50.
[82] *Ibid*. s. 407 (1A), as added by 1980 Act, s. 50.
[83] *Ibid*. s. 407 (1B).

with in respect of two or more complaints on the same day, any periods of imprisonment in default of payment should not cumulatively exceed the summary court maximum, which was 90 days.[84] The provision in section 407 (1B) of the 1975 Act appears to alter that rule by providing that, if, for example, a court on the same day imposed periods of imprisonment in respect of two fines of £750, for offences in separate complaints, the maximum period of imprisonment which could be imposed would be six months, rather than 90 days.[85]

2–104   Where a period of imprisonment has been imposed in default of payment of a fine and an instalment is not paid at the time ordered, or part only of the fine has been paid within the time allowed, the offender becomes liable to imprisonment for a period proportionate to the amount of the fine then outstanding.[86]

2–105   When a period of imprisonment is imposed subsequent to a default of payment of part of a fine, part having already been paid, the maximum period of imprisonment to be imposed should bear to the period that might have been imposed in respect of the whole fine the same proportion as the outstanding balance bears to the original fine.[87] The statutory provision in this regard is not very clearly expressed, but it is submitted that the foregoing represents its meaning. The provision was presumably added by the 1980 Act because, prior to that time, there was some uncertainty about whether, when imposing a period of imprisonment at a stage when part of a fine had already been paid, the court should state a period appropriate to the whole of the original fine, leaving it to administrative action to calculate the proportion thereof applicable to the unpaid balance, or do the calculation itself and state the period applicable only to that balance.

2–106   If in any sentence or extract of sentence the period of imprisonment inserted in default of payment of a fine is in excess of that competent under the 1975 Act, as amended, such period is to be reduced to the maximum permissible; and the judge who pronounced the sentence has power to order the sentence or extract to be corrected accordingly.[88]

2–107   All warrants of imprisonment for payment of a fine must

---

[84] See, for example, *Kesson* v. *Heatly*, 1964 J.C. 40.
[85] For further discussion of this, see para. 8–41 *et seq.*
[86] 1975 Act, s. 407 (1C).
[87] *Ibid.* s. 407 (1D).
[88] *Ibid.* s. 407 (2).

specify a period at the expiry of which the person sentenced is to be discharged, notwithstanding that the fine has not been paid.[89]

-108   A person committed to prison or detention for failure to pay a fine may make payment to the governor of the prison of all or part of the outstanding amount due by him. If only part payment is made the term of imprisonment is to be reduced by the same proportion that the payment made bears to the amount outstanding when the period of imprisonment commenced. However, the day on which any sum is paid is not to be regarded as a day served by the prisoner as part of his sentence.[90] This proviso avoids the abuse whereby a fine defaulter could, at no inconsiderable public expense, spend only a few hours in prison and then secure his release by payment of a lesser amount than would have prevented his being taken to prison in the first place.

Recovery by civil diligence

-109   A court may order recovery of a fine by civil diligence. This may be ordered at any time after a fine has been imposed, including after imprisonment in default of payment has been ordered, provided that imprisonment has not in fact taken place. Equally, imprisonment may be imposed at a later stage notwithstanding that recovery by civil diligence has previously been ordered.[91] In that event, of course, the order for imprisonment could not be carried into effect if the civil diligence was effective in producing payment of the fine, or if the fine was otherwise paid.

-110   Where civil diligence is ordered there should be added to the finding of the court imposing the fine the words "and decrees and ordains instant execution by arrestment and also execution to pass hereon by poinding and sale, after a charge of ten free days." Execution is to be in the same manner as if the proceedings were on an extract decree in a summary cause.[91]

-111   Civil diligence is the only means of recovering a fine imposed in proceedings taken against a company, association, incorporation or body of trustees.[92] It has been little used against individuals partly because, until the passing of the 1980 Act, a decision to recover in this way was final and could not be followed by the imposition of

---

[89] 1975 Act, s. 408.
[90] *Ibid.* s. 409 (1), as amended by 1980 Act, 7th Sched, para. 65.
[91] *Ibid.* s. 411, as amended by 1980 Act, s. 52.
[92] *Ibid.* s. 333.

imprisonment, even if the diligence was unsuccessful. No doubt, also, the cumbersome state of the Scots law of diligence at the present time has partly contributed to the courts' reluctance to use this method of recovery. In the case of *Moffat* v. *Shaw* (1896) 2 Adam 57 Lord McLaren laid down a distinct principle for the guidance of judges in the inferior courts. In that case a question arose as to the use of civil diligence in place of imprisonment, in a case under the Vaccination Act 1863. His Lordship said: "In the enforcement of the penalty the statute requires that the more humane and more effective alternative of imprisonment for a short period should be adopted in preference to the civil remedy of poinding, which might be ruinous to a poor man." Whether that approach would necessarily find favour to-day is perhaps open to doubt. Indeed, in these more affluent times, it may well be that civil diligence, backed as it now is by the possibility of a sentence of imprisonment, should be seen as a more attractive means of recovery than has hitherto been the case.

Persons to whom fines are to be paid

2–112　　　　Any fine imposed in the High Court is payable to H.M. Exchequer.[93] Otherwise, all fines and expenses are to be paid to the clerk of court, to be accounted for by him to the person entitled to them.[94] However, where a warrant has been issued for the apprehension of an offender for non-payment of a fine, he may pay the fine in full to a constable. In that event the warrant will not be enforced, and the constable is obliged to remit the fine to the clerk of court.[95] Similarly, any part payment of a fine made to the governor of a prison under section 409 of the 1975 Act must be remitted by him to the clerk of the court in which the conviction was obtained.[96]

CAUTION

2–113　Summary courts have power on convicting of a common law offence to ordain an offender to find caution for good behaviour for any period not exceeding 12 months, in the case of the sheriff court, and six months, in the case of the district court. This may be ordered in lieu of, or in addition to, imprisonment or a fine. The maximum

---

[93] 1975 Act, s. 203.
[94] *Ibid.* s. 412.
[95] *Ibid.* s. 401 (3), as added by 1980 Act, 7th Sched., para. 63.
[96] *Ibid.* 7th Sched.

amount of caution which may be required is £200 in the case of the district court, and the prescribed sum (at present £1,000) in the case of the sheriff court.[97] In either case the Secretary of State has power by order to alter these maximum amounts to take account of a change in the value of money.

–114 Imprisonment may be awarded for failure to find caution,[97] and since caution is not mentioned in section 400 of the 1975 Act it would seem that a supervision order pending payment is not competent. Caution may be found by consignation of the amount with the clerk of court, or by bond of caution, which may be signed by the mark of the cautioner. Where caution becomes liable to forfeiture, that may be granted by the court on the motion of the prosecutor and, where necessary, warrant may be granted for its recovery. In the event of the cautioner failing to pay the amount due under his bond within six days of receiving a charge to that effect, the court may order him to be imprisoned for the maximum period applicable under section 407 of the 1975 Act, or may grant time for payment, or may order recovery by civil diligence.[98] "Good behaviour" is not defined in the Act, but in practice it is generally taken to mean no more than refraining from committing further offences. Consequently, forfeiture will generally be ordered only where the offender has committed a further offence during the relevant period. Because of the current delays in many courts in bringing cases to trial, difficulties can arise if an offence alleged to have been committed during the relevant period is not to be the subject of a trial until after that period has expired. It is submitted that, in such a case, the court would be entitled, where consignation had taken place, to retain the sum concerned until the outcome of the trial became known.

2–115 When caution is to be found other than by way of a bond of caution similar procedures apply as in the case of fines to the allowance of time for payment, and recovery in the event of non-payment. However, no provision is made for the payment of caution by instalments, and that is therefore not competent.

COMPENSATION ORDERS

2–116 Where a person is convicted of an offence a court, except when granting an absolute discharge or making a probation order or

---

[97] 1975 Act, ss. 284, 289, as amended by 1980 Act, 7th Sched., para. 50.
[98] *Ibid*. s. 303.

deferring sentence, instead of or in addition to dealing with the offender in any other way, may make a compensation order requiring him to pay compensation for any personal injury, loss or damage caused (whether directly or indirectly) by the acts which constituted the offence.[99] In solemn proceedings there is no limit to the amount of such an order.[1] In summary proceedings a sheriff or stipendiary magistrate may make a compensation order in respect of each offence to an amount not exceeding the prescribed sum within the meaning of section 289B of the 1975 Act. The limit in the case of the district court is £200.[2]

2–117   Where, in the case of an offence involving the dishonest appropriation, or the unlawful taking and using, of property or a contravention of section 175 (1) of the Road Traffic Act 1972, the property is recovered, but has been damaged while out of the owner's possession, that damage (however and by whomsoever it was in fact caused) shall be treated for the purpose of making a compensation order as having been caused by the acts which constituted the offence.[3]

2–118   In two cases a compensation order may not be made. These are:

(a)   in respect of loss suffered in consequence of the death of any person, and

(b)   in respect of injury, loss or damage due to an accident arising out of the presence of a motor vehicle on a road, except such damage as is treated, as in para. 2–117 above, as having been caused by the convicted person's acts.[4]

2–119   In determining whether to make a compensation order against any person and in determining the amount of any such order, the court must take into consideration that person's means so far as known to the court. However, where the person is serving, or is to serve, a period of imprisonment or detention, no account is to be taken, in assessing such means, of earnings contingent upon his obtaining employment after release.[5] Where a court considers that

---

[99] 1980 Act, s. 58 (1); for a discussion of the use of compensation orders see para. 10–72 *et seq*.

   [1] *Ibid*. s. 59 (2).
   [2] *Ibid*. s. 59 (3).
   [3] *Ibid*. s. 58 (2).
   [4] *Ibid*. s. 58 (3).
   [5] *Ibid*. s. 59 (1).

it would be appropriate to impose a fine and to make a compensation order, but the convicted person has insufficient means to pay both, the court should prefer a compensation order.[6]

-120   Where a person has been both fined and had a compensation order made against him in respect of the same offence or different offences in the same proceedings, the compensation order takes precedence over the fine in respect of payments made by the offender.[7] Payments under a compensation order are to be made to the clerk of court who has to account for them to the person entitled thereto, but only the court has power to enforce compensation orders.[8] All of the provisions in the 1975 Act relative to the payment, remission, transfer and enforcement of fines apply, subject to any necessary modifications, to compensation orders. However, a court may impose imprisonment in respect of a fine and decline to impose imprisonment in respect of a compensation order, but not vice versa, and, where a court imposes imprisonment both in respect of a fine and of a compensation order the amounts are to be aggregated for the purpose of calculating the maximum period allowed.[9]

-121   At any time before a compensation order has been complied with or fully complied with a court of summary jurisdiction in Scotland to which the order has been transferred, or the court which made the order, or (where that court was the High Court) the appropriate sheriff court, may, on the application of the offender, discharge the compensation order or reduce the amount that remains to be paid. This may be done if it appears to the court either that the injury, loss or damage has been held in civil proceedings to be less than it was taken to be for the purposes of the order, or that property, the loss of which was reflected in the order, has been recovered.[10]

---

[6] 1980 Act, s. 61.
[7] *Ibid.* s. 62.
[8] *Ibid.* s. 60.
[9] *Ibid.* s. 66.
[10] *Ibid.* s. 64.

CHAPTER 3

CUSTODIAL DISPOSALS

INTRODUCTION

3–01 With the exception of the rarely used power enjoyed by a summary court to order detention in the precincts of a court or in legalised police cells,[1] the only custodial sentence for persons of the age of 21 or over is now imprisonment. The only custodial sentence for persons who are not less than 16 but under 21 years of age is detention. The obsolescent sentences of preventive detention and corrective training were finally swept away by the 1980 Act,[2] and specific types of imprisonment, namely penal servitude and imprisonment with hard labour, had previously been abolished by the Criminal Justice (Scotland) Act 1949.[3] Any enactment conferring a power to pass a sentence of penal servitude or imprisonment with hard labour is to be construed as conferring power to pass a sentence of imprisonment for a term not exceeding the term for which a sentence of the former kind could have been passed prior to 12 June 1950: but this is not to be construed as permitting a court other than the High Court to pass a sentence of imprisonment for a term exceeding two years.[4]

MAXIMUM SENTENCES

High Court

3–02 Except where otherwise provided by a particular statute under which an accused is convicted, the High Court has no upper limit to its power to impose imprisonment or detention, and it may impose a sentence of any determinate period, or for life. Apart from the life sentence, no other indeterminate sentence is competent. A person convicted of murder, unless he is under the age of 21,[5] must be sentenced to imprisonment for life.[6] On sentencing any person convicted of murder a judge may make a recommendation as to the minimum period which should elapse before, under section 61 of the Criminal Justice Act 1967, the Secretary of State releases that

---

[1] See *infra*, paras. 3–06 and 3–07.
[2] s. 83 (3) and Sched. 8.
[3] s. 16, now 1975 Act, s. 221.
[4] *Ibid.* subss. (1) and (2).
[5] See *infra*, para. 3–09.
[6] 1975 Act, s. 205 (1), as amended by 1980 Act, s. 43.

person on licence.[7] When making such a recommendation the judge must state his reasons for so recommending.[8] Notwithstanding the proviso to section 228 (1) of the 1975 Act, such a recommendation may be made the subject of an appeal, and may be dealt with on appeal in the same manner as any other sentence.[9]

Sheriff court under solemn jurisdiction

‌–03   The maximum period of imprisonment or detention that may be imposed on indictment in the sheriff court is two years.[10] However, if the sheriff holds that any competent sentence which he can impose is inadequate so that the question of sentence is appropriate for the High Court, there is a power of remit to that court for sentence.[11]

Sheriff court under summary jurisdiction

‌–04   A sheriff, when sitting summarily, has power on convicting a person of a common law offence to impose imprisonment for any period not exceeding three months.[12] Where that power is exercised it is incompetent to impose a fine in addition.[13] The above period of three months may be increased to six months where a person is convicted of (a) a second or subsequent offence inferring dishonest appropriation of property, or attempt thereat, or (b) a second or subsequent offence inferring personal violence.[14] A charge of breach of the peace, even where it involves threats of violence and malicious damage, is not an offence inferring personal violence for this purpose.[15]

District court

‌–05   A district court has power on convicting a person of a common law offence to impose imprisonment for any period not exceeding 60 days.[16] The same limit applies in relation to statutory offences,

---

[7] 1975 Act, S. 205A (1), as added by 1980 Act, s. 43; for a description of the role of the Parole Board in advising on the release of life sentence prisoners, see para. 11–23 *et seq.*
[8] *Ibid.* s. 205A (2).
[9] *Ibid.* s. 205A (3); generally, on appeals against sentence, see Chap. 9.
[10] *Ibid.* s. 2 (2).
[11] *Ibid.* s. 104 (1), as amended by 1980 Act, Sched. 4, para. 15; and see Chap. 8 for the procedure to be followed.
[12] 1975 Act, s. 289 (*d*).
[13] *McGunnigal* v. *Copeland*, 1972 S.L.T. (Notes) 70.
[14] 1975 Act, s. 290.
[15] *Adair* v. *Morton*, 1972 S.L.T. (Notes) 70.
[16] 1975 Act, s. 284.

and it is not competent for a statutory offence to be tried in the district court where the maximum penalty which may be imposed for that offence exceeds 60 days imprisonment or a fine of £200 or both.[17]

DETENTION IN PRECINCTS OF COURT

3–06 Where a court of summary jurisdiction has power to impose imprisonment on an offender it may, in lieu of so doing, order that he be detained within the precincts of the court or at any police station till such hour, not later than eight in the evening on the day on which he is convicted, as the court may direct. Before making such an order the court must take into consideration the distance between the proposed place of detention and the offender's residence (if known to, or ascertainable by, the court) and must not make any such order as would deprive the offender of a reasonable opportunity of returning to his residence on the day on which the order is made.[18] It is believed that this power is little, if at all, used, and its contemporary usefulness may be doubted.

NO IMPRISONMENT FOR LESS THAN FIVE DAYS

3–07 No person may be sentenced to imprisonment by a court of summary jurisdiction for a period of less than five days.[19] Where a court of summary jurisdiction has power to impose imprisonment on an offender it may sentence the offender to be detained, for such period not exceeding four days as the court thinks fit, in what are known as legalised police cells.[20] The principal provision for such legalised cells is contained in the Prisons (Scotland) Act 1952,[21] and the main purpose of such provision is to ensure that, mainly in the more remote areas, prisoners can be detained in secure conditions for periods of up to 30 days before, during, and after a trial. As a short custodial sentence under section 425 of the 1975 Act it is thought that detention in legalised police cells is little used. It may not be used in the case of females unless provision is made for their supervision by female officers.[22]

---

[17] 1980 Act, s. 7 (1).
[18] 1975 Act, s. 424.
[19] *Ibid.* s. 425 (1).
[20] *Ibid.* s. 425 (2) to (4).
[21] s. 14.
[22] 1975 Act, s. 425 (5).

CONSIDERATION OF TIME SPENT IN CUSTODY

1–08 A court, in passing a sentence of imprisonment or detention on a person for any offence, must, in determining the period of imprisonment or detention, have regard to any period of time spent in custody by that person on remand awaiting trial or sentence.[23]

YOUNG OFFENDERS

Sentence for murder

1–09 Where a person convicted of murder is under the age of 18 years he must not be sentenced to imprisonment for life but to be detained without limit of time. When so sentenced he is liable to be detained in such place, and under such conditions, as the Secretary of State may direct.[24] Where a person convicted of murder has attained the age of 18 years but is under the age of 21 years he must not be sentenced to imprisonment for life but to be detained in a young offenders' institution. Such a person is liable to be detained for life.[25] The power to make a recommendation in relation to a person convicted of murder as to the minimum period which should elapse before the Secretary of State releases that person on licence applies equally to young offenders as it does to adult offenders.[26]

Sentence in cases other than murder

1–10 It is not competent to impose imprisonment on a person under 21 years of age:[27] and, with the abolition of the separate sentences of borstal training and detention centre training by the 1980 Act, a sentence of detention is now the only competent custodial sentence that may be imposed on a person who is not less than 16 but under 21 years of age. Detention (whether by way of sentence or otherwise) may be imposed where, but for the above prohibition, the court would have power to impose a period of imprisonment. The period of such detention must not exceed the maximum period of imprisonment which might otherwise have been imposed.[28] The slightly obscure phrase "whether by way of sentence or otherwise" takes

---

[23] 1975 Act, ss. 218, 431; for a discussion of the effect of this provision see *infra*, Chap. 8.

[24] *Ibid.* s. 205 (2), as amended by 1980 Act, s. 43.

[25] *Ibid.* s. 205 (3).

[26] *Ibid.* s. 205A, as added by 1980 Act, s. 43; and see *supra*, para. 3–02.

[27] *Ibid.* ss. 207 (1) and 415 (1), as amended by 1980 Act, s. 45 (1).

[28] *Ibid.* ss. 207 (2) and 415 (2).

account of the amended definition of "sentence" in the 1975 Act[29] and distinguishes between a period of detention imposed under a direct sentence in respect of a crime or offence, and a period of detention imposed in default of payment of any sum of money or for contempt of court.

3–11   Detention, whether upon a direct sentence, or in default of payment of a sum of money, or for contempt of court, must not be imposed unless the court is of the opinion that no other method of dealing with the person is appropriate: and the court must state its reasons for that opinion, and, except in the case of the High Court, those reasons must be entered in the record of proceedings.[30] To enable the court to form such an opinion it must obtain (from an officer of a local authority or otherwise) such information as it can about the offender's circumstances. It must also take into account any information before it concerning the offender's character and physical and mental condition.[31] In practice this means that a court must at least obtain a social inquiry report before imposing a sentence of detention. Information obtained only from the Crown or the defence is not sufficient.[32] The court is obliged to consider anything contained in a social inquiry report, but is not obliged to follow any recommendations therein.[33]

Place where detention to be served

3–12   In a case where a court by way of a direct sentence imposes detention on a male person for a period of at least 28 days but not exceeding four months, the court must order that the detention be in a detention centre. In any other case it must order that the detention be in a young offenders' institution.[34] That means that detention in a young offenders' institution must be ordered:

    (a)   in all cases of a direct sentence imposed on a male offender where the period of detention is for less than 28 days or for more than four months;

    (b)   in all cases of a direct sentence imposed on a female offender, regardless of the length of the sentence; and

---

[29] 1975 Act, s. 462 (1), as amended by 1980 Act, Sched. 7, para. 76 (c).
[30] *Ibid* ss. 207 (3) and 415 (3).
[31] *Ibid.* ss. 207 (4) and 415 (4), as amended by 1980 Act, s. 45 (1).
[32] *Auld* v. *Herron*, 1969 J.C. 4.
[33] *Scott* v. *MacDonald*, 1961 S.L.T. 257; *Kyle* v. *Cruickshank*, 1961 J.C. 1; *Hogg* v. *Heatlie*, 1962 S.L.T. 39.
[34] 1975 Act, ss. 207 (5) and 415 (5), as amended by 1980 Act, s. 45 (1).

(c)   in all cases where the detention is imposed in default of payment of a sum of money or for contempt of court.

-13   Where detention in a detention centre would be required under the foregoing provisions but the court is of the opinion that:

(a)   the convicted person is physically or mentally unfit to be detained in a detention centre; or

(b)   for any special reason a young offenders' institution is a more appropriate place of detention,

it may order the detention to be in a young offenders' institution. In the latter case the court must state the special reason and, except in the case of the High Court, that reason must be entered in the record of the proceedings.[35] Unlike the now repealed provisions of the 1975 Act relative to borstal training,[36] the 1980 Act contains no provision which obliges the court to call for, or the Secretary of State to provide, a report on an offender's physical and mental condition. Instead, the court is merely required to take into account any information before it concerning these matters.[37] The effect of this, it is submitted, will be that, if the court, either from the information supplied by the Crown or defence or contained in a social inquiry report, or from its own observation of the offender, has no reason to suppose that the offender is unfit for detention in a detention centre, it may pass such a sentence without further inquiry. In any other case, however, it would be appropriate to adjourn the case to obtain either a medical or psychiatric report. In any event, where the Secretary of State is satisfied that a person is physically or mentally unfit to be detained in a detention centre, he may transfer that person to a young offenders' institution.[38]

Where offender already in a detention centre

-14   Where detention is imposed (a) for a period of less than 28 days, and/or (b) other than by way of direct sentence, but the convicted person is already detained in a detention centre, the detention is to be in a detention centre, notwithstanding the terms of the order made by the court.[39]

Concurrent and consecutive periods of detention

-15   Periods of detention imposed at the same time and ordered to

---

[35] 1975 Act, ss. 207 (6) and 415 (6), as amended by 1980 Act, s. 45 (1).
[36] *Ibid.* ss. 204 (2) and 414 (2).
[37] See *supra*, para. 3–11.
[38] 1975 Act, ss. 207 (10) and 415 (10), as amended by 1980 Act, s. 45 (1).
[39] *Ibid.* ss. 207 (7) and 415 (7), as amended by 1980 Act, s. 45 (1).

be consecutive are to be treated as a single period of detention.[40] This provision is of obvious significance only in relation to direct sentences of detention where the consequence would be, for example, that a court would require to order that consecutive periods of three months and two months detention should be served in a young offenders' institution since, treated as a single period of detention, they amount to more than four months. What is not clear from the statutory provisions is what the court should do if, at the same time, it orders consecutive periods of detention, one of, say, two months on a direct sentence, and one of 14 days in default of payment of a fine. Taken separately, these would require to be ordered to be served in a detention centre and in a young offenders' institution respectively,[41] and, taken together, they amount to a period which, as a direct sentence, would fall to be served in a detention centre; but can that be ordered where one of the elements in the total sentence is of a kind where the statute expressly prohibits such an order? It is submitted that, until an authoritative decision is given on this matter, it may be appropriate to allow the direct sentence to play the dominant role, and in the example given above to order detention in a detention centre. A possible justification for this course is that the sentence imposed in default of payment of the fine can at any time be extinguished by payment of the unpaid balance of the fine. Where a person is serving a period of detention in a detention centre when a period of detention is ordered which is:

(a) consecutive to the period being served, and the periods together total more than five months; or

(b) concurrent with the period being served and is for more than five months,

the convicted person will, notwithstanding the terms of any order made by the court when imposing the period of detention, be transferred to a young offenders' institution to serve the remainder of that total period or, as the case may be, of those concurrent periods.[42]

Recall to young offenders' institution on reconviction

3–16 Where a person who has been sentenced to detention under either section 207 or section 415 of the 1975 Act, and who is under

---

[40] 1975 Act, ss. 207 (8) and 415 (8).

[41] See *supra*, para. 3–12.

[42] 1975 Act, ss. 207 (9) and 415 (9), as amended by 1980 Act, s. 45 (1).

supervision following on his release, is convicted of an offence punishable with imprisonment, the court may make an order for his recall. This power is not available where the person is subject to a licence granted under section 60 (1) or section 61 of the Criminal Justice Act 1967.[43] Any such order for recall has the like effect as an order for recall made by the Secretary of State under section 12 of the Criminal Justice (Scotland) Act 1963, that is to say the recall may be for a period not exceeding three months.[44] It is thought that courts rarely, if ever, make use of this power preferring, if a custodial sentence is to be imposed, to impose a direct sentence of detention for whatever period seems appropriate.

RESTRICTIONS ON PASSING SENTENCES OF IMPRISONMENT OR DETENTION

Imprisonment of person not previously so dealt with

‑17   A court must not pass a sentence of imprisonment on a person of or over 21 years of age who has not been previously sentenced to imprisonment or detention by a court in any part of the United Kingdom unless the court considers that no other method of dealing with him is appropriate. For the purpose of determining whether any other method of dealing with such a person is appropriate the court must obtain (from an officer of a local authority or otherwise) such information as it can about the offender's circumstances. It must also take into account any information before it concerning the offender's character and physical and mental condition.[45]

‑18   The foregoing provisions replace prior legislation restricting the imprisonment of first offenders, and now restrict the imprisonment of any adult, whether a first offender or not, who has not previously been sentenced to imprisonment or detention. It is to be noted that the restriction applies where a court is passing a *sentence* of imprisonment, and where the offender has not previously been *sentenced* to imprisonment or detention. Consequently, the restriction does not apply where imprisonment is being imposed in default of payment of a sum of money or for contempt of court, but does apply where any previous imprisonment or detention was imposed for either of these reasons.[46] A possible difficulty may be thought to

---

[43] 1975 Act, ss. 212 (1) and 421 (1), as amended by 1980 Act, Sched. 7, paras. 38 and 67.

[44] Compare *infra*, para. 11–33.

[45] 1980 Act, s. 42 (1); and see *supra*, para. 3–11 and cases referred to therein.

[46] 1975 Act, s. 462 (1), definition of "sentence" as amended by 1980 Act, Sched. 7, para. 76 (*e*); *cf. Sullivan* v. *McLeod*, 1980 S.L.T. (Notes) 99.

arise where a person has not been sentenced to imprisonment or detention prior to the date of the current offence, so that any schedule of previous convictions does not disclose such a sentence, but it transpires that he has subsequently received such a sentence, and may indeed still be undergoing it at the date in question. It is submitted that the wording of section 42 (1) is such that its restrictions would not apply in such a case since the reference to a previous sentence of imprisonment is not restricted in any way as to the date of that sentence save that it must be previous to the new sentence being imposed. It might nonetheless be wise, where a person is presently undergoing a sentence of imprisonment or detention, for the court to ascertain whether or not that sentence, or the conviction to which it relates, is under appeal and, if it is, to proceed as if section 42 (1) did apply; for, if the appeal were to be successful, it could be argued that the spirit if not the letter of the section had not been taken into account in the later case.

3–19   Where a court of summary jurisdiction passes a sentence of imprisonment on any person to whom the above restrictions apply, the court must state the reason for its opinion that no other method of dealing with him is appropriate, and must have that reason entered in the record of the proceedings.[47]

3–20   For the purpose of determining whether a person has been previously sentenced to imprisonment or detention by a court in any part of the United Kingdom the court should (a) disregard a previous sentence of imprisonment which, having been suspended, has not taken effect under section 23 of the Powers of Criminal Courts Act 1973 or under section 19 of the Treatment of Offenders Act (Northern Ireland) 1968, and (b) construe detention as meaning (i) in relation to Scotland, detention in a young offenders' institution or detention centre, (ii) in relation to England and Wales, borstal training or detention in a detention centre, and (iii) in relation to Northern Ireland, detention in a young offenders' centre.[48] The absence of any reference in (i) above to borstal training would seem to imply that a previous sentence of borstal training in Scotland is not to be taken as a previous sentence of detention, with the result that in such a case the court would be

---

[47] 1980 Act, s. 42 (2).
[48] *Ibid.* s. 41 (2) as applied by s. 42 (3).

bound to comply with the restrictions imposed by section 42 (1) of the 1980 Act.

21 The foregoing restrictions do not affect the power of a court to pass sentence on any person for an offence the sentence for which is fixed by law.[49]

Imprisonment or detention of person not legally represented

22 A court must not pass a sentence of imprisonment or of detention in respect of any offence, nor impose imprisonment or detention under section 396 (2) of the 1975 Act in respect of failure to pay a fine, on an accused who is not legally represented in that court and has not been previously sentenced to imprisonment or detention by a court in any part of the United Kingdom,[50] unless the accused either (a) applied for legal aid and the application was refused on the ground that he was not financially eligible, or (b) having been informed of his right to apply for legal aid, and having had the opportunity, failed to do so.[51] Section 396 (2) of the 1975 Act provides for the situation where, on the occasion of the imposition of a fine, a court refuses time to pay and imposes imprisonment or detention when the offender fails to pay. The above restriction, accordingly, does not apply in any other circumstances where a court imposes imprisonment or detention in default of payment of a fine. Difficulties may arise in cases falling under head (b) above if an accused claims that he was not informed of his right to apply for legal aid, and the contrary cannot be satisfactorily established. Probably the best course in such an event would be for the court to defer sentence for a short period to enable the accused then to apply for legal aid should he wish to do so.

23 As with the restriction on imprisoning persons not previously sentenced to imprisonment or detention, the above restriction does not affect the power of a court to pass sentence on any person for an offence the sentence for which is fixed by law.[52]

24 In relation to the above restriction "legal aid" means legal aid for the purposes of any part of the proceedings before the court, and

---

[49] 1980 Act, s. 41 (3) as applied by s. 42 (3).
[50] These words have the meaning described *supra*, in para. 3–20.
[51] 1980 Act, s. 41 (1).
[52] *Ibid.* s. 41 (3).

"legally represented" means represented by counsel or a solicitor at some stage after the accused is found guilty and before he is dealt with by the passing of a sentence of, or by the imposition of, imprisonment or detention.[53]

CHILDREN

3–25 The subject of children, and the imposition of custodial sentences on children, is dealt with in Chapter 5.

---

[53] 1980 Act, s. 41 (4).

CHAPTER 4

MENTALLY DISORDERED OFFENDERS

Duty on prosecutor
Remit to sheriff court

01   Where it appears to the prosecutor in any court before which a person is charged with an offence that the person may be suffering from mental disorder, the prosecutor must bring before the court such evidence as may be available of the mental condition of that person.[1] If the person is charged before a court of summary jurisdiction other than a sheriff court, and the offence charged is one punishable with imprisonment, then, if it appears to the court that the person may be suffering from mental disorder, he must be remitted to the sheriff court in the manner provided by section 286 of the 1975 Act.[2] Mental disorder means mental illness or mental deficiency however caused or manifested.[3]

Remand in hospital

02   Where a court remands or commits for trial a person charged with any offence who appears to the court to be suffering from mental disorder, and the court is satisfied that a hospital is available for his admission and suitable for his detention, the court may, instead of remanding him in custody, commit him to that hospital.[4] Such an order may only be made on the written or oral evidence of a medical practitioner.[5] No provision is made, however, requiring that medical practitioner to possess any special qualification under the Mental Health (Scotland) Act 1960.[6] When such an order is made the hospital must be specified in the warrant and, if the responsible medical officer is satisfied that the person concerned is suffering from mental disorder of a nature or degree which warrants his admission to a hospital under Part IV of the 1960 Act,[7] he must be detained there for the period for which he is remanded or the period of committal, unless previously liberated in due course of

---

[1] 1975 Act, ss. 175 (2), 376 (5).
[2] *Ibid.* s. 376 (4); and see *Herron* v. *McCrimmon*, 1969 S.L.T.(Sh.Ct.) 37.
[3] 1960 Act, s. 6.
[4] 1975 Act, ss. 25 (1), 330 (1); for remands other than for trial, see *infra*, para. 8–14.
[5] *Ibid.* ss. 25 (4), 330 (4).
[6] *cf. infra*, para. 4–11.

law.[8] When the responsible medical officer has examined the person so detained he must report the result of that examination to the court. If the report is to the effect that the person is not suffering from mental disorder of the above nature or degree the court may commit him to any appropriate prison or other institution or otherwise deal with him according to law.[9] The responsible medical officer is any medical practitioner on the staff of the hospital authorised to act as such by the board of management.[10]

Insanity

(a) In bar of trial

4–03 Insanity at the time of a trial is a bar to the trial taking place if the effect of the insanity is to render the accused unfit either to tender a rational plea, or properly to instruct his defence.[11] It is outwith the scope of this work to examine what may or may not amount to insanity in any particular case. However, the procedures which may lead up to a disposal in a case of insanity in bar of trial fall to be mentioned.

4–04 The plea of insanity in bar of trial is normally taken by the defence, in which case it should be intimated as a special defence.[12] It may, however, be put in issue by the prosecutor, or by the court itself. There is authority[13] that the question whether or not an accused is capable of pleading may be left to the jury, but the normal practice is for the court to conduct an inquiry before the accused is called on to plead. If, as a result of that inquiry, the court concludes that an accused is fit to plead, it is not then competent to put that matter to a jury.[14] Evidence at a preliminary inquiry is normally led from two or more psychiatrists who have each independently examined the accused. Where it appears to a court that it is not

---

[7] In general, admission under Part IV of the Act is restricted to those suffering from mental disorder where the disorder is (a) mental deficiency such that the person is incapable of living an independent life or of guarding himself against serious exploitation, or (b) a mental illness other than a persistent disorder which is manifested only by abnormally aggressive or seriously irresponsible conduct. Patients under the age of 21, however, may be detained if they suffer from any mental disorder that requires or is susceptible to treatment (1960 Act, s. 23 (1)).

[8] 1975 Act, ss. 25 (2), 330 (2).

[9] Ibid. ss. 25 (3), 330 (3).

[10] 1960 Act, ss. 53 (1), 111 (1).

[11] Hume, ii. 143, Macdonald, 9, 10, 271, Gordon, 10.42 et seq.; and see H.M.A. v. Brown (1907) 5 Adam 312.

[12] H.M.A. v. Brown, supra; H.M.A. v. Cunningham, 1963 J.C. 80.

[13] H.M.A. v. Brown, supra.

[14] Russell v. H.M.A., 1946 J.C. 37.

practicable or appropriate for the accused to be brought before it for the purpose of determining whether he is insane in bar of trial, the court may order that the case be proceeded with in his absence provided that no objection to such a course is taken by or on behalf of the accused.[15]

4-05 Where any person charged on indictment is found insane so that the trial cannot proceed, or if in the course of the trial it appears to the jury that he is insane, the court must direct a finding to that effect to be recorded.[16] In such a case the court must then order that the person concerned is to be detained in a state hospital, or such other hospital as for special reasons the court may specify.[17] Such an order has the same effect as a hospital order under section 175 of the 1975 Act (see *infra*) together with an order restricting the person's discharge, made without limitation of time.[18] The order will remain in force until the restriction is removed by the Secretary of State. He must be satisfied that the restriction is no longer required for the protection of the public.[19]

4-06 In general the rules relating to insanity in bar of trial apply equally to a person charged summarily in the sheriff court.[20] Where the court is satisfied that the person is insane so that his trial cannot proceed, the court must direct a finding to that effect, and the reasons for that finding, to be recorded. The court then deals with the person by the making of a hospital order under section 376 (2) of the 1975 Act.[21] It is not competent for a person to found on a plea of insanity in bar of trial unless, before the first witness for the prosecution is called, he gives notice to the prosecutor of the plea and of the witnesses by whom he proposes to maintain it. Upon such notice being given the court must, if the prosecutor so moves, adjourn the case.[22] A summary court has the same power as a court of solemn jurisdiction to inquire into an accused person's sanity in his absence (see *supra*, para. 4–04).[23]

4-07 A person who has been found insane in bar of trial, and has

---

[15] 1975 Act, ss. 174 (5), 375 (4).
[16] *Ibid.* s. 174 (1); but see *H.M.A.* v. *Brown and Foss*, 1966 S.L.T. 341.
[17] *Ibid.* s. 174 (3).
[18] *Ibid.* s. 174 (4).
[19] 1960 Act, s. 61 (1).
[20] 1975 Act, s. 375 (1).
[21] *Ibid.* s. 375 (2); *Barr* v. *Herron*, 1968 J.C. 20; *Bain* v. *Smith*, High Court, 19 February 1980.
[22] *Ibid.* s. 375 (3).
[23] *Ibid.* s. 375 (4).

been dealt with accordingly, has not thereby tholed his assize. Should he recover his sanity he may again be put on trial.[24]

(b) At the time of commission of the offence

4-08   When a person is charged on indictment and is found to have committed the act libelled, but to have been insane at the time, he may not be convicted. The jury should be directed to find whether the person was insane at the time, and to declare whether the person has been acquitted by them on account of that insanity.[25] If insanity at the time of commission of the offence is being founded on by the accused he must lodge a special defence to that effect.[26] Where a jury declares that it has acquitted a person on account of his insanity at the time of committing the offence, the court should proceed in the same manner as if the accused had been found insane in bar of trial, that is by ordering his detention in a state hospital, or such other hospital as for special reasons the court may specify.[27]

4-09   Curiously, there are no express statutory provisions to deal with the case where a person is charged summarily in the sheriff court and is found to have committed the act alleged but to have been insane at the time. Section 376 (3) of the 1975 Act provides that, where a person is so charged and the court would have power, on convicting him, to make an order under section 376 (1), then, if the court is satisfied that the person did the act or made the omission charged, it may, if it thinks fit, make such an order without convicting him. This has been construed[28] as meaning that, if a court is satisfied that an offender committed the act charged, but was insane at the time, it should acquit him and proceed to make a hospital or guardianship order. It is submitted that this interpretation of section 376 (3) is not really tenable. The section itself makes no mention of insanity, and does not purport to deal with a situation where the accused person was suffering from mental disorder at the time of the commission of the offence as distinct from the time when he appears before the court. Furthermore, to make an order "without convicting" a person is not the same as to acquit that person.[29]

---

[24] *H.M.A.* v. *Bickerstaff*, 1926 J.C. 65.

[25] 1975 Act, s. 174 (2); *H.M.A.* v. *Mitchell*, 1951 J.C. 53.

[26] *H.M.A.* v. *Cunningham, supra.*

[27] 1975 Act, s. 174 (3).

[28] See, *e.g.* Renton & Brown, para. 20–17.

[29] Compare, for example, the statutory provisions relating to absolute discharge and probation in 1975 Act, ss. 383, 384.

10 It is submitted, accordingly, that there is no statutory provision to deal with the situation where an accused person in a summary prosecution establishes that he was insane at the time of commission of the alleged offence. Nor, it is also submitted, has there ever been any such statutory provision. The provisions to be found in the Lunatics (Scotland) Act 1857, the Criminal Justice (Scotland) Act 1949, and the Mental Health (Scotland) Act 1960 all relate to cases on indictment only and are silent with regard to summary procedure. Inquiries through the Crown Office suggest that the normal practice in cases where it is known that a defence of insanity at the time of commission of the offence is likely to be put forward (and they are very rare) is either to take no proceedings at all or, if it appears to be in the public interest, to proceed by way of petition. There is no statutory provision requiring a defence of insanity at the time of commission of the offence to be intimated before a trial begins,[30] and in such a case, if the defence were established, a question would arise as to how the case should be disposed of. It is submitted that the proper course would simply be to find the accused not guilty on the ground that his insanity prevented him from having the necessary *mens rea*. In the absence of statutory provision it would not be competent to proceed to make any kind of hospital order (and see *infra,* para. 9–90).

Hospital orders and guardianship orders

11 Where a person is convicted in the High Court or the sheriff court of an offence, other than an offence the sentence for which is fixed by law, punishable by that court with imprisonment, the court may, subject to certain conditions, make an order (a "hospital order") authorising his admission to and detention in such hospital as may be specified in the order, or place him under the guardianship of such a local authority or such other person approved by a local authority as may be so specified (a "guardianship order"). The conditions are:

(a) the court must be satisfied, on the written or oral evidence of two medical practitioners that the offender is suffering from mental disorder of a nature or degree which, in the case of a person under 21 years of age, would warrant his admission to hospital or his

---

[30] Compare 1975 Act, ss. 339 and 375 (3); and see *Lambie* v. *H.M.A.*, 1973 J.C. 53.

reception into guardianshi;) under Part IV of the 1960 Act;[31] and

(b) the court must be of the opinion, having regard to all the circumstances including the nature of the offence and the character and antecedents of the offender, and to the other available methods of dealing with him, that the most suitable method of disposing of the case is by means of such an order.[32]

Of the two medical practitioners at least one must be approved for the purposes of section 27 of the 1960 Act by a health board as having special experience in the diagnosis or treatment of mental disorder.[33] The power to make an order is exercisable by the High Court in cases remitted to it from the sheriff court as well as in cases originating in that court.[34] A hospital order should not be made unless the court is satisfied that the hospital in question is available for the person's admission within 28 days of the making of such an order.[35] Similarly, a guardianship order should not be made unless the court is satisfied that the local authority, or any other person involved, is willing to receive the offender into guardianship.[36]

4–12 A state hospital should not be specified in a hospital order unless the court is satisfied that the offender, on account of his dangerous, violent and criminal propensities, requires treatment under conditions of special security, and cannot suitably be cared for in a hospital other than a state hospital. Evidence to that effect must be given by the medical practitioners whose evidence is taken into account when deciding whether or not to make a hospital order.[37]

4–13 A hospital order or guardianship order must specify the form of mental disorder, being mental illness or mental deficiency or both, from which the offender is found by the court to be suffering. No such order may be made unless the offender is described by each of the medical practitioners whose evidence is taken into account as suffering from the same form of mental disorder, whether or not he

---

[31] See *supra*, note 7.
[32] 1975 Act, ss. 175 (1), 376 (1).
[33] *Ibid.* ss. 176 (1), 377 (1).
[34] *Ibid.* s. 175 (1).
[35] *Ibid.* ss. 175 (3), 376 (6).
[36] *Ibid.* ss. 175 (5), 376 (8).
[37] *Ibid.* ss. 175 (4), 376 (7).

is also described by either of them as suffering from the other form.[38]

14 Where a hospital order or guardianship order is made the court may not pass sentence of imprisonment (which includes any sentence or order for detention), or impose a fine or make a probation order. It may, however, make any other order which it would otherwise have power to make.[39] That is to say, it may for example make an order for forfeiture of an article, or for disqualification for holding or obtaining a driving licence.

15 The court by which a hospital order is made may give such directions as it thinks fit for the conveyance of the patient to a place of safety and his detention therein pending his admission to the hospital within the period of 28 days mentioned above. However, a direction for the conveyance of a patient to a residential establishment provided by a local authority under Part IV of the Social Work (Scotland) Act 1968 must not be given unless the court is satisfied that the authority is willing to receive the patient therein.[40]

Medical evidence

16 Apart from the requirement that has already been noted concerning the qualifications of at least one of the medical practitioners (see *supra*, para. 4–11), there are certain other statutory requirements in relation to medical evidence taken into account for the purpose of making a hospital order, or a guardianship order.

17 A report in writing purporting to be signed by a medical practitioner may be received in evidence without proof of the signature or qualifications of the practitioner. The court may, however, in any case require that the practitioner by whom such a report was signed be called to give oral evidence.[41]

18 Where a written report is tendered in evidence otherwise than by or on behalf of the accused, a copy of it must be given to his counsel or solicitor. If the accused is unrepresented, the substance of the report must be disclosed to him or, where he is a child under

---

[38] 1975 Act, ss. 175 (6), 376 (9).
[39] *Ibid.* ss. 175 (7), 376(10).
[40] *Ibid.* ss. 177, 378.
[41] *Ibid.* ss. 176 (2), 377 (2).

16 years of age, to his parent or guardian if present in court. In any case the accused may require that the practitioner by whom the report was signed be called to give oral evidence. Furthermore, evidence to rebut that contained in the report may be called by or on behalf of the accused. Where the court is of opinion that further time is necessary in the interests of the accused for consideration of a report or its substance the case must be adjourned.[42]

4–19   For the purpose of calling evidence to rebut the evidence contained in a report that has been tendered otherwise than by or on behalf of the accused, arrangements may be made by him or on his behalf, where he is detained in a hospital, for his examination by any medical practitioner. Any such examination may be made in private.[43]

Restriction on discharge from hospital

4–20   Where a hospital order is made and it appears to the court, having regard to the nature of the offence, the antecedents of the person concerned, and the risk that as a result of his mental disorder he would commit offences if set at large, that it is necessary for the protection of the public so to do, the court may make an order restricting that person's discharge. Such an order may be made either without limit of time or during such period as may be specified in the order.[44] Such an order must not be made unless the medical practitioner approved by the health board for the purposes of section 27 of the 1960 Act has given evidence orally before the court.[45]

4–21   An order restricting discharge has the effect of subjecting the patient to the special restrictions set out in section 60 (3) of the 1960 Act. These are:

(a)   none of the provisions of Part IV of that Act relating to the duration, renewal and expiration of authority for the detention of patients apply, and the patient continues to be liable to be detained until he is absolutely discharged by the Secretary of State;

(b)   power to grant leave of absence to the patient, and power to transfer the patient to another hospital may

---

[42] 1975 Act. ss. 176 (3). 377 (3).
[43] *Ibid.* ss. 176 (4), 377 (4).
[44] *Ibid.* ss. 178 (1), 379 (1).
[42] 1975 Act, ss. 176 (3), 377 (3).

be exercised only with the consent of the Secretary of State; and

(c) the power to take an absconding patient into custody and to return him to hospital may be exercised at any time, and cannot be defeated by the length of time that the patient contrives to remain at large.[46]

22 Where an order restricting discharge is in force it is not competent to make a guardianship order in respect of the same person. Where, under section 58 (4) of the 1960 Act the hospital order containing the order restricting discharge ceases to have effect upon the making of another hospital order, that subsequent order is to have the same effect in relation to the order restricting discharge as the previous hospital order. It is however competent in such a case for the court making the subsequent order to make another order restricting discharge to have effect on the expiration of the previous such order.[47]

---

[46] Compare 1960 Act, s. 36 (3).
[47] 1975 Act, ss. 178 (3), 379 (3).

CHAPTER 5

CHILDREN

Definition of "child"

5–01   For the purposes of the 1975 Act the word "child" has, with a few exceptions, the meaning assigned to it by section 30 of the 1968 Act.[1] A child is there stated to mean:

(a)   a child who has not attained the age of 16 years;

(b)   a child over the age of 16 years who has not attained the age of 18 years and in respect of whom a supervision requirement of a children's hearing is in force under Part III of the 1968 Act; and

(c)   a child whose case has been referred to a children's hearing in pursuance of Part V of that Act. That is, generally, a child whose case has been transferred from a juvenile court in England or Wales.

Prosecution of children

5–02   Since the coming into force of the 1968 Act most children who have committed offences are dealt with by being referred to a children's hearing, and therefore do not appear in court. Indeed, no child may be prosecuted for any offence except on the instructions of the Lord Advocate, or at his instance; and any such prosecution is competent only in the High Court or the sheriff court.[2] In practice children under the age of 16 are rarely prosecuted unless the offence is sufficiently serious to merit being taken on indictment, though they may on occasions be prosecuted summarily when the offence is one where the prosecutor wishes to seek some particular penalty which cannot be imposed by a children's hearing, such as forfeiture or disqualification for holding or obtaining a driving licence. Prosecution is more common in the case of children between the ages of 16 and 18 who are subject to a supervision requirement. On occasions a child may be prosecuted, either summarily or on indictment, along with an adult in respect of an offence or offences alleged to have been committed by them jointly. However, it is not obligatory to prosecute a child in such circumstances,[3] and the matter is one for the discretion of the prosecutor.

---

[1] 1975 Act, s. 462.

[2] 1968 Act, s. 31(1).

[3] *Ibid.* Sched. 2, para. 10, repealing s. 50 of the Children and Young Persons (Scotland) Act 1937.

Finding of guilt

–03   The words "conviction" and "sentence" must not be used in relation to children dealt with summarily. Instead they are to be replaced by "a finding of guilt" and "an order made upon such a finding".[4] Every court in dealing with a child who is brought before it as an offender must have regard to the welfare of the child and must, in a proper case, take steps for removing him from undesirable surroundings.[5]

Remit to children's hearing

–04   Where a child who is not subject to a supervision requirement is charged with an offence and pleads guilty to, or is found guilty of, that offence the court, instead of making an order on that plea or finding, may remit the case to the reporter of the local authority to arrange for the disposal of the case by a children's hearing. Alternatively, the court may request the reporter to arrange a children's hearing for the purpose of obtaining their advice as to the treatment of the child.[6] In that event the court, after consideration of the advice received, may either dispose of the case itself or remit the case to the hearing for disposal.[7]

–05   Where a child who is subject to a supervision requirement is charged with an offence and pleads guilty to, or is found guilty of, that offence the High Court may, and the sheriff court must, request the reporter to arrange a children's hearing for the purpose of obtaining their advice. Where that is done the case may be disposed of in either of the ways mentioned above.[8]

–06   A summary court may also follow the same procedure in the case of a person who is not subject to a supervision requirement but who is over the age of 16 and is not within six months of attaining the age of 18. If, however, in such a case the court wishes to remit the case to the hearing for disposal, it may only do so where the hearing have so advised.[9]

–07   Where a court has remitted a case to the reporter the jurisdiction of the court in respect of the child or person ceases, and his case stands referred to a children's hearing.[10]

---

[4] 1975 Act, s. 429.
[5] *Ibid.* ss. 172, 371.
[6] *Ibid.* ss. 173 (1), 372 (1).
[7] *Ibid.* ss. 173 (2), 372 (2).
[8] *Ibid.* s. 173 (3), as amended by 1980 Act, Sched. 7, para. 35, and s. 372 (3).
[9] *Ibid.* s. 373.
[10] *Ibid.* ss. 173 (4), 372 (4).

5–08   None of the foregoing disposals applies to a case in respect of an offence the sentence for which is fixed by law.[11]

5–09   Where a court decides, with or without a prior remit for advice, to deal with a case involving a child itself, its powers of disposal will depend on the age of the child. If the child is over the age of 16 all of the powers of disposal applicable to young offenders will be available to the court. These are dealt with elsewhere in this volume. If, however, the child is under the age of 16 some, but not all, of these powers will be available. The following are the powers that are applicable to such children.

Non-custodial disposals

5–10   A court may deal with a child by an absolute discharge, by an admonition, by the making of a probation order, or by the imposition of a fine. Further, a court may defer making an order in respect of a child just as it may defer sentence in the case of an older offender. Although in general the above powers may be exercised in the manner appropriate to older offenders, two special features applicable to children should be noted. In the first place, where a social inquiry report has been prepared for the assistance of the court and the child is not represented by counsel or solicitor, a copy of the report need not be given to the child but one must be given to his parent or guardian if present in court.[12] In the second place, where a child has been fined and would, if he were an adult, be liable to be imprisoned in default of payment, the court may, if it considers that none of the other methods by which the case may legally be dealt with is suitable, order that the child be detained for such period, not exceeding one month, as may be specified in the order in a place chosen by the local authority in whose area the court is situated.[13] It should be added that, since a child is by definition also a person under the age of 21, the general restrictions applicable in such cases before any form of detention can be ordered in default of payment of a fine will also apply.[14] It is submitted that section 41 (1) of the 1980 Act (restriction on imprisonment of person not legally represented) will also apply in the case of a child.

5–11   Prior to the passing of the 1968 Act it was competent to deal with cases involving children by fining the parent, or by ordering the

[11] 1975 Act, ss. 173 (5), 372 (5).
[12] *Ibid.* ss. 192, 393.
[13] *Ibid.* s. 406 (made applicable to fines on indictment by 1980 Act, s. 47 (2)).
[14] See *supra*, para. 2–92.

parent to give security for his co-operation in securing the child's good behaviour. These are now no longer competent.[15]

Custodial disposals

-12 Where any person under the age of 18 is convicted of murder he must be sentenced to be detained without limit of time, and is liable to be detained in such place, and under such conditions, as the Secretary of State may direct.[16]

-13 Apart from the foregoing case, where a child is convicted on indictment and the court is of opinion that no other method of dealing with him is appropriate, it may sentence him to be detained for a period which must be specified in the sentence. During that period the child is liable to be detained in such place and on such conditions as the Secretary of State may direct.[17]

-14 Where a child is charged summarily before the sheriff and pleads guilty, or is found guilty, the sheriff may order the child to be committed for such period not exceeding two years as may be specified in the order to such a place as the Secretary of State may direct for the purpose of undergoing residential training. Where such an order is made the child is liable during that period to be detained in that place subject to such conditions as the Secretary of State may direct.[18]

---

[15] 1968 Act, Sched. 2, para. 17, Sched. 9, and 1975 Act, Sched. 10.

[16] 1975 Act, s. 205 (2), as amended by 1980 Act, s. 43.

[17] *Ibid.* s. 206 (1), as amended by 1980 Act, s. 44.

[18] *Ibid.* s. 413.

CHAPTER 6

ROAD TRAFFIC OFFENCES

6–01 It is not the intention in this chapter to attempt to set out the financial and custodial penalties which are available to courts dealing with road traffic offences. These are many and various, and are moreover subject to frequent change by the passage of new legislation. For those who seek to know the maximum penalty for a particular offence there is really no alternative to a diligent study of the relevant statutes. Instead, this chapter will concentrate mainly on the two orders which are peculiar to road traffic cases, and which have generated over the years a considerable volume of judicial decision — and on occasions misunderstanding: these are endorsement and disqualification. The problems engendered by these matters have been added to recently by the new "totting-up" provisions introduced by the Transport Act 1981. The effect of these provisions is far from clear and in many instances must await authoritative judicial interpretation. The passage of the Act through Parliament occurred after this chapter was in its first draft and, at the time of going to press, no date has been fixed for the introduction of the relevant provisions. Consequently, since the parts of this chapter affected by the changes may for a little time have a continuing relevance, it has not been completely revised. All that has been done is to note those portions which will be repealed or amended by the new provisions and, as an appendix to the chapter, to set out the principal new provisions themselves together with some tentative comment as to their interpretation and effect.

6–02 Although in many instances the rules governing endorsement and disqualification are the same, there are also important differences and these must always be kept clearly in mind. Thus, although disqualification may sometimes be obligatory, and sometimes discretionary, endorsement, where appropriate at all, is always obligatory. So too, although a court may sometimes order endorsement without disqualification, it may never order disqualification without endorsement. Again, although in one instance ("totting-up" cases) a court may refrain from disqualification if mitigating circumstances are present, in all other obligatory disqualification cases, and always in cases of endorsement, it may refrain from making the order only if special reasons are established.

ENDORSEMENT

Offences involving obligatory endorsement

03   The offences which involve obligatory endorsement are set out in the Fourth Schedule to the Road Traffic Act 1972. That Act has been extensively amended by subsequent legislation including the Road Traffic Act 1974, and care must always be taken to keep these subsequent amendments in mind. The general scheme of Part I of the Fourth Schedule is to set out in columns the various offences created by the Act, and to indicate as appropriate those where endorsement is obligatory. In some instances the word "obligatory" in relation to a particular offence is qualified in some way. In such cases endorsement is obligatory only if the condition or conditions referred to in the qualification are satisfied. That does not mean, however, that endorsement becomes discretionary if the conditions are not satisfied. There is no statutory provision for discretionary endorsement and, if there is to be no obligatory endorsement, there should be no endorsement at all.

04   The following are the cases where the word "obligatory" is qualified:

(a)   Failing to comply with traffic directions (1972 Act, s. 22). Endorsement is obligatory if the offence is committed in respect of a motor vehicle by a failure to comply with a direction of a constable or an indication given by a sign specified in regulations.

(b)   Leaving vehicles in dangerous positions (1972 Act, s. 24). Endorsement is obligatory if the offence is committed in respect of a motor vehicle.

(c)   Contravention of construction and use regulations (1972 Act, s. 40 (5)). Endorsement is obligatory if the offence is committed by using, or causing or permitting the use of, any motor vehicle or trailer so as to cause, or to be likely to cause, danger by the condition of the vehicle or its parts or accessories, the number of passengers carried by it, or the weight, distribution, packing or adjustment of its load. Endorsement is also obligatory in the case of a breach of a requirement as to brakes, steering-gear, or tyres, where the vehicle is used for any purpose for which it is so unsuitable as to cause or be likely to cause danger, or in respect of an offence of carrying on a goods vehicle a load which, by reason of its insecurity or position, is likely to cause danger. However, there should be no endorsement where the offender proves that he did not know, and had no reasonable cause to suspect that the facts of the case were such that the offence would be committed.

(d)   Driving without a licence (1972 Act, s. 84 (1)). Endorsement is obligatory where the offence is committed by driving a motor vehicle in a case where either no licence authorising the driving could have been granted to the offender or, if a provisional (but no other) licence to drive could have been granted to him, the driving would not have complied with the conditions thereof.

6–05   Other offences involving obligatory endorsement are set out in Parts II and III of the Fourth Schedule. Some of these are offences only under English law. Those which are offences in Scotland are:

(1)   Culpable homicide by the driver of a motor vehicle;

(2)   Stealing or attempting to steal a motor vehicle;

(3)   An offence under section 13 (4) of the Road Traffic Regulation Act 1967 (contravention of traffic regulations on special roads) committed in respect of a motor vehicle otherwise than by unlawfully stopping or allowing the vehicle to remain at rest on a part of a special road on which vehicles are in certain circumstances permitted to remain at rest;

(4)   An offence under section 23 (5) of the same Act (contravention of pedestrian crossing regulations) committed in respect of a motor vehicle;

(5)   An offence under section 25 (2) of the same Act (failure to obey a sign exhibited by school crossing patrol) committed in respect of a motor vehicle;

(6)   An offence under section 26 (6) or 26A (5) of the same Act (contravention of order prohibiting or restricting use of street playground by vehicles) committed in respect of a motor vehicle; and

(7)   An offence punishable by virtue of section 78A of the same Act (speeding offences under that and other Acts).

Endorsement of licence

-06   Where a person is convicted of an offence involving obligatory endorsement as above described the court must order that particulars of the conviction, and, if the court orders him to be disqualified, particulars of the disqualification, should be endorsed on any licence held by him. Particulars of any conviction or disqualification so endorsed may be produced as prima facie evidence of the conviction or disqualification.[1] If no order for disqualification is made the conviction need not be endorsed if the court is satisfied that there are special reasons for not doing so.[2] The wording of these requirements has been amended by the 1981 Act to reflect the changes introduced by section 19 of that Act (Sched. 9, paras. 6 and 7; and see appendix to this chapter).

-07   Although the Act refers to endorsement of "any" licence held by the offender, it is submitted that this can refer only to full or provisional licences issued under the 1972 Act.[3] Thus an endorsement may not be made on a heavy goods vehicle licence, or a foreign licence. However, whether an offender is at the time of conviction the holder of a licence under the 1972 Act or not, an order for endorsement operates as an order that any licence he may then hold or may subsequently obtain shall be so endorsed.[4] Consequently, although no actual endorsement may be made on, for example, a foreign driving licence, the order should still be made since it may later prove to be of significance in relation to a "totting-up" disqualification.

Production of licence

-08   When a person who is the holder of a licence is prosecuted for an offence involving obligatory endorsement he must produce it to the court. He may do this in one of three ways — by causing it to be delivered to the clerk of court not later than the day before the date of the hearing, by posting it by registered or recorded delivery so as to reach the clerk of court not later than the day before the hearing,

---

[1] 1972 Act, s. 101 (1).
[2] *Ibid.* s. 101 (2); for "special reasons" see *infra*, paras. 6–27 to 6–32.
[3] See definition of "licence" in 1972 Act, s. 110.
[4] 1972 Act, s. 101 (3).

or by having it with him at the hearing. If he is convicted of the offence the court must, before making any order for endorsement, require the licence to be produced to it,[5] and, if the offender fails to do so, a constable may require him to produce it and, upon its being produced, may seize it and deliver it to the court (1972 Act, s. 161 (3A), as added by 1981 Act, s. 22). The requirement to have a licence produced, which was introduced by the Road Traffic Act 1972, has caused some uncertainty as to the procedure which should be followed when an offender pleads guilty by letter but has not complied with any of the requirements as to production of his licence. If, notwithstanding his written plea of guilty, he still attends court in person, there is no problem: he can then be required to produce his licence. But what if he does not attend court? The papers which accompany the complaint that is sent to a person charged with an offence involving obligatory endorsement contain instructions about production of the licence, and the view is held in some quarters that this amounts to a "requirement" to produce the licence, with the result that, if the licence is not produced, the court may nonetheless proceed to sentence the offender in absence, and to order endorsement of his licence. It is submitted that this view is erroneous. The obligation on the court to require production of the licence arises only if the offender is convicted, and that cannot take place until the hearing of the case in court, which will inevitably be some time after the prosecutor has sent the complaint and the accompanying instructions to the accused person. Consequently, it is submitted that the proper practice in such cases is to record the conviction and to defer sentence for a week or two so that the requirement to produce his licence can be intimated to the offender. If, at the adjourned diet, he has still failed to produce his licence the court may then order its endorsement, and the consequences of non-production will come into effect.

Consequences of non-production

6–09   If an offender fails to produce his licence in any of the ways described above he is guilty of an offence unless he satisfies the court that he has applied for a new licence and has not received it. If he fails so to satisfy the court his licence must be suspended from the time when its production was required until it is produced to the court, and it is, while suspended, of no effect.[5] The consequence of

---

[5] 1972 Act, s. 101 (4).

this is that a person who drives a motor vehicle while his licence is so suspended will be guilty of an offence under section 84 of the 1972 Act. Quite frequently an offender who has failed to produce his licence will say, by way of explanation, that he has lost it. Not only is this not an excuse sanctioned by the statute, but it may well be no more than a device to prevent the court from seeing the endorsements which the licence may contain. It is submitted that in such a case the proper course is to suspend the offender's licence until it is produced to the court: if it is genuinely lost the offender will then have to apply for a new licence, and produce it as soon as it is received.

Examination of licence

6–10   Where a person is convicted of an offence involving obligatory endorsement and his licence is produced to the court, then in determining what order to make the court may take into consideration particulars of any previous conviction or disqualification endorsed on the licence.[6] This power is not affected by the provisions of what are now section 311 (1) (notice of penalties) and section 357 (1) (schedule of previous convictions) of the Criminal Procedure (Scotland) Act 1975.[7] Thus, if the necessary conditions are satisfied the court may order a "totting-up" disqualification notwithstanding that the prosecutor has not himself libelled the relevant previous convictions, and has not served the appropriate notice of penalties.[8] Since, under the 1981 Act, the date when an offence was committed gains a new significance, examination of an offender's licence becomes even more important, that not being information that is contained in a schedule of previous convictions. So too, where an offender is liable to a minimum three year disqualification in respect of a second or subsequent drink/driving offence committed within 10 years (see *infra*, para. 6–16), that disqualification may be imposed notwithstanding that the notice of penalties served by the prosecutor gives notice of liability to a minimum of only one year's disqualification.[9]

Absolute discharge and probation orders

6–11   It is now competent to make an order for endorsement and,

---

[6] 1972 Act, s. 101 (4A).
[7] *Ibid.* s. 101 (8).
[8] *Urry* v. *Gibb*, 1979 S.L.T. (Notes) 19.
[9] *Campbell* v. *McLeod*, 1975 S.L.T. (Notes) 6.

where appropriate, for disqualification, in cases where a person is granted an absolute discharge or made the subject of a probation order. Notwithstanding the provisions of sections 191 and 392 of the Criminal Procedure (Scotland) Act 1975, such a person is to be treated as if he had been convicted for the purposes of sections 93 (disqualification) and 101 (endorsement) of the 1972 Act.[10] By a curious oversight the foregoing provisions, introduced by the 1980 Act, appear to have been the work of a draughtsman who was unaware that the 1972 Act had already been amended and added to by the Road Traffic Act 1974. Consequently, there are now two subsections (8) to each of sections 93 and 101 of the 1972 Act!

Disqualification and endorsement as penalties

6–12   If, *per incuriam*, a prosecutor fails to serve a notice of penalties on a person who is subsequently convicted of an offence involving obligatory endorsement, there is clear authority for the proposition that, if the offence also attracts obligatory or discretionary disqualification, an order for such disqualification may not be made.[11] Disqualification is a penalty and, as such, notice of its possible imposition must be given. There may, however, be some doubt about whether endorsement should similarly be regarded as a penalty. Although that view has been expressed in England,[12] there is some Scottish authority for the proposition that endorsement is merely a recording of a conviction and not a penalty in its own right.[13] The significance of an endorsement, of course, is that it may count then, or upon a subsequent conviction, as a qualifying endorsement for a possible "totting-up" disqualification. Such a disqualification is, of course, a true penalty but, as has been seen, the effect of subsections (4A) and (8) of section 101 is that it may be imposed in the absence of a notice of penalties. Standing that, there seems a certain illogicality in holding that the ordering of the relevant endorsements themselves can only proceed upon a proper notice of penalties. However, the matter is one which awaits an authoritative decision in Scotland.

General   DISQUALIFICATION

6–13   Orders for disqualification fall generally into two categories: those where the disqualification is obligatory, and those where the

---

[10] 1972 Act, ss. 93 (8) and 101 (8), as added by 1980 Act, s. 55.
[11] *Coogans* v. *MacDonald*, 1954 J.C. 98.
[12] *Bell* v. *Ingham* [1968] 2 All E.R. 333.
[13] *Pirie* v. *Rivard*, 1976 S.L.T. (Sh. Ct.) 59.

disqualification is discretionary. With the exception of a "totting-up" disqualification all offences involving disqualification are also offences involving obligatory endorsement. The scheme of the 1972 Act in relation to disqualification is similar to that in relation to endorsement; that is to say that the appropriate column of Part I of Schedule 4 shows, as appropriate, those offences in respect of which disqualification is either obligatory or discretionary. As with endorsements certain of those entries are qualified by conditions or circumstances relating to the offence. Certain other offences involving obligatory and discretionary disqualification are listed in Parts II and III of the Schedule.

Obligatory disqualification

-14   Where a person is convicted of an offence involving obligatory disqualification the court must order him to be disqualified for such period not less than 12 months as the court thinks fit unless the court for special reasons thinks fit to order him to be disqualified for a shorter period or not to order him to be disqualified.[14] It follows from the wording of this subsection in the Act that, in such cases, the court may order the offender to be disqualified for more than 12 months if it thinks fit.

-15   The offences involving obligatory disqualification are as follows:

(1)   Culpable homicide by the driver of a vehicle (Part II of Schedule 4);

(2)   Causing death by reckless driving (section 1);

(3)   Reckless driving if committed within three years after a previous conviction of an offence either under section 1 or 2 (section 2);

(4)   Driving or attempting to drive when unfit through drink or drugs (section 5 (1));

(5)   Driving or attempting to drive with more than the permitted blood/alcohol level (section 6 (1));

(6)   Failing to provide a specimen of blood or urine for a laboratory test where it is shown that at the relevant time the offender was driving or attempting to drive a motor vehicle (section 9 (3)), (now section 8 (7), by virtue of the amendments made by the 1981 Act);

(7)   Motor racing and speed trials on highways (section 14).

---

[14] 1972 Act, s. 93 (1).

6–16   Where a person is convicted of one of the offences numbered (4), (5) or (6) in the preceding paragraph, and he has within the 10 years immediately preceding the commission of that offence been convicted of any such offence, he must, in the absence of special reasons, be disqualified for a minimum period of three years.[15] By virtue of section 93 (8) of the 1972 Act (added by section 55 of the 1980 Act) the obligation to disqualify for at least three years will arise even where, on the previous occasion, the offender was granted an absolute discharge or placed on probation. That apart, it is to be noted that, so far as the previous offence is concerned, the section refers only to the offender having been convicted. It would appear to follow, therefore, that a minimum three year disqualification must be imposed even where, on the previous occasion, no disqualification was ordered because of special reasons. It is also to be noted that the period of 10 years is calculated back from the date of *commission* of the second offence, though, so far as the earlier offence is concerned, the qualifying date is the date of *conviction*. Thus an offender could be liable to a three year disqualification even where more than 10 years had elapsed between the dates of commission of the two relevant offences.

Discretionary disqualification

6–17   Apart from the offences noted *supra*, para. 6–15, all other offences involving obligatory endorsement also involve discretionary disqualification. In such cases the court may order the offender to be disqualified for such period as it thinks fit.[16] The various qualifications noted in relation to endorsement (*supra*, para. 6–4) also apply in relation to discretionary disqualification.

"Totting-up" disqualification

(The whole system of "totting-up" disqualification has been radically altered by the provisions of section 19 of the 1981 Act. What follows in the next nine paragraphs describes the practice as it was prior to the introduction of that Act. For the new provisions reference should be made to the appendix to this chapter.)

6–18   Where a person convicted of an offence involving obligatory or

---

[15] 1972 Act, s. 93 (4).
[16] *Ibid*. s. 93 (2).

discretionary disqualification has within the three years immediately preceding the commission of the offence been convicted on not less than two occasions of any such offence, and particulars of the convictions have been ordered to be endorsed on his licence, the court must order him to be disqualified for such period not less than six months as the court thinks fit.[17] This is popularly known as a "totting-up" disqualification. In such a case the court may order the offender to be disqualified for a shorter period or may refrain from disqualifying him at all if it is satisfied, having regard to all the circumstances, that there are grounds for mitigating the normal consequences of the conviction.[17]

-19   Although the wording of section 93 (3) is similar to that in section 93 (4) (compulsory three year disqualification), it is to be noted that the former subsection refers to previous convictions particulars of which "have been ordered to be endorsed". It follows that a previous conviction will not qualify where, for special reasons, no order for endorsement was made. Furthermore, under section 93 (3) the previous convictions must have occurred "on not less than two occasions". That is to say, an offender will not be liable to a totting-up disqualification if he has two previous endorsed convictions but both were incurred on the same occasion.[18] It should be noted that the subsection 93 (8) added by the 1980 Act applies also to cases falling under section 93 (3). Thus, a previous offence may qualify even if it was dealt with by an absolute discharge or by the making of a probation order, provided that endorsement of the offender's licence was ordered at the same time. Furthermore, unless there are mitigating circumstances, the third offence will attract the compulsory six months disqualification even where it itself is being dealt with by an absolute discharge or probation.

-20   The period of any disqualification imposed under section 93 (3) must be in addition to any other period of disqualification imposed (whether previously or on the same occasion).[19] This is the only exception to what is otherwise the normal rule, namely that a disqualification, obligatory or discretionary, cannot be made consecutive to any other period of disqualification, nor may it be postponed in any way at all.[20] Thus, for example, if a court is

---

[17] 1972 Act, s. 93 (3); for mitigating factors see *infra*, paras. 6–22 to 6–26.
[18] *cf. R.* v. *Rogers* [1953] 1 All E.R. 206.
[19] 1972 Act, s. 93 (5).
[20] *Williamson* v. *MacMillan*, 1962 S.L.T. 63.

sentencing an offender for a contravention of section 99 (*b*) (driving while disqualified) and it wishes to increase the existing period of disqualification, it may only do so by ordering a period of disqualification which will itself extend beyond the termination of the existing disqualification. So too — and this is not an uncommon situation — if a court is asked to postpone a period of disqualification for a short time, to allow the offender to carry out an important business trip, or even simply to drive his car home after the hearing, there is no power to accede to that request. The answer in such a case, if the court is disposed to be sympathetic, is to defer sentence for the appropriate period and then to impose the disqualification together with any other penalty thereafter (see also *infra*, paras. 6–48 and 9–42).

6–21   Where a "totting-up" disqualification is being imposed it must be made to run consecutively to any existing disqualification, or to any new disqualification imposed at the same time as the totting-up. Thus, for example, if an offender falls under the "totting-up" provisions by reason of having committed an offence involving obligatory disqualification, he must be disqualified for at least 12 months in respect of that offence, and for a further six months under section 93(3), making at least 18 months in all. Furthermore, it has been held in England[21] that if, on the occasion when section 93(3) comes into operation, the offender is convicted of more than one offence involving obligatory or discretionary disqualification, he should be disqualified for consecutive periods of six months in respect of each offence. It is submitted that this is a correct view since section 93 (3) refers to a person being convicted of "an offence" rather than "offences". However, the question has not been decided in Scotland and it is understood that it is common practice to treat the complaint, which may include several charges, as qualifying for the section 93 (3) disqualification rather than the individual charges themselves. Even if not strictly correct such an approach can perhaps be justified on the basis that the court might readily find mitigating reasons for not imposing a multiplicity of consecutive disqualifications. However it should be noted that liability to a "totting-up" disqualification is not extinguished once it has been incurred.[22] A person may commit a number of "third" offences on different occasions within the three year period, and

---

[21] *R.* v. *McNulty* [1964] 3 All E.R. 713.
[22] *Fearon* v. *Sydney* [1966] 2 All E.R. 694.

may be convicted in respect of them on different dates and perhaps in different courts. In each case he will be liable to a "totting-up" disqualification and, if imposed, that will require to be consecutive to any other "totting-up" disqualification imposed previously.

Mitigating circumstances

–22   Where an offender comes under the provisions of section 93 (3) the court must order him to be disqualified for such period not less than six months as the court thinks fit, unless the court is satisfied, having regard to all the circumstances, that there are grounds for mitigating the normal consequences of the conviction. In that event the court may order him to be disqualified for a shorter period, or may make no order for disqualification. The wording of the subsection makes it clear that, in distinction to cases where special reasons must be found, the court is given a wide discretion to consider mitigating factors. Furthermore, unlike special reasons, these may be factors relating to the offender rather than to the offence. The distinction has been expressed by the High Court of Justiciary as follows:

"This clear distinction in language between subs. (3) and subs. (1) suggests very plainly that the ambit of the discretion entrusted to a sheriff in the cases falling within subs. (3) is materially wider than the limited discretion which is reposed in the sheriff in cases falling within subs. (1)".[23]

–23   In considering the use of this discretion it must be borne in mind that the primary purpose of section 93 (3) is not to penalise serious offences. That can and, it is submitted, should be done by imposing an appropriate disqualification for the offence itself under subsection (1) or subsection (2). The purpose of section 93 (3) is to deter and, where that fails, punish those who repetitively violate the Road Traffic Act. Thus the previous offences, and indeed the instant offence, which bring an offender under the subsection may themselves all be comparatively minor. That in itself, it is submitted, should rarely if ever be regarded as a mitigating circumstance.[24] So too, the fact that the first of the qualifying convictions occurred very close to the commencement of the three year period is not a relevant mitigating factor.[25] Furthermore, the

[23] *Smith* v. *Craddock*, 1979 J.C. 66.
[24] *Baker* v. *Cole* [1971] 3 All E.R. 680, *per* Lord Parker C.J. at 681; *Lambie* v. *Woodage* [1972] 2 All E.R. 462.
[25] *McNab* v. *Smith*, High Court, 9 November 1977.

use of the phrase "all the circumstances" in section 93 (3) indicates that it is the duty of the court, when considering the exercise of its discretion in such cases, to have regard *inter alia* to all previous convictions incurred by the offender, and not merely to those falling within the three year period.[26]

6–24   Probably the factor most frequently advanced in mitigation of the consequences of section 93 (3) is hardship, either to the offender himself, or indirectly to others such as his wife and family. As was said in *Smith* v. *Craddock*,[23] "it would be difficult, if not indeed impossible as well as undesirable, to attempt to lay down rigid rules or guidelines as to the degree of hardship in individual cases, personal, circumstantial or professional which would entitle a sheriff to exercise this very important discretion." While not seeking to differ from that view, some comment may be helpful on the hardship submissions which are most frequently encountered in court.

6–25   Most often these will relate to the loss of employment which will ensue if the offender is disqualified. It is submitted that such an argument should always be examined with care, bearing in mind that a person who drives for a living does not thereby have a licence to break the law with impunity.[27] Furthermore, examination of the facts may sometimes reveal that the offender will not in fact become unemployed if disqualified, but that his employer will, for a period, keep him on in a different, albeit less well paid, capacity. Subject to all of the foregoing, hardship to the offender or his family as a result of a disqualification bringing about loss of employment is a factor which the court is plainly entitled to consider.

6–26   In cases involving professional drivers it is sometimes argued, as a subsidiary to a hardship argument, that such people drive very high mileages in a year and are therefore more likely than others to accumulate endorsements. It is submitted that such an argument is unsound and ought not to be taken into account by the court. In the first place there is no statutory authority for linking a "totting-up" liability to distance covered rather than time elapsed, and in the second place, and in any event, it is a fallacy to assume that road traffic offences are occasioned merely by exposure to driving rather than by lack of proper care and attention. Lastly, it may be said that a professional driver ought to be setting a higher, rather than a lower, standard than the average motorist.

---

[26] *McNab* v. *Pyper*, High Court, 14 December 1977.
[27] *McNab* v. *McDonald*, High Court, 9 November 1977.

Special reasons

27   In cases involving obligatory endorsement or obligatory disqualification the court may refrain from making the appropriate order only where there are special reasons for not doing so. Whether it is disqualification or merely endorsement that is in issue the criteria are the same and, it is submitted, it is not open to a court to apply a less stringent test in the latter case than in the former one. For these reasons any decided cases dealing with special reasons for not disqualifying are relevant to cases involving endorsement only, and vice versa.

28   What will amount to special reasons is essentially a question of law but will always depend first and foremost on the facts of the particular case; and the number of decided cases on the subject amply demonstrates the wide variety of circumstances that can and do arise. However, several principles which must be applied in such cases are now clearly established. The most fundamental is that, for a reason to be special, it must be special to the particular offence itself and not to the offender.[28] Furthermore, factors giving rise to the detection of the offence (*e.g.* a "random check") as opposed to its commission will not amount to a special reason.[29]

29   It follows that, in distinction to cases falling under section 93 (3) or section 19 of the 1981 Act, considerations of hardship affecting the offender or his family or others can never be a special reason. Thus, the possible loss of a university place is not a special reason.[30] Nor is it a special reason that a disqualification may cause public prejudice where the offender is an officer supervising the organisation of the Territorial Army throughout a county.[31] Furthermore, it is not a special reason that an offender has an otherwise good driving record.[32]

30   So far as factors pertaining to the offence itself are concerned it has been held, in a careless driving case, that a special reason may be found where there has only been a small degree of carelessness.[33] However, the case of *Smith* v. *Henderson* has been disapproved in England,[34] and it is submitted that it might not readily now be followed in Scotland. Where a sheriff purported to find special

---

[28] *Adair* v. *Munn,* 1940 J.C. 69; *Whittall* v. *Kirby* [1946] 2 All E.R. 552.
[29] *Smith* v. *Peaston*, High Court, 16 September 1977.
[30] *Carnegie* v. *Clark*, 1947 J.C. 74.
[31] *McFadyean* v. *Burbon*, 1954 J.C. 18.
[32] *Muir* v. *Sutherland,* 1940 J.C. 66.
[33] *Smith* v. *Henderson*, 1950 J.C. 48.
[34] *Nicholson* v. *Brown* [1974] R.T.R. 177.

reasons for not endorsing in a case under the Pelican Crossings Regulations on the basis that the offence was trivial, and there had been no evidence that it had caused actual danger to anyone, it was held on appeal that he had erred; the offence was an absolute one and was designed to protect the public from potential as distinct from actual danger.[35] So too, in relation to an offence under section 6 (1) (driving with more than the permitted amount of alcohol) it is not a special reason for not disqualifying that the offender had only a very small excess over the limit.[36]

6–31   It may be a special reason for not disqualifying in a drink/driving case that the offender did not know, and had no reasonable grounds for suspecting, that he was committing the offence.[37] This is probably more difficult to establish in an unfitness case (section 5) than in a case of exceeding the prescribed limit (section 6). In the latter case a not uncommon assertion is that the offender was given a "laced" drink. If accepted, that will amount to a special reason for not disqualifying.[38] Before such a plea can be accepted, however, it must be established, firstly, that the offender did not know and had no reasonable grounds for suspecting that his drink had been "laced", and, secondly, that the alcohol surreptitiously provided was responsible for the excess over the prescribed limit. The latter requirement may prove difficult to establish in cases where it is proved, or the offender admits, that he knew he was consuming some alcohol, but asserts that more was added without his knowledge.

6–32   If a person drives in circumstances which would normally attract an obligatory disqualification (*e.g.* with more than the permitted amount of alcohol), or an obligatory endorsement, but does so because of a sudden emergency, that may amount to a special reason for not disqualifying him or not endorsing his licence.[39] However, in such cases the emergency should be shown to be such as to provide a compelling reason for the offender having driven, and it must be shown that he had no real alternative but to do so.[40]

---

[35] *Tudhope* v. *Birbeck*, 1979 S.L.T. (Notes) 47.

[36] *Herron* v. *Sharif*, 1974 S.L.T. (Notes) 63; *Delaroy-Hall* v. *Tadman* [1969] 2 Q.B. 208.

[37] *Brewer* v. *Metropolitan Police Commissioner* [1969] 1 All E.R. 513.

[38] *Skinner* v. *Ayton*, 1977 S.L.T. (Sh.Ct.) 48, following *Pugsley* v. *Hunter* [1973] 1 W.L.R. 578.

[39] *Graham* v. *Annan*, 1980 S.L.T. 29; *Brown* v. *Dyerson* [1969] 1 Q.B. 45.

[40] *Copeland* v. *Sweeney*, 1977 S.L.T. (Sh.Ct.) 28.

PROCEDURE

Attendance of offender in court

-33   In Scotland it is not obligatory for a court to require the attendance in court of an offender when an order for disqualification is being made. Indeed, in cases where the offender resides a long distance from the court where the order is to be made, it would seem unnecessarily oppressive to require his attendance, particularly if the court is satisfied that he has received the appropriate notice of penalties and it is not proposed to impose more than the minimum disqualification called for by the statute. Such cases apart, however, it is submitted that it is good practice to require an offender to attend court when a disqualification is to be imposed. There are principally two reasons for this. In the first place, if the disqualification is imposed in the offender's presence it is not thereafter open to him to assert (in answer perhaps to a charge of driving while disqualified) that he was unaware that the disqualification had been imposed. In the second place — and this applies particularly if the court is considering the imposition of a discretionary disqualification — it permits the offender, who may not fully have appreciated the seriousness of his offence, to put forward submissions in mitigation.

Previous convictions and notices of penalties

-34   As has already been observed it is open to a court, when considering sentence, to have regard to previous convictions endorsed on an offender's licence notwithstanding that these may not have been libelled by the prosecutor, and indeed to proceed to impose a "totting-up" disqualification notwithstanding that the appropriate notice of penalties has not been served.[41] So too, in a case falling under section 93 (4) (compulsory three year disqualification) it is open to the court to impose the appropriate disqualification notwithstanding that the notice of penalties served by the prosecutor warns only of a liability for a disqualification of "not less than twelve months".[42]

Statement of grounds for not disqualifying or endorsing

-35   In any case where a court exercises its power under section 93 or 101 not to order any disqualification or endorsement, or to order

---

[41] 1972 Act, s. 101 (4A) and (8); *Urry* v. *Gibb*, 1979 S.L.T. (Notes) 19.
[42] *Campbell* v. *McLeod*, 1975 S.L.T. (Notes) 6.

disqualification for a shorter period than would otherwise be required, it must state the grounds for doing so in open court, and if it is a court of summary jurisdiction, it must cause these grounds to be entered in the record of proceedings.[43] It has been said that a failure to comply with this requirement may put a refusal to disqualify in peril.[44]

Procedure in "special reasons" cases

6–36   The existence of special reasons for not disqualifying or not endorsing as the case may be should not be put in issue *ex proprio motu* by the court; it is for the accused to plead, and establish if he can, that such reasons are present.[45] The principal reason for this is that the Crown may otherwise be given no proper opportunity to argue that special reasons should not be found. Furthermore, if in a case involving obligatory disqualification or endorsement, an accused does not proffer special reasons at the time of sentence, he may not do so later.[46] If the facts which are to be founded on as establishing the special reasons are not admitted by the prosecutor, evidence should be led by and, if necessary, on behalf of the accused in an attempt to prove them.[47] Such proof is required on a balance of probabilities.[48] In such a proof it is open to the prosecutor to cross-examine the accused and his witnesses and, if so advised, to lead evidence in rebuttal. If no evidence is led and the court is faced with conflicting statements from the prosecutor and the accused, neither should be preferred: all such statements should simply be ignored.[49]

6–37   In cases where disqualification is discretionary only, and submissions are made that there are special reasons for not ordering endorsement, it is important that the court should approach its task correctly. Where, in such a case, a sheriff decided that special reasons for not endorsing had not been established, and then went on not only to order endorsement but also to impose a period of disqualification, it was held that he had dealt with matters in the

---

[43] 1972 Act, s. 105 (1); *McNab* v. *Pyper*, High Court, 14 December 1977.

[44] *McNab* v. *Pyper, supra; cf. Winslow* v. *Farrell*, 1965 J.C. 49, but see also *Bruce* v. *Hogg*, 1966 J.C. 33.

[45] *McLeod* v. *Scoular*, 1974 J.C. 28; *Tudhope* v. *Birbeck, supra; McNab* v. *Feeney*, 1980 S.L.T. (Notes) 52.

[46] *Hynd* v. *Clark*, 1954 S.L.T. 85.

[47] *McLeod* v. *Scoular, supra.*

[48] *Farrell* v. *Moir*, 1974 S.L.T. (Sh. Ct.) 89.

[49] *Galloway* v. *Adair*, 1947 J.C. 7; *Barn* v. *Smith*, 1978 J.C. 17.

wrong order.[50] What should have been done was to decide what monetary penalty was appropriate and whether any period of disqualification ought to be ordered in the circumstances established in the proof in mitigation of penalty; only after a proper decision had been reached on these matters should the question of endorsement have been considered. The need to follow such a course arises because, if the court in its discretion decides to order disqualification, endorsement must then follow. It is only where the court has decided not to disqualify that it may then competently consider whether or not there are special reasons for not endorsing.

DISQUALIFICATION UNTIL PASSING OF DRIVING TEST

38 Where a person is convicted of an offence involving obligatory or discretionary disqualification the court may, whether or not he has previously passed the driving test, order him to be disqualified until he has, since the date of the order, passed the test. Such an order may be made whether or not any other order of disqualification has been made.[51] Where such an order is made, and provided that the offender is not subject to any other period of disqualification, he is entitled to hold a provisional licence and to drive in accordance with its conditions.[52] A disqualification until the driving test is passed is expressly excluded from the categories of disqualification that may subsequently be removed by the court which made the order.[53]

39 It has been held in England[54] that a disqualification until the driving test is passed should not be imposed as a punishment, but should be imposed where to do so is in the public interest. In general, it is submitted, there are three types of case where the court should consider such a disqualification. The first is where the offender is inexperienced and the circumstances of the case tend to cast doubts on his driving competence.[55] The second is where a substantial fixed period of disqualification is being imposed. In modern traffic conditions a lengthy interruption in a driver's experience is undesirable, and in such a case the person concerned should, in the public interest, be required to demonstrate that he is once again competent to drive. The third case is where the convicted

---

[50] *Graham* v. *Annan, supra.*
[51] 1972 Act, s. 93 (7).
[52] *Ibid.* s. 98 (3).
[53] *Ibid.* s. 95 (5); see *infra*, paras. 6–42 to 6–47.
[54] *R.* v. *Donnelly* [1975] R.T.R. 243.
[55] *R.* v. *Lobley* [1974] R.T.R. 550; *R.* v. *Heslop* [1978] R.T.R. 441.

driver is elderly or infirm and there is reason to suppose that his ability to drive safely is diminishing.[56] Such cases should always be regarded sympathetically, but bearing in mind that the public interest is paramount.

AIDERS AND ABETTORS

6–40 Those who aid, abet, counsel or procure, or incite to the commission of an offence involving obligatory disqualification may themselves be disqualified, if convicted. In such cases, however, their offence is to be regarded as one involving discretionary disqualification.[57]

EFFECT OF DISQUALIFICATION

6–41 Where the holder of a licence is disqualified by an order of a court, his licence is suspended so long as the disqualification continues in force, and during the time of suspension is of no effect.[58] If a person who is disqualified obtains a licence, he is guilty of an offence,[59] and any such licence is of no effect.[60] As previously noted, however, a person who is disqualified until he passes a driving test, and who is not otherwise disqualified, may obtain and hold a provisional licence.[61] A person who holds a foreign driving licence is, if disqualified by a court in Great Britain, forbidden to drive on roads in Great Britain even though his foreign licence is still valid,[62] and he will be guilty of an offence under section 99 (*b*) of the 1972 Act if he does drive during the relevant period.

REMOVAL OF DISQUALIFICATION

6–42 A disqualification may in certain circumstances be removed by the court which made the original order. The person disqualified must apply to the court, but no application may be made before the expiry of certain periods, depending on the length of the disqualification concerned. These periods are:

    (a)   two years, if the disqualification is for less than four years;

---

[56] *Ashworth* v. *Johnston* [1959] Crim. L.R. 735.
[57] 1972 Act, s. 93 (6).
[58] *Ibid*. s. 98 (1).
[59] *Ibid*. s. 99 (*a*).
[60] *Ibid*. s. 98 (2).
[61] *Ibid*. s. 98 (3).
[62] Motor Vehicles (International Circulation) Order 1957, art. 2 (S.I. 1957 No. 1074, as substituted by S.I. 1962 No. 1344); and see *supra*, para. 6–7.

(b)   one half of the period of disqualification, if it is for less than 10 years but not less than four years;

(c)   five years in any other case.

In determining the relevant period any time after the conviction during which the disqualification was suspended or the person was not disqualified (*e.g.* pending an appeal) must be disregarded.[63] It is submitted that (c) above would include cases where the disqualification was for life.

43   Where an application is made to it the court may, as it thinks proper, either by order remove the disqualification or refuse the application. In exercising that discretion the court must have regard to the character of the person disqualified and his conduct subsequent to the order, the nature of the offence, and any other circumstances of the case.[64] The prosecutor will normally submit information to the court regarding the applicant's conduct subsequent to the order. It is to be noted that, where an order is made removing a disqualification, the removal is "from such date as may be specified in the order".[64] That means that a court is not obliged to remove a disqualification with instant effect; it may, if it thinks fit, postpone the removal to a later date.

44   Where an application is refused a further application may be made after the expiry of a period of not less than three months.[65] There is no limitation on the number of applications that may be made provided the three months interval is observed.

45   As has already been noted, a disqualification until a driving test is passed may not be removed.[66] However, if such a disqualification has been imposed in addition to one for a determinate period, the latter may be removed although the former must remain in operation.[67]

Removal of "totting-up" disqualification

46   A disqualification under section 93 (3) of the 1972 Act, or section 19 of the 1981 Act, although it may be for any period, will frequently be for less than two years and therefore may not be removed.[68] Where, under section 93 (5) of the 1972 Act, it was

---

[63] 1972 Act, s. 95 (2).
[64] *Ibid.* s. 95 (1).
[65] *Ibid.* s. 95 (3).
[66] *Ibid.* s. 95 (5).
[67] *R.* v. *Nuttall* [1971] Crim. L.R. 485.
[68] 1972 Act, s. 95 (2).

imposed in addition to another period of disqualification so that the *cumulo* disqualification exceeded two years, it formerly fell to be regarded as a separate, additional disqualification which could not be removed.[69] That rule has now been changed by section 20 of the 1981 Act which provides that any such consecutive periods of disqualification are to be treated as one continuous period of disqualification in determining whether an application for removal of disqualification may be made under section 95. Accordingly, such an application will now be competent provided that the total period involved exceeds two years.

Removal of obligatory three year disqualification

6–47   Where a person has been disqualified for at least three years under section 93 (4) for a second or subsequent drink/driving offence within 10 years, there is no prohibition against his applying for removal of the disqualification at any time after the expiry of two years. It is submitted, however, that in such a case, where the original period of disqualification was mandatory, there should be particularly compelling reasons before a court will exercise its discretion to remove the disqualification.[70]

APPEAL AGAINST DISQUALIFICATION

6–48   A person disqualified by an order of a court in Scotland may appeal against the order in the same manner as against a sentence, and the court by or before which he was convicted may, if it thinks fit, pending the appeal suspend the disqualification.[71] In determining the expiration of the period for which a person is disqualified by an order of a court made in consequence of a conviction, any time after the conviction during which the disqualification was suspended or he was not disqualified is to be disregarded.[72] The foregoing provision relating to suspension of a disqualification pending an appeal appears to be at odds with section 264 (1) of the 1975 Act which provides, in relation to solemn procedure only, that where, upon conviction of any person, any disqualification, forfeiture or disability attaches to such person by reason of such conviction, they are not to attach for the period of two weeks from the date of the verdict nor, in the event of appeal proceedings being commenced,

---

[69] *R.* v. *Lambeth Metropolitan Magistrate, ex parte Everett* [1968] 1 Q.B. 446.
[70] *Damer* v. *Davison* [1976] R.T.R. 44.
[71] 1972 Act, s. 94 (3), as amended by 1980 Act, Sched. 7, para. 23.
[72] *Ibid.* s. 94 (4).

until the appeal, if it is proceeded with, is determined. There is no comparable provision in relation to summary appeals and, although "disqualification" is not expressly defined in the 1975 Act, it may be doubted whether the above provision is intended to cover disqualifications under the Road Traffic Acts: indeed, the provision, which was first introduced by the Act of Adjournal 1926, probably relates only to, for example, disqualifications for holding certain offices or permits.[73]

NOTIFICATION OF DISEASE OR DISABILITY

49 If, in any proceedings for an offence committed in respect of a motor vehicle, it appears to the court that the accused may be suffering from any disease or physical disability which would be likely to cause the driving by him of a motor vehicle to be a source of danger to the public, the court must notify the Secretary of State. Such a notice must be sent in such manner and to such address and contain such particulars as the Secretary of State may determine.[74] This obligation to notify the Secretary of State would appear to arise even in cases where the accused is not convicted.

---

[73] Compare *supra*, para. 6–20 and *infra*, para. 9-42.
[74] 1972 Act, s. 92.

APPENDIX TO CHAPTER 6

CERTAIN PROVISIONS OF THE TRANSPORT ACT 1981

INTRODUCTION

1. Part IV of the Transport Act 1981, together with Schedules 7 and 8, and the consequential and minor amendments contained in Schedule 9, substantially alter many of the provisions of the 1972 Act. Schedule 8 amends sections 6 to 12 of the 1972 Act and makes significant changes to the law concerning drink related offences. These sections are, however, outwith the scope of this book.

2. For the purposes of this book the most significant changes effected by the other parts of the 1981 Act mentioned above concern what have been referred to in Chapter 6 as "totting-up" disqualifications. From the coming into effect of the 1981 Act the old provisions, contained in sections 93(3) and 93(5) of the 1972 Act, are repealed and are replaced by a system whereby, in certain circumstances, an endorsement on a driving licence will show a number of penalty points (the precise number depending on the nature of the offence or offences of which the person is convicted), and, in certain circumstances, the person concerned will become liable to disqualification when the total number of points to be taken into account reaches 12 or more. The length of the period for which the person is liable to be disqualified is dependent, among other things, on whether or not any previous disqualification or disqualifications are also to be taken into account.

3. The provisions giving effect to this new procedure are complex and, in some instances, less clear than one might have wished. They will no doubt prove to be a fruitful source of appeals to the High Court and, in the meantime, one can do no more than offer some tentative and preliminary comment. In what follows the relevant subsections are set out verbatim with, in each case, a following commentary.

THE TRANSPORT ACT 1981

PART IV

ROAD SAFETY

Disqualification for repeated offences.

19.—(1) Where a person is convicted of an offence involving obligatory or discretionary disqualification and the court does not order him to be disqualified (whether on that or any other conviction) but orders particulars of the conviction to be endorsed under section 101 of the 1972 Act, the endorsement ordered shall include—

(a) particulars of the offence, including the date when it was committed; and

(b) the number of penalty points shown in respect of the offence in Schedule 7 to this Act (or, where a range of numbers is so shown, a number falling within the range);

but if a person is convicted of two or more such offences the number of penalty points to be endorsed in respect of those of them that were committed on the same occasion shall be the number or highest number that would be endorsed on a conviction of one of those offences.

Commentary:

(i) An endorsement showing an appropriate number of penalty points is to be made on a person's licence only where the court does not order him to be disqualified. If an order for disqualification is made, that disqualification is to be endorsed on the licence as at present, but no points are to be endorsed. Although not entirely clear from the subsection itself, this appears from the amendment to section 101 (1) of the 1972 Act contained in para. 6 of Schedule 9 to the 1981 Act. However, where a person is disqualified the court is to add to any other qualifying points on the licence the points that would have been added but for the disqualification so as to see whether the total reaches 12 or more (see *infra* section 19 (3)).

(ii) The significance of the phrase "(whether on that or any other conviction)" is not immediately clear. Presumably it means that, if a person is convicted simultaneously of several offences and is disqualified in respect of one of them, no penalty points are to be endorsed in respect of any of the offences.

(iii) An endorsement showing a number of penalty points is also to show the date when the offence was committed. The date of commission of an offence is of critical importance under the points system (see *infra*, section 19 (3)) and, since that date is not shown on the schedule of previous convictions in use in Scottish courts, it will in future be essential that courts should have an offender's licence available for inspection in all cases.

(iv) The closing words of the subsection could give rise to some difficulty. The immediate meaning is clear. Thus, for example, if a person is convicted under the same complaint of contraventions of sections 3, 84 (1), and 143 of the 1972 Act, all committed on the same occasion, the number of penalty points to be endorsed will be a maximum of eight, notwithstanding the multiplicity of offences. However, it is not uncommon for a person to be charged and convicted, under the same complaint, of offences which were committed on different occasions. The fact that the subsection specifically restricts the number of points when the offences were committed on the *same* occasion suggests that this restriction is not to apply when the offences were committed on *different* occasions. Thus, two offences under section 143, committed on different occasions, would appear to attract a total of up to 16 penalty points. It is to be noted that the foregoing comments beg a possible question as to the meaning of the phrase "same occasion". If, for example, a motorist commits an offence under section 3, involving an accident, and thereafter, in contravention of section 25 (2), fails to report the accident to the police within 24 hours, is that latter offence to be taken as having been committed on the same, or on a different, occasion? It is tentatively submitted that the word "occasion" may properly be construed as relating to a course of events which have their common origin in the same act of driving or management of the motor vehicle.

(v) A closely related problem also falls to be noted. It is not uncommon, in cases where a person has been charged with some road traffic offences and has also given a blood sample for analysis, for the charges to be dealt with in separate complaints which may call in court on different days. The complaint with the non-drink offences may well call in court first and, if these offences are relatively minor albeit endorseable, no question of disqualification may arise at that stage, and the court may simply proceed to endorse the appropriate number of points on the offender's licence. If, however, the offender had also been charged with, and convicted of, the drink related offence in the same complaint, and had been disqualified in respect of that offence, it would not then have been competent for the court to endorse any points on the licence (see *supra,* note (i)). It may not be possible to avoid this sort of situation arising from time to time. However, three comments may be made. Firstly, the fact that it can arise, and may give rise to some difficulty, may persuade prosecutors to take steps to have all offences that occurred on the same occasion dealt with in the same complaint in future. Secondly, even where the situation that has been described does arise, it would seem that the offender will not be prejudiced thereby since, by virtue of section 19 (3) (b) (infra), the subsequent disqualification will in effect cancel out the previously endorsed points. Thirdly, since separate complaints may call before the court in the opposite order to that envisaged in the above example, judges, prosecutors and defending counsel or solicitors will have to be alive to the possibility that an offender may have already been disqualified in respect of another offence committed on the same occasion. In cases where that is so, it is submitted that it would not be competent to endorse any points on the occasion when the court subsequently came to deal with the complaint containing the minor, endorseable offences.

(2) Where a person is convicted of an offence involving obligatory or discretionary disqualification and the penalty points to be taken into account under subsection (3) number twelve or more, the court shall order him to be disqualified for not less than the minimum period defined in subsection (4) unless the court is satisfied, having regard to all the circumstances not excluded by subsection (6), that there are grounds for mitigating the normal consequences of the conviction and thinks fit to order him to be disqualified for a shorter period or not to order him to be disqualified.

Commentary:

This subsection fixes 12 or more as the critical number of penalty points for disqualification to become obligatory unless mitigating circumstances are present. There are two important differences from the comparable provision in section 93 (3) of the 1972 Act. In the first place, the minimum period for such disqualification is variable, depending on certain circumstances (see *infra*, section 19 (4)); and, in the second place, statutory limitations are now set on the court's exercise of its discretion in determining whether or not mitigating circumstances are present (see *infra*, section 19 (6)).

(3) The penalty points to be taken into account on the occasion of a person's conviction are—
(a) any that on that occasion will be ordered to be endorsed on any licence

held by him or would be so ordered if he were not then ordered to be disqualified; and

(b) any that were on a previous occasion ordered to be so endorsed, unless the offender has since that occasion and before the conviction been disqualified, whether under subsection (2) or under section 93 of the 1972 Act;

but if any of the offences was committed more than three years before another the penalty points in respect of that offence shall not be added to those in respect of the other.

Commentary:

(i) When a person is convicted of an endorseable offence the points to be taken into account include any that on that occasion will be ordered to be endorsed or would be so ordered if he were not then ordered to be disqualified. Thus, for example, if a person already has seven qualifying points on his licence and is convicted of careless driving, but is not disqualified for that offence, the court may endorse five points in respect of that conviction: the total points will then amount to 12 and the person will be liable to disqualification under section 19 (2). If, in the same situation the court imposes a disqualification in respect of the conviction for careless driving, it will not order endorsement of the five points but will take them into account with the same consequence so far as a "totting-up" disqualification is concerned. It is to be noted, however, that, in terms of Part I of Schedule 7, the number of points appropriate to an offence where disqualification is obligatory in the absence of special reasons is only four. Consequently, if in the example given above the person had been convicted of such an offence rather than careless driving, the number of points to be added, whether the person was disqualified or not, would take the total to only 11, so that a "totting-up" disqualification would not be incurred.

(ii) In addition to the foregoing the court is to take into account any points that were "on a previous occasion" ordered to be endorsed. Although that phrase is expressed in the singular, it is suggested that courts are not thereby obliged to consider only one, single, previous occasion of endorsement. That would defeat the whole object of the provisions which is to deal with those who offend repetitively. Courts will, it is submitted, take account of all the relevant points previously endorsed, whether or not they were all so endorsed on the same occasion.

(iii) Previous endorsements are not to be taken into account where, since the occasion of any such endorsement and before the current conviction, the offender has been disqualified, whether under section 19 (2) of the 1981 Act or under section 93 of the 1972 Act. This provision represents a considerable innovation on previous practice. It means that, once a person has been disqualified, whether under a "totting-up" provision or otherwise, any previous endorsed points cease to be relevant, even where they fall within the appropriate period of time. Under section 19 (4), however, any such disqualification itself is now to be taken into account as a factor in determining the length of a "totting-up" disqualification (but, see *infra*, commentary (i) on section 19 (4)).

(iv) The period of time within which previously endorsed points will qualify to be taken into account is to be determined by reference to the date of commission of the offence in question rather than the date of conviction. Since the date of commission of an offence is not shown on a schedule of previous convictions it will be essential, for this subsection to be complied with, that courts should examine an offender's driving licence in all cases. This will, of course, exacerbate some of the problems referred to *supra* in paras. 6-8 and 6-9.

> (4) The minimum period referred to in subsection (2) is—
> (*a*) six months if no previous disqualification imposed on the offender is to be taken into account; and
> (*b*) one year if one, and two years if more than one, such disqualification is to be taken into account;
> and a previous disqualification imposed on an offender is to be taken into account if it was imposed within the three years immediately preceding the commission of the latest offence in respect of which penalty points are taken into account under subsection (3).

Commentary:
(i) This subsection prescribes the minimum period of disqualification that is to be imposed in the absence of mitigating circumstances. If no previous disqualification is to be taken into account the period will, as previously, be six months. However, that period is to be increased to one year if a previous disqualification is taken into account, and to two years if two or more such disqualifications are taken into account. Bearing in mind the

provision in section 19 (3) (*b*) that points endorsed prior to a disqualification are not to be taken into account thereafter, it might be thought that the effect of this provision is that a person will immediately become liable to a "totting-up" disqualification where he has one or more previous disqualifications within the relevant period. It is submitted that this is not so. Under section 19 (2) the essential, and indeed only, requirement before a person becomes liable to such a disqualification is that points numbering 12 or more should fall to be taken into account and, since no points will be endorsed where a person is disqualified, it follows that, if a person's previous record consists only of offences for which he was disqualified, there will be no points to be taken into account apart from any that fall to be endorsed in respect of the current offence. Some examples may serve to illustrate the position:

Example 1:
In January 1979 A commits an offence in respect of which his licence is subsequently endorsed. Under the transitional provisions of the 1981 Act (*infra,* section 19 (7) (*a*)) that endorsement would now count for three points. In January 1980 he commits, and is subsequently disqualified in respect of, an offence attracting obligatory disqualification. No points will be endorsed in respect of that conviction (section 19 (1)), and by virtue of section 19 (3) (*b*) the effect of that disqualification is that the three points attributable to the earlier endorsement cannot be taken into account in the event of a subsequent conviction. Finally, late in 1981, he is convicted of an offence for which he is not disqualified but in respect of which five points fall to be endorsed on his licence. Since five is the total number of points to be taken into account on the occasion of that conviction, he is not liable to a "totting-up" disqualification, notwithstanding the earlier disqualification.

Example 2:
In January 1980 A is disqualified in respect of an offence attracting obligatory disqualification. As before, no points are endorsed in respect of that conviction. Within the following year he commits, and is convicted of, further offences in respect of which he is not disqualified but a total of seven points are endorsed on his licence.

When, late in 1981, he is convicted of a further offence in respect of which five points fall to be endorsed on his licence, he will not only become liable to a "totting-up" disqualification, having by then acquired a total of 12 points to be taken into account, but will be liable to a minimum disqualification of one year, since the previous disqualification will then fall to be taken into account also.

(ii) Although, in the examples given above, the earlier disqualification was taken to be in respect of an offence attracting obligatory disqualification, it is submitted that, for the purposes of section 19 (4), any previous disqualification, including one under "totting-up" provisions, or in respect of an offence for which disqualification is only discretionary, may fall to be taken into account.

(iii) The time limit within which previous disqualifications fall to be taken into account for the purpose of section 19 (4) is different from the time limit for endorsed points under section 19 (3). A disqualification is to be taken into account if it was *imposed* within the three years immediately preceding the commission of the latest offence in respect of which points are taken into account.

(iv) Section 19 (4) does not state whether a "totting-up" disqualification is to be in addition to any other period of disqualification imposed (whether then or on a previous occasion) on the offender, nor is there any provision dealing with that matter elsewhere in the section. At first sight it would seem unlikely that the legislature should have chosen to vary the previous practice in this respect, and it could be argued that the deterrent effects of the provisions would be much reduced if repeating offenders were, in the event of a subsequent disqualification, to be no worse off than first offenders. It is tentatively submitted, however, that the effect of the provisions is that a "totting-up" disqualification should commence to run on the day on which it is imposed, that is to say it should be concurrent with any other disqualification, whether imposed then or previously. When the Transport Bill was first presented to the House of Commons it contained an express provision that, if a court simultaneously imposed a direct disqualification and a "totting-up" disqualification, the two periods were to be concurrent. That provision was subsequently excluded from the Act and, while that could be taken as indicating that the legislature intended the opposite effect, it is equally consistent with the view that the express provision was simply thought to be otiose and unnecessary. That the latter is the more correct view is confirmed by two considerations. In the first place it is well established that, in the absence of express statutory provision, a period of disqualification may not be postponed in any way (*Williamson* v. *MacMillan*, 1962 S.L.T. 63). In the second place, section 20 of the 1981 Act provides that, for the purpose of determining whether an application may be made under section 95 of the 1972 Act for removal of a disqualification, a "totting-up" disqualification under section 93 (5) of that Act is to be treated as being continuous with any other period of disqualification so as to make a single period. There can plainly be no reason why disqualifications under section 93 (5) should, for the foregoing purpose, be treated differently from disqualifications under section 19 of the 1981 Act, and the fact that only section 93 (5) disqualifications are referred to in section 20 of the 1981 Act indicates that a similar provision is unnecesary in relation to section 19 disqualifications. That, of course, is the case only if section 19 disqualifications are to be concurrent with, rather than consecutive to, other disqualifications imposed on the offender.

> (5) Where an offender is convicted on the same occasion of more than one offence involving obligatory or discretionary disqualification—
> (a) not more than one disqualification shall be imposed on him under subsection (2); and
> (b) in determining the period of the disqualification the court shall take into account all the offences; and
> (c) for the purposes of any appeal any disqualification imposed under subsection (2) shall be treated as an order made on the conviction of each of the offences.

Commentary:
  (i) The provisions of head (a) of this subsection seem reasonably clear, and alter the rule that seems to have been applied, at least in England, in relation to disqualifications under section 93 (3) of the 1972 Act (see *supra,* para. 6–21). These provisions are also consistent with the view that "totting-up" disqualifications are now to be concurrent with other disqualifications. The provisions of head (c) also seem reasonably clear and, taken with head (a), mean, for example, that, if a person appeals successfully against his conviction on one of several offences, any "totting-up" disqualifica-

tion will still stand in respect of the other offences unless, of course, it is itself successfully appealed against.

(ii) The purpose of the provision in head (b) is not immediately clear. Perhaps, since the periods of disqualification prescribed by section 19 (4) are *minimum* periods, it means no more than that the court should consider the possibility of increasing these periods where a person is convicted on the same occasion of more than one offence.

(iii) A problem may arise under this subsection in cases where, at the first calling of a complaint or indictment containing several endorseable offences, the accused pleads guilty to some of the charges and not guilty to others. Often, in such cases, sentence will be deferred in respect of the pleas of guilty until the date of trial. If the accused is then found guilty in respect of the charges that have gone to trial it may be said that his conviction on these charges has taken place on a different occasion from his conviction on the charges to which he originally pled guilty. If that view is correct then subsection (5) would not apply since only the sentencing would be taking place on the same occasion. It is submitted, however, that the sense of the subsection is such that the accused in such a case would fall to be treated as if the convictions had all occurred on the same occasion.

> (6) No account is to be taken under subsection (2) of—
> (a) any circumstances that are alleged to make the offence or any of the offences not a serious one;
> (b) hardship, other than exceptional hardship; or
> (c) any circumstances which, within the three years immediately preceding the conviction, have been taken into account under that subsection in ordering the offender to be disqualified for a shorter period or not ordering him to be disqualified.

Commentary:

This subsection limits in certain important respects the discretion which the court may exercise in determining whether or not there are mitigating circumstances in "totting-up" cases. No account is now to be taken of three matters:

(i) "any circumstances that are alleged to make the offence or any of the offences not a serious one". Although this restriction, as expressed, appears to apply only to the offence or offences of which a person is convicted at the time when he becomes liable to disqualification under section 19 (2), it is submitted that the same consideration should apply to the earlier offences in respect of which the endorsed points are being taken into account (*cf, supra,* para. 6–23). Indeed, the scheme of Schedule 7 is such that different numbers of points will be endorsed for different types of offence and, in certain cases where a discretion is allowed in fixing the number of points, the relative seriousness of the offence will already have been taken into account.

(ii) "hardship, other than exceptional hardship". It is not clear how courts will interpret this provision, and of course much will depend on the circumstances of each case. Plainly, however, the intention is to restrict the number of persons who may at present avoid a "totting-up" disqualification; and, since loss of employment is probably the most frequently advanced "hardship" argument, it may be that that alone will no longer be sufficient to amount to a mitigating circumstance (*cf. supra,* para 6–24 *et seq.*). Indeed it could be argued with some force that the word "exceptional" is not merely a synonym for "severe", but imports a degree of hardship that would be altogether out of the ordinary.

(iii) "any circumstances which . . . or not ordering him to be disqualified". While the purpose of this provision is clear, it is very difficult to say how it can be operated in practice. There are at least two major, related problems. The first, and most obvious, is that of ascertaining what circumstances were taken into account in ordering an offender to be disqualified for a shorter period or not ordering him to be disqualified at all. It should generally be obvious from an offender's licence, or from a schedule of previous convictions, that such a decision has been taken on a previous occasion, but neither the licence nor the schedule will disclose what prompted that decision; and of course, while that previous decision may have been taken by the same court as is considering the possibility of a "totting-up" disqualification, it may equally have been taken in a sheriff court at the other end of Scotland, or even in a magistrates' court in Plymouth or Brighton. Some offenders themselves may seek to indicate the circumstances that were taken into account on the previous occasion, but most courts would probably be unwilling, and unwise, to accept such information as accurate without further verification. The only alternative, however, would seem to be to apply to the court which actually made the decision for a note of the reasons. If that court was a magistrates' court or, in Scotland, a court of summary jurisdiction it should, under section 105 (1) of the 1972 Act (as amended by the 1981 Act, Sched. 9, para. 13), have recorded on the record of proceedings the grounds for its decision, and it should be able to provide a note of these. It must be said, however, that this will be a cumbersome and time-consuming procedure and will not, in any event, be available where the previous decision was taken in a higher court.

Even if such an inquiry is successful in producing some information, it may do no more than to reveal the second obvious problem which is whether the circumstances which are to be disregarded must be precisely the same as those which were taken into account on the previous occasion. If, as is likely in many cases, the information disclosed by the sort of inquiry suggested above amounts to no more than that the earlier decision was taken on the ground of "hardship to the offender", is that to exclude in the current case any plea that is also based on hardship? Even if more details about the earlier case can be obtained, the same sort of question will remain. If, for example, in the earlier case the mitigating circumstance was that the offender required his car to drive his sick wife to and from hospital, is a similar plea to be excluded on the next occasion notwithstanding that his wife is more gravely ill than previously and now requires to attend hospital more frequently; but may the plea be heard on the second occasion if, in addition to conveying his sick wife to hospital, the offender has also come under the necessity of taking his disabled daughter to and from hospital; or will both of these pleas fall to be rejected on the subsequent occasion on the basis that they both involve the same, or substantially the same, type of mitigating circumstance, namely hardship to the offender's family? Time alone will tell how courts will operate this provision — assuming, of course, that they can ever obtain the necessary information to enable them to operate it at all. It may, however, be ventured that courts will generally wish to take a fairly liberal view of the provision, and will not wish to exclude genuinely mitigating circumstances simply because they would fall to be disregarded if a strict interpretation were taken.

(7) For the purposes of this section—

(a) an order for endorsement which was made before the commencement of this section counts as an order made in pursuance of subsection (1) for the endorsement of 3 penalty points, unless a disqualification was imposed on the offender on that or any subsequent occasion; and

(b) circumstances which have been taken into account under section 93 (3) of the 1972 Act in ordering an offender to be disqualified for a shorter period or not ordering him to be disqualified shall be treated as having been so taken into account under subsection (2) of this section.

Commentary:

(i) The consequence of this transitional provision is that persons with pre-1981 Act endorsements on their licence may, in some cases, be less at risk and, in some cases, be more at risk of a "totting-up" disqualification than they would have been had those earlier endorsements attracted the number of points provided for in Schedule 7. Standing the provisions contained in the proviso to section 19 (1), it is submitted that, where a person has two or more pre-1981 Act endorsements in respect of offences committed on the same occasion, only three points in all should be counted in respect of all such endorsements.

(ii) Subsection 7 (*b*) contains a similar provision to that in subsection 6 (*c*), and the same comments must be made.

(8) The Secretary of State may by order made by statutory instrument—
(*a*) alter the number of penalty points shown in Schedule 7 in respect of an offence (or, where a range of numbers is shown, alter that range); and
(*b*) provide for different numbers to be so shown in respect of the same offence committed in different circumstances;
but no such order shall be made unless a draft of it has been laid before Parliament and approved by resolution of each House of Parliament.

Commentary:

No commentary is necessary in respect of this subsection.

Section 19 (9) does not apply to Scotland.

Removal of disqualification.
20. Where, in pursuance of section 93 (5) of the 1972 Act, a period of disqualification was imposed on an offender in addition to any other period or periods then, for the purpose of determining whether an application may be made under section 95 of that Act for the removal of either or any of the disqualifications the periods shall be treated as one continuous period of disqualification.

Commentary:

Reference should be made to the commentary (iv) to section 19 (4).

Offender escaping consequences of endorseable offence by deception.

    21. —(1) Where—

(a) in dealing with a person convicted of an endorseable offence a court was deceived regarding any circumstances that were or might have been taken into account in deciding whether or for how long to disqualify him; and

(b) the deception constituted or was due to an offence committed by that person;

then, if he is convicted of that offence, the court by or before which he is convicted shall have the same powers and duties regarding an order for disqualification as had the court which dealt with him for the endorseable offence but shall in dealing with him take into account any order made on his conviction of the endorseable offence.

    (2) In this section "endorseable offence" means an offence involving obligatory or discretionary disqualification.

Commentary:

This section extends the circumstances in which a court may make an order for disqualification to include a person's conviction of a non-road traffic offence of the kind envisaged in the section. Presumably such offences will be principally uttering, perjury, or the perversion of the course of justice. In dealing with the offender for such an offence the court is to take into account any order made on his conviction of the endorseable offence. Thus, for example, if an offender successfully concealed the existence of a relevant previous disqualification from a court that was imposing a disqualification under section 19 (2) with the result that he was disqualified for only six months rather than a year, the court, on his subsequent conviction for uttering or whatever, would have to take that six months disqualification into account and if, for example, three months of it had expired by the date of the subsequent conviction, the court would then impose a disqualification for nine months.

SCHEDULE 7

POINTS TO BE ENDORSED

PART I

OFFENCES WHERE DISQUALIFICATION OBLIGATORY EXCEPT FOR SPECIAL REASONS

Description of offence	Number of penalty points
Any offence involving obligatory disqualification (within the meaning of Part III of Road Traffic Act 1972).	4

Part II

Offences where Disqualification Discretionary

A—Offences under Road Traffic Act 1972

Section of 1972 Act creating offence	Description	Number of penalty points
2	Reckless driving...	10
3	Careless or inconsiderate driving......................	2—5
5(2)	Being in charge of motor vehicle when unfit through drink or drugs.	10
6(1)(*b*)	Being in charge of motor vehicle with alcohol above prescribed limit.	10
7(4)	Failure to provide specimen for breath test	4
8(7)	Failing to provide specimen for analysis	10
16	Carrying passenger on motor cycle contrary to section 16.	1
22	Failing to comply with traffic directions..............	3
24	Leaving vehicle in dangerous position................	3
25(4)	Failing to stop after accident...........................	5—9
25(4)	Failing to give particulars or report accident	4—9
40(5)	Contravention of construction and use regulations.	3
84(1)	Driving without licence	2
88(6)	Failing to comply with conditions of licence.........	2
91(1)	Driving with uncorrected defective eyesight........	2
91(2)	Refusing to submit to test of eyesight.................	2
99(*b*)	Driving while disqualified as under age	2
99(*b*)	Driving while disqualified by order of court.........	6
143	Using, or causing or permitting use of, motor vehicle uninsured and unsecured against third-party risks.	4—8
175	Taking in Scotland a motor vehicle without consent or lawful authority or driving, or allowing oneself to be carried in, a motor vehicle so taken.	8

B—Offences under other Acts
(or, where stated, attempts)

Act and section creating offence or providing for its punishment	Description	Number of penalty points
Road Traffic Regulation Act 1967 s. 13(4).	Contravention of traffic regulations on special roads.	3
Road Traffic Regulation Act 1967 s. 23(5).	Contravention of pedestrian crossing regulations.	3
Road Traffic Regulation Act 1967 s. 25(2).	Failure to obey sign exhibited by school crossing patrol.	3
Road Traffic Regulation Act 1967 s. 26(6), s. 26A(5).	Contravention of order prohibiting or restricting use of street playground by vehicles.	2
Road Traffic Regulation Act 1967 s. 78A.	Exceeding a speed limit....................	3
Theft Act 1968 s. 12	Taking or attempting to take conveyance without consent or lawful authority or driving or attempting to drive a motor vehicle so taken or allowing oneself to be carried in a motor vehicle so taken.	8
Theft Act 1968 s. 25	Going equipped for stealing with reference to theft or taking of motor vehicle.	8

C—Thefts and attempted thefts

Description of offence	Number of penalty points
Stealing or attempting to steal motor vehicle.......	8

Note: The descriptions of offences under A and B above indicate only their general nature.

CHAPTER 7

MISCELLANEOUS DISPOSALS

FORFEITURE

01 Where a person is convicted of an offence on indictment and the court which passes sentence is satisfied that any property which was in his possession or under his control at the time of his apprehension:

(a)   has been used for the purpose of committing, or facilitating the commission of, any offence, or

(b)   was intended by him to be used for that purpose,

that property is liable to forfeiture, and any property so forfeited is to be disposed of as the court may direct.[1] It is to be noted that the above power extends to property used or intended to be used for the commission of *any* offence, and not merely the offence of which a person is convicted. The reference to "facilitating the commission" of an offence includes a reference to the taking of any steps after it has been committed for the purpose of disposing of any property to which it relates or of avoiding apprehension or detection.[2]

02   Where a person is convicted of any offence by a court of summary jurisdiction the same provisions apply as in the case of a person convicted on indictment.[3] Formerly, the somewhat different provisions applicable to summary procedure applied not only where a person was convicted but also expressly to cases where a probation order was made. The replacement of the old section 436 of the 1975 Act by the provisions contained in section 223 appears to remove that power, so that forfeiture of articles may not now be ordered where a summary case is disposed of by the making of a probation order.

03   The powers of forfeiture described above are available to the court in relation both to common law and statutory offences. However, many statutes contain their own specific provisions for forfeiture. Examples are the Prevention of Crime Act 1953, the Salmon and Freshwater Fisheries (Protection) (Scotland) Act 1951, and the Misuse of Drugs Act 1971. It is submitted that, where the

---

[1] 1975 Act, s. 223 (1).

[2] *Ibid.* s. 223 (2).

[3] *Ibid.* s. 436, as amended by 1980 Act, Sched. 7, para. 71.

powers provided under a particular statute are different from those provided by the 1975 Act, the court should use the powers contained in the statute under which the person concerned is charged. In either case, where a statutory offence is involved, there can be no order for forfeiture unless that is mentioned in the notice of penalties served on the accused.[4]

7-04   The power to order forfeiture is most commonly used in relation to articles such as weapons, firearms, dangerous drugs, a housebreaker's tools, and so on. It has been held, however, that the court has power to order the destruction of indecent or obscene books which were exhibited to view in contravention of section 380 (3) of the Burgh Police (Scotland) Act 1892.[5] A power to order forfeiture also implies the right to seize the articles concerned.[6] Without express statutory authority, however, it is not competent to order the forfeiture of a motor car used as a conveyance to and from the scene of an offence against a fishing statute.[7]

7-05   There are sometimes problems when the article which the court wishes to forfeit does not belong to the offender himself. Thus a third party, whose boat was ordered to be forfeited, successfully petitioned the High Court for recall of the forfeiture.[8] So too, it was held, in a prosecution under the Wireless Telegraphy Act 1949 for using a receiver without a licence, to be incompetent to order the forfeiture of the television set in question where it was the subject of a rental agreement.[9] In *Lloyds & Scottish Finance Ltd.* v. *H.M.A.*,[10] however, a somewhat different approach was taken. In that case a person was charged on indictment with theft, and pleaded guilty to reset. At the time of the offence he had used a motor vehicle which was the subject of a hire-purchase agreement. Forfeiture of the vehicle was ordered with a direction that it be sold by public auction. The finance company, as owners of the vehicle, sought to have the High Court quash the order for forfeiture and suspend the order for sale. In the event the order for forfeiture was not quashed, but the order for sale was varied to enable the value of the vehicle to be paid

---

[4] *Duffy* v. *Lakie*, 1962 S.L.T. 31.

[5] *Galletly* v. *Laird*, 1952 J.C. 16.

[6] *Mauchline* v. *Stevenson* (1878) 4 Couper 20.

[7] *Simpson* v. *Fraser & Others*, 1948 J.C. 1.

[8] *Loch Lomond Sailings Ltd.* v. *Hawthorn*, 1962 J.C. 8.

[9] *Semple & Sons* v. *MacDonald*, 1963 J.C. 90. (Such a forfeiture is now competent under s. 11 (4) of the Wireless Telegraphy Act 1967, but see *infra* case in note 10).

[10] 1974 J.C. 24.

to the finance company. The decision in this case was largely influenced by the fact that section 23 of the Criminal Justice Act 1972 (which contains the forfeiture provision that is now section 223 of the 1975 Act) provided, on one view in relation to English cases only, for third parties being able to claim an interest in forfeited goods for up to six months after the date of the order. The High Court saw no reason why the same right should not exist in Scotland, and indeed urged courts to have in mind the interests of third parties when making forfeiture orders. It is suggested that the case of *Lloyds & Scottish Finance* may also be distinguished from the others to which reference has been made in that the offender had, under the hire-purchase agreement, a quantifiable interest in the vehicle of which he could properly be deprived by forfeiture, whereas there is no such interest in cases involving mere rental.

-06   Where an order for forfeiture has been made, the court or any justice of the peace may, if satisfied on information on oath:

   (a)   that there is reasonable cause to believe that the article is to be found in any place or premises; and

   (b)   that admission to the place or premises has been refused or that a refusal of such admission is apprehended,

issue a warrant of search.[11]

EXPENSES

-07   In cases on indictment expenses may be awarded only in the extremely rare case of a private prosecution. Such prosecutions are, however, sometimes brought under summary procedure and are then subject to the provisions set out in section 435 of the 1975 Act (as amended by section 46 (1) (*e*) of the 1980 Act). These are:

   (a)   expenses may be awarded to or against a private prosecutor but must not be awarded against any person prosecuting in the public interest unless the statute or order under which the prosecution is brought expressly or impliedly authorises such an award;[12]

   (b)   the finding regarding expenses must be stated in the sentence or judgment disposing of the case;

   (c)   expenses awarded to the prosecutor are to be restricted

[11] 1975 Act, ss. 224, 437.
[12] *Mackirdy* v. *McKendrick* (1897) 2 Adam 435; *Lockwood* v. *Chartered Institute of Patent Agents* (1912) 7 Adam 14.

to the fees set forth in Schedule 3 to the Summary
Jurisdiction (Scotland) Act 1954;[13]

(d)   the court may award expenses against the accused
without imposing any fine or may direct the expenses
incurred by the prosecutor, whether public or private,
to be met wholly or partly out of any fine imposed;

(e)   expenses awarded against the accused, where the fine
or fines imposed do not exceed £200, shall not exceed
£50;

Provided that if it appears to the court that the reasonable expenses of the prosecutor's witnesses together
with the other expenses exceed the sum of £50, the
court may direct the expenses of those witnesses to be
paid wholly or partly out of the fine;

(f)   where a child is himself ordered by a sheriff sitting
summarily to pay expenses in addition to a fine, the
amount of the expenses so ordered to be paid must in
no case exceed the amount of the fine;

(g)   any expenses awarded are recoverable by civil
diligence.[14]

7–08   The table of fees referred to in (c) above does not apply where
expenses are awarded against a prosecutor, and in such a case the
account may be remitted for taxation.[15] Where there are two or
more accused the amount of expenses awarded against each must
not exceed the permitted limit, although the total expenses may do
so.[16]

CONTEMPT OF COURT

7–09   Every court has an inherent power to punish those who are in
contempt of court. Formerly, at least in the High Court or the Court
of Session, the punishment took the form of a sentence of imprisonment for an indefinite period.[17] In more recent times, however, the
normal practice has been to impose a determinate sentence either in
the form of a term of imprisonment,[18] or a fine,[19] and, by virtue of
section 15 (1) of the Contempt of Court Act 1981, any sentence of
imprisonment must now be for a fixed term.

---

[13] Now Act of Adjournal (Fees in the Inferior Courts) 1972.
[14] *Ross* v. *Stirling* (1869) 1 Couper 336.
[15] *J. & G. Cox Ltd.* v. *Lindsay*, 1907 S.C. 96.
[16] *Tough & Ross* v. *Mitchell* (1886) 1 White 79.
[17] *Muir* v. *Milligan* (1868) 6 M. 1125; *Leys* v. *Leys* (1886) 13 R. 1223.
[18] *Wylie & Anor.* v. *H.M.A.*, 1966 S.L.T. 149.
[19] *H.M.A.* v. *Airs*, 1975 J.C. 64.

-10   A book primarily concerned with sentencing is not the place to discuss at length what is or is not contempt of court. That is fully dealt with in other textbooks.[20] It may, however, be helpful to give some indication of the circumstances in which the problem of sentencing for contempt is most frequently encountered. In this context it must be borne in mind that the need to sentence for contempt may arise in two quite distinct types of case. The first is where the offender has in fact been proceeded against, normally by the Lord Advocate, for the contempt in question. A summary prosecution for contempt is competent but rare. In such cases the offender's guilt will either be admitted or established by evidence in the normal way, and the sentencing problem for the court will be essentially the same as in any other case. The second type of case arises where the court itself proposes summarily to find the offender guilty of the contempt. In such cases difficulties may arise as to whether or not the court should deal with the matter itself, or leave it to be dealt with by the prosecutor and, if dealing with it itself, what level of sentence is competent and appropriate. Certain procedural difficulties are also encountered on occasions.

-11   Contempt by a witness in a summary prosecution is to some extent dealt with by statute. Section 344 of the 1975 Act (as amended by section 46 (1) (c) of the 1980 Act) provides:

"(1) If a witness in a summary prosecution shall wilfully fail to attend after being duly cited, or unlawfully refuse to be sworn, or after the oath has been administered to him refuse to answer any question which the court may allow, or to produce documents in his possession when required by the court, or shall prevaricate in his evidence, he shall be deemed guilty of contempt of court and be liable to be summarily punished forthwith for such contempt by a fine not exceeding £50 or by imprisonment for any period not exceeding 21 days.

(2) Where such punishment as aforesaid is summarily imposed, the clerk of court shall enter in the record of the proceedings the acts constituting the contempt or the statements forming the prevarication.

(3) The foregoing provisions of this section shall be without prejudice to the prosecutor proceeding by way of formal complaint for any such contempt where such summary punishment, as above mentioned, is not imposed.

---

[20] See, for example, Gordon, *Criminal Law*, 2nd ed., Chap. 51.

(4) Any witness who, after being duly cited in accordance with section 315 of this Act —

(a) fails without reasonable excuse, after receiving at least 24 hours' notice, to attend for precognition by a prosecutor at the time and place mentioned in the citation served on him, or

(b) refuses when so cited to give information within his knowledge regarding any matter relative to the commission of the offence in relation to which such precognition is taken,

shall be liable to the like punishment as is provided in the foregoing provisions of this section."

It is submitted that, where a prosecutor proceeds by way of summary complaint as provided for in subsection (3) the court's powers of punishment will then be the normal summary ones in respect of a common law offence, and will not be restricted to those set out in subsection (1).

7–12   There are no comparable statutory provisions relative to contempt in cases on indictment and, as can be seen, the provisions in summary procedure relate only to certain classes of contempt and only two categories of offender. In all other cases, therefore, the matter must be dealt with according to the common law of contempt. Generally, any improper or disorderly behaviour in court may be treated as contempt, and it is for the presiding judge to decide whether any particular conduct amounts to contempt of court. Where, however, the conduct itself constitutes a substantial crime or offence, such as an attempt to pervert the course of justice, prevarication, or the carrying of an offensive weapon, the judge will normally seek to ascertain whether the prosecutor proposes to bring criminal proceedings against the offender before dealing himself with the matter as a contempt of court.

7–13   The following are some examples of conduct which may be treated as contempt of court:

(a)   drunkenness in court by an accused, a witness, a juror or a spectator;[21]

(b)   insulting language to the judge;[22] in such a case the court should be slow to regard criticism as contempt unless it is clearly disrespectful or likely to interfere

---

[21] *Alex. MacLean* (1838) 2 Swin. 185; *John Allan* (1826) Shaw 172; *Jas. Wemyss* (1840) Bell's *Notes* 165; *Eliz. Yates* (1847) Ark. 238.
[22] *Robt. Clark or Williamson* (1829) Shaw 215.

with the proper administration of justice; it should be recognised that "disappointed litigants sometimes feel aggrieved and that some of them are ill-tempered, and that they may say or write things which are foolish and reprehensible"; consequently the contempt process should not "degenerate into an oppressive or vindictive abuse of the court's powers";[23]

(c)   failure to attend court when duly cited as a witness or an accused;[24] to amount to contempt such failure must be wilful: it is submitted that a failure by an accused person to attend for his trial may still be treated as contempt notwithstanding that such person has been granted bail under the Bail etc. (Scotland) Act 1980, and is thereby liable to prosecution in respect of that failure;

(d)   prevarication by witnesses;[25]

(e)   refusal by a witness to take an oath or affirmation, or to answer questions.[26]

14   When contempt occurs, difficulties may arise as to the appropriate procedure to be followed. In 1975 Lord Justice-General Emslie circulated to all judges a memorandum setting out a suggested procedure, and that has formed the basis for practice in all subsequent cases. With the permission of the Lord Justice-General, that memorandum is printed as an appendix to this chapter. In dealing with cases of contempt the court must bear in mind that the desirability of dealing with the matter expeditiously must be balanced against the need to allow the offender to consider, and perhaps take advice on, his position, and, where the contempt occurs in the course of a jury trial, the need to avoid the risk of creating any prejudice in the mind of the jury. So far as the formal finding of guilt is concerned this may properly, in the case of contempt by a spectator, be made as soon as the contempt has been committed. In a jury trial, however, the best course is to delay making the formal finding until at least the jury has retired to consider its verdict. Thereafter, unless the contempt is of a trivial nature, further consideration should be deferred to enable the offender to have the opportunity of obtaining professional advice (and, if necessary, legal aid), and considering his position. The

---

[23] *Milburn*, 1946 S.C. 301, *per* L.P. Normand at 315.
[24] *H.M.A.* v. *Bell*, 1936 J.C. 89; *Pirie* v. *Hawthorn*, 1962 J.C. 69.
[25] Hume, i. 380; Alison, i. 484; *MacLeod* v. *Speirs* (1884) 5 Couper 387.
[26] *Wylie & Another* v. *H.M.A.*, 1966 S.L.T. 149; *H.M.A.* v. *Airs, supra.*

period of deferment will depend on circumstances, including perhaps the desirability of obtaining a social inquiry report, and will be at the discretion of the judge. At the adjourned diet the offender should be given a full opportunity of apologising for his conduct, and of making a statement in mitigation.[27] These will, of course, be given such weight as they merit when sentence is being determined. If a custodial sentence is imposed it may be made consecutive to any sentence then being served by the offender , but such a sentence is not eligible for parole.[28]

7–15   Until the passing of the Contempt of Court Act 1981 there were no statutory provisions, other than those mentioned *supra* in para. 7-11, setting out the penalties which may be imposed in respect of a contempt of court. The Act now provides (by section 15 (2)) that the maximum penalty which may be imposed by way of imprisonment or fine for contempt of court in Scottish proceedings is two years imprisonment or a fine or both. That power is, however, restricted in that (a) where the contempt is dealt with by a sheriff in the course of or in connection with proceedings other than criminal proceedings on indictment, the maximum penalty is not to exceed three months imprisonment or a fine of £500 or both, and (b) where the contempt is dealt with by a district court the penalty is not to exceed sixty days imprisonment or a fine of £200 or both. In addition, the relevant provisions in the 1975 Act (a) restricting the detention of young offenders, (b) relating to persons suffering from mental disorder, and (c) relating to the remit by a district court to the sheriff court of persons suffering from mental disorder, apply to persons found guilty of contempt of court.

Offences Against Children

7–16   Any court by or before which a person is convicted of having committed any offence:

    (a)   under section 21 of the Children and Young Persons (Scotland) Act 1937;

    (b)   mentioned in Schedule 1 to the 1975 Act; or

    (c)   in respect of a female person aged 17 years or over which constitutes the crime of incest,

may refer (i) the child in respect of whom the offence mentioned in paragraph (a) or (b) above has been committed; or (ii) any child who is, or who is likely to become, a member of the same household

---

[27] *Royle* v. *Gray*, 1973 S.L.T. 31.
[28] *Petition Manson*, High Court, 27 May 1977.

as the person who has committed the offence mentioned in paragraph (b) or (c) above, to the reporter.[29] The offences mentioned in Schedule 1 to the 1975 Act (as amended by Schedule 1 to the Sexual Offences (Scotland) Act 1976) are:

(a)   any offence under the Sexual Offences (Scotland) Act 1976;

(b)   any offence in respect of a child under the age of 17 years which constitutes the crime of incest;

(c)   any offence under section 12, 15, 22 or 33 of the Children and Young Persons (Scotland) Act 1937; and

(d)   any other offence involving bodily injury to a child under the age of 17 years.

INCAPACITIES AND DISQUALIFICATIONS

17   Under various statutes courts are empowered, in addition to other penalties, to make orders declaring offenders to be incapable of holding certain offices, or disqualifying them for holding certain permits or licences. Such powers are always to be found in the statutes creating the particular offences. Two examples will illustrate this. For a contravention of section 1 of the Public Bodies Corrupt Practices Act 1889, an offender is liable to be adjudged incapable of holding any public office for five years from the date of conviction (or for ever in the case of a second or subsequent conviction). In addition such an offender may be ordered to forfeit any office held by him at the date of conviction, and to forfeit any claim he may have to a pension as an employee of a public body. Again, in a more modern statute, section 11 of the Betting, Gaming and Lotteries Act 1963 provides that if the holder of a bookmaker's permit or a betting agency permit is convicted of certain offences the court may forfeit his permit. Forfeiture in such a case involves disqualification for holding a permit of either description for five years or such shorter time as the court may specify.

REVOCATION OF PAROLE LICENCE

18   The Criminal Justice Act 1967 provided for the creation of a Parole Board for Scotland, and gave power to the Secretary of State to release certain prisoners, including those serving life sentences, on licence on the recommendation of the board.[30] Certain courts are

---

[29] 1975 Act, ss. 168, 364, as amended by 1980 Act, Sched. 7, paras. 38, 57.

[30] ss. 60 (1) and 61; more generally on parole see para. 11–23 et seq.

empowered, in certain circumstances, to revoke such licences.

7–19   If a person who is subject to a licence under section 60 or 61 of the Act is convicted by the High Court or by a sheriff, whether summarily or on indictment, of an offence punishable on indictment with imprisonment, the court by which he is convicted may, whether or not it passes any other sentence on him, revoke the licence.[31] When the provisions of section 62 (8) of the Criminal Justice Act 1967 were incorporated as sections 213 (1) and 422 (1) of the 1975 Act the restriction in the use of this power to the High Court or the sheriff court was omitted. Nonetheless, it is submitted that this has not altered the previous provision, so that this power may not be exercised by a district court. The Parole Board itself has certain powers to recommend the recall of persons who are convicted while on licence but, it is submitted, it is not good practice for a court which is considering a disposal other than revocation of the licence to defer sentence on an offender in order to see whether or not the board will recommend his recall: only the court can indicate the view it takes of the offence by passing sentence and, until it does so, the board has no basis on which to exercise its discretion. Consequently the court should impose whatever sentence it deems proper without regard to any action that may subsequently be taken by the Parole Board.

Effects of revocation

7–20   On the revocation of the licence of any person he is liable to be detained in pursuance of his sentence and, if at large, is to be deemed to be unlawfully at large.[32] In a case where a section 60 (non-life sentence) licence is revoked the Secretary of State must not thereafter release that person on licence before the expiration of one year from the date of revocation or before the expiration of one third of the period during which the licence would have remained in force, whichever is the later.[33]

RECOMMENDATION FOR DEPORTATION

7–21   The right of entry into and abode in the United Kingdom is presently regulated by the Immigration Act 1971 though some alterations to the relevant definitions may be made by the British Nationality Bill, presently before Parliament. Under the 1971 Act

---

[31] 1975 Act, ss. 213 (1), 422 (1).
[32] Criminal Justice Act 1967, s. 62 (9).
[33] *Ibid.* s. 62 (10).

persons who are not patrial (*i.e.* not having the right of abode in the United Kingdom) are liable to deportation in certain circumstances. One of these is where their deportation is recommended by a court which, in Scotland, must be either the High Court or the sheriff court.[34]

22   A person who is non-patrial is liable to deportation from the United Kingdom if, after he has attained the age of 17, he is convicted of an offence for which he is punishable with imprisonment and on his conviction he is recommended for deportation by a court empowered to do so.[35] However, the court must not recommend a person for deportation unless he has been given not less than seven days notice in writing stating that a person is not liable to deportation if he is patrial, describing the persons who are patrial and stating, so far as material, the effect of section 3 (8) (onus on person to prove that he is patrial) and section 7 (exemption from deportation for certain existing residents). The court has power to adjourn, after convicting an offender, for the purpose of enabling a notice to be given to him or, if a notice was given to him less than seven days previously, to allow the necessary seven days to elapse.[36] A recommendation for deportation may be made in respect of an offender who is sentenced to imprisonment for life.[37]

23   The question whether an offence is one for which a person is punishable with imprisonment is to be determined without regard to any enactment restricting the imprisonment of young or first offenders. Furthermore, for the purposes of deportation a person who, on being charged with an offence, is found to have committed it, shall, notwithstanding any enactment to the contrary and notwithstanding that the court does not proceed to conviction, be regarded as a person convicted of the offence. References in the Act to conviction are to be construed accordingly.[38]

Procedure

24   Where a court is considering making a recommendation for deportation, and the offender has been served with the notice required by section 6 (2) of the Act, he should be given an opportunity to give evidence on matters affecting his eligibility for

---

[34] Immigration Act 1971, s. 6 (2).
[35] *Ibid.* s. 3 (6).
[36] *Ibid.* s. 6 (2).
[37] *Ibid.* s. 6 (4).
[38] *Ibid.* s. 6 (3).

deportation as set out in the notice. If a recommendation is then made, a certificate of recommendation should be sent as soon as possible to the Home Office, along with a copy of any social inquiry report that was considered by the court. If a person has been convicted of an offence under section 24 (1) (*a*) or (*b*) of the Act (illegal entry, overstaying or breach of conditions), but the court decides not to make a recommendation for deportation, the Home Secretary should, when possible, be informed of the reasons for the court's decision.

7–25   Where a person is recommended for deportation by a court he must be detained in custody pending the making of a deportation order unless the court directs otherwise, or unless the Home Secretary subsequently directs his release.[39] It is suggested that in determining whether or not to release such a person the court should apply the normal considerations applicable to a grant or refusal of bail.

Exclusion From Licensed Premises

7–26   Where a court by or before which a person is convicted of an offence committed on licensed premises is satisfied that in committing that offence he resorted to violence or offered or threatened to resort to violence, the court may make an exclusion order prohibiting him from entering those premises or any other specified premises without the express consent of the licensee of the premises or his servant or agent.[40] In summary proceedings the word "convicted" is to be construed, where the court makes a probation order or grants an absolute discharge, as a reference to the court's being satisfied that the person committed the offence.[41]

7–27   An exclusion order may be made either in addition to any sentence which is imposed in respect of the offence of which the person is convicted, or in addition to a probation order or an absolute discharge (notwithstanding the normal provisions relating to them and to their effect). An exclusion order may not be made in any circumstances other than those mentioned.[42] Unless the order is terminated as described below, it is to have effect for such period as is specified in the order, being not less than three months or more

---

[39] Immigration Act 1971, Sched. 3, para 2 (1).
[40] Licensed Premises (Exclusion of Certain Persons) Act 1980, s. 1 (1).
[41] *Ibid.* s. 4 (2).
[42] *Ibid.* s. 1 (2) (*a*) and (*c*).

than two years.[43] Where a court makes an exclusion order, or an order terminating or varying an exclusion order, the clerk of the court must send a copy of the order to the licensee of the premises to which the order relates.[44]

8   Without prejudice to any other right to expel a person from premises, the licensee of licensed premises or his servant or agent may expel from those premises any person who has entered or whom he reasonably suspects of having entered the premises in breach of an exclusion order. A constable must, on the demand of the licensee or his servant or agent, help to expel any person whom the constable reasonably suspects of having entered the premises in breach of an exclusion order.[45]

9   A person who enters any premises in breach of an exclusion order is guilty of an offence and is liable, on conviction in a court of summary jurisdiction, to a fine not exceeding £200 or to imprisonment for a term not exceeding one month or both.[46] The court by which a person is convicted of an offence as just described is required to consider whether or not the exclusion order should continue in force. The court may, if it thinks fit, by order terminate the exclusion order or vary it by deleting the name of any specified premises. An exclusion order is not otherwise to be affected by a person's conviction for such an offence.[47]

0   In relation to all of the foregoing the term "licensed premises" means premises in respect of which a licence under the Licensing (Scotland) Act 1976 is in force, but does not include premises in respect of which an off-sales licence or a licence under Part III of the 1976 Act (licences for seamen's canteens) is in force.[48]

1   Two points may be noted in relation to the foregoing provisions. The first is whether or not they can be applied in a case where a person is convicted of a breach of the peace committed on licensed premises. It has been held[49] that a charge of breach of the peace, even where it involves threats of violence and malicious damage, is not an offence inferring personal violence for the purpose of enabling a sheriff summary court to impose more than a

---

[43] Licensed Premises (Exclusion of Certain Persons) Act 1980, s. 1 (3).
[44] *Ibid.* s. 4 (3).
[45] *Ibid.* s. 3.
[46] *Ibid.* s. 2 (1).
[47] *Ibid.* s. 2 (2).
[48] *Ibid.* s. 4 (1).
[49] *Adair* v. *Morton*, 1972 S.L.T. (Notes) 70.

three months sentence of imprisonment.[50] The present Act, however, describes the particulars of a qualifying offence in a specific and factual way, and it is accordingly submitted that an exclusion order may be made where a person is convicted of a breach of the peace, provided that the court is satisfied that, in committing the offence, the offender "resorted to violence or offered or threatened to resort to violence".

7–32   The second point is one relating to practice. The Act contains no provision enabling the licensee of any premises concerned to state to the court whether or not he would wish an exclusion order to be made: and of course such a provision would be contrary to normal and accepted practice in statutes relating to sentencing powers. On the other hand, an exclusion order is plainly intended to be not so much a penalty imposed on the offender as a benefit conferred on the licensee concerned: and it is clear from the terms of section 1(1) of the Act that the licensee may waive that benefit if he so wishes. Now there is little point in a court making an exclusion order if it is not to be enforced by the licensee, and this suggests that it may be prudent for a court, where circumstances permit, to seek to ascertain his views before such an order is made.

---

[50] See para. 3–4.

MEMORANDUM TO JUDGES ISSUED BY
LORD JUSTICE-GENERAL IN 1975

1. As a consequence of the decision of the Court in *H.M. Advocate* v. *Airs*, 1975 J.C. 64, judges may welcome further guidance as to the procedure to be adopted when the conduct of any party during a trial constitutes, in the opinion of the presiding judge, a contempt of the Court.

2. Only the presiding judge can decide if conduct amounts to contempt. If he is of that opinion, he should normally make the appropriate judicial finding at the appropriate time and, as a matter of record, this finding should be entered in the minutes.

3. The appropriate time to make the judicial finding will vary according to circumstances. In the case of contempt by a spectator, for example, the finding may properly be made at once. In the case, however, of contempt by a witness or by a party to the proceedings in a trial, criminal or civil, before a jury, it is important to avoid the risk of creating prejudice in the mind of the jury and the best course will be to delay making the formal finding until at least the jury has retired at the conclusion of the trial.

4. Thereafter in every case it is for the judge to decide whether the circumstances warrant an exception to the normal rule that the trial judge ought personally to deal with the contempt of the Court over which he is presiding.

5. If there is to be no exception to the general rule, the judge should not, however, deal with the offender, including a spectator, forthwith. Although an act of contempt should be dealt with expeditiously, it is much more important that it be dealt with — and be seen to be dealt with — objectively. When the judge has made a finding of contempt he should defer further consideration to enable the offender to have the opportunity of obtaining professional advice (and if need be legal aid) and considering his position. The period of deferment will depend upon the circumstances. It would be a matter for judicial determination, in the light of the circumstances of each

case, whether the offender should be detained in custody until the adjourned diet, or released either with or without Bail. If the offender is under 21 the judge ought also to bear in mind the propriety of obtaining a Social Inquiry Report.

6. At the adjourned diet the offender should be given a full opportunity of apologising for his conduct, and of making a statement in mitigation. If a custodial sentence is then imposed, it should normally be made to run consecutively to any sentence the offender is currently serving, and this would be a factor in determining severity.

7. If on the other hand the judge feels that the case is of such an exceptional nature that he cannot properly deal with it himself he should, after making the formal finding of contempt, remit the case to the High Court at Edinburgh, on a specified diet, either detaining or releasing the offender as he might think appropriate.

8. If the offence be one of prevarication, the judge should normally ascertain whether the Crown intends to bring criminal proceedings against the offender before deciding to deal with the matter himself as a contempt.

CHAPTER 8

PROCEDURE

INTRODUCTION

1   While it is essential that the correct procedures should be observed by judges and by clerks of court when a sentence is being passed, since otherwise the sentence may be put at risk, the rules governing these procedures are detailed and complex and are, moreover, to be found partly in the common law, partly in a variety of statutes, and partly in directions contained in judgments issued by the appeal court. Consequently the task of finding one's way successfully to the correct procedure in any particular case is not an easy one. This chapter is an attempt to make that path a little simpler to follow.

PROCEDURE IMMEDIATELY AFTER GUILT ESTABLISHED

2   Once an offender has pled guilty or has been found guilty by the verdict of a jury or the finding of a court, it is the court's duty to consider and pass sentence provided that it is moved to do so by the prosecutor, and provided that it may competently do so.[1] Unless the court is unable competently to proceed any further it may not "make no order".[2] In cases on indictment the prosecutor must formally move for sentence. If he does not do so, no sentence may be pronounced,[3] and the accused should be discharged from the dock. The motion may, however, be inferred from the prosecutor's actings as where he lays before the court a schedule of previous convictions.[4] In summary cases no formal motion for sentence is required, but here too a prosecutor will normally take some action consistent with asking for sentence by, for example, submitting a notice of penalties or a schedule of previous convictions. However, should he do none of these things, and if the case is not one where a notice of penalties is required, the court may, in contrast to cases on indictment, still proceed to sentence.

Plea of guilty

3   Where there has been a plea of guilty the prosecutor will narrate the circumstances of the offence and the accused, or his

---

[1] See *infra*, para. 8–07.
[2] *Skeen* v. *Sullivan*, 1980 S.L.T. (Notes) 11.
[3] Macdonald, 348; Hume, ii, 470; Alison, ii, 653; Bell's *Notes*, 300.
[4] *Noon* v. *H.M.A.*, 1960 J.C. 52.

counsel or solicitor, who must in all cases be given an opportunity to address the court in mitigation,[5] will normally give the accused's version of these circumstances. If there is any dispute between the prosecution and the defence concerning any material facts, and if no evidence is led, the proper course for the court is to ignore such disputed facts.[6] This may, of course, give rise to problems. The defence statement of facts may be so inconsistent with that given by the prosecution as to negate the plea of guilty. In that event, if the plea of guilty is not withdrawn, the proper course, it is submitted, is for the court to refuse to proceed on the plea of guilty and to have a plea of not guilty recorded so that the case can proceed to trial. Where that course is followed it may be desirable to ensure that the trial is taken by a different judge. Again, disputes on matters of fact, while not negating the plea of guilty, may be so extensive or material that, if he is to ignore these facts, the judge will be left with insufficient to form a satisfactory basis for a decision on sentence. There is no authority to determine the proper procedure in such a case, but it is submitted that it would be open to a judge to require evidence to be led before pronouncing sentence. Similar problems may also arise in summary cases where an accused has pled guilty by letter and has tendered an explanation which is in some respects inconsistent with the account given by the prosecutor. The proper course in such a case is for the judge to put the accused's explanation to the prosecutor to see if the two accounts can be reconciled; very often they can. However, if they cannot, and the inconsistency is, or may be, material, the case should be continued to a later date so that the accused may appear personally. If the case is one where the court is considering the possibility of making a compensation order, and any dispute relates to, for example, the value of stolen or damaged property, the court may wish to continue the case to have the true value established. However, courts should, it is submitted, be reluctant to spend too much time on ascertaining the *quantum* of loss for such purposes (see para. 10–75).

Previous convictions

8–04   Where a person is convicted of an offence, the court may have regard to any previous conviction in respect of that person in deciding on the disposal of the case.[7] Previous convictions should be

---

[5] *Falconer* v. *Jessop*, 1975 S.L.T. (Notes) 78.
[6] *Galloway* v. *Adair*, 1947 J.C. 7; *Barn* v. *Smith*, 1978 J.C. 17.
[7] 1975 Act, ss. 159 (2), 356 (2).

contained in a notice prepared by the prosecutor, and that notice must conform to, and have been served on the accused in accordance with, the relevant statutory provisions.[8] When moving for sentence in cases on indictment, or after a plea or finding of guilt in summary cases, the prosecutor lays this notice before the court. In solemn procedure, any conviction contained in the notice is held to apply to the accused unless he gives prior written intimation objecting to such a conviction on the ground that it does not apply to him or is otherwise inadmissible.[9] In summary procedure, where a plea of guilty is tendered in writing the accused is deemed to admit any previous conviction set forth in the notice, unless he expressly denies it in the writing by which that plea is tendered: in any other case the judge or the clerk of court must ask the accused whether he admits the previous conviction.[10] In both solemn and summary procedure, if a previous conviction is not admitted, the prosecutor may either withdraw it, or he may lead evidence in order to prove it. Since, in a summary case, the prosecutor may not know in advance that a previous conviction is to be challenged, he should normally be allowed an opportunity, by adjournment if necessary, to adduce the necessary evidence to prove the conviction. A previous conviction may be proved, *inter alia*, by an extract conviction, by witnesses including an official of any prison in which the accused may have been confined on such conviction, and by fingerprint evidence.[11]

–05 Certain detailed rules relating to previous convictions fall to be noted. A previous conviction must be one dated prior to the date of the current offence.[12] A previous conviction cannot be libelled if it is under appeal.[13] It has also been held to be improper for a prosecutor in moving for sentence to refer to offences not included in the notice of previous convictions.[14] While that, and the rule that a previous conviction must be one dated prior to the current offence, are strictly correct, it would clearly be absurd if a court was not, in appropriate circumstances, informed of a conviction that has occurred subsequent to the current offence and which could not therefore be included in the notice. The most obvious example of this is where the offender has, since the current offence, been

---

[8] 1975 Act, ss. 68, 161 and 357.
[9] *Ibid* s. 68 (2)-(4).
[10] *Ibid* s. 357 (1), as amended by the 1980 Act, s. 40.
[11] *Ibid* ss. 162, 163, 164, 357, 358.
[12] H.M.A. v. *John Graham* (1842) 1 Brown 445.
[13] *McCall* v. *Mitchell* (1911) 6 Adam 303.
[14] *Ramsay* v. *H.M.A.*, 1959 J.C. 86; *Adair* v. *Hill*, 1943 J.C. 9.

sentenced to a long period of imprisonment. In such a case, if the court were not to be informed of this, it might take a course which would be wholly inconsistent with the term of imprisonment, such as asking for a social inquiry report with a view to considering a probation order. Another example is where the accused has, since the current offence, been placed on probation. In such a case it is obviously desirable for the court to be aware of this if it is to make a sensible decision in the case under consideration. Yet another example is the case where a young offender has a history of appearances before children's hearings. If not mentioned, the court has, it is submitted, a right to inquire about this. In fact it is now common practice for prosecutors and defence counsel or solicitors to bring this sort of information to the court's attention. Apart from its obvious good sense two other factors make this sort of practice desirable. One is that such convictions and children's hearing appearances are often mentioned in social inquiry reports and, as the use of such reports becomes greater, so does the opportunity for the court to become aware of such matters. Moreover, it is now clear that a court is entitled to have regard to convictions disclosed in a report, even although these have not been libelled by the prosecutor.[15] Where convictions are disclosed in a report it is proper practice for the court to give the accused an opportunity to admit or deny them. The second factor, which is special to road traffic cases, is that where a person is convicted of an offence involving obligatory endorsement and his driving licence is produced to the court, then in determining what order to make the court may take into consideration particulars of any previous conviction or disqualification endorsed on the licence.[16] This power is not affected by the provisions of section 357 (1) of the 1975 Act relating to previous convictions, and consequently the court may take such previous convictions into consideration notwithstanding that they have not been libelled by the prosecutor.[17]

8–06   Two other matters relating to previous convictions require to be noticed. Firstly, a previous conviction libelled must apply to the accused; thus, it is incompetent in a complaint against the representative of a company as an individual to libel a conviction

[15] *Sharp* v. *Stevenson*, 1945 S.L.T. (Notes) 79; *Sillars* v. *Copeland*, 1966 S.L.T. 89.
[16] Road Traffic Act 1972, s. 101 (4A).
[17] *Ibid.* s. 101 (8); and see *Whyte* v. *Hogg*, High Court, 10 December 1975; *Urry* v. *Gibb*, 1979 S.L.T. (Notes) 19.

obtained against the company in its corporate capacity.[18] Secondly, it has been observed[19] that, where a judge considers a previous conviction, he should look at the conviction and the sentence alone and should not take into account the details that led thereto. There is in Scotland no modern reported statement to the same effect and, with the growing insistence in recent times on providing a court with the maximum information concerning an offender and his background, it may be doubted whether the view expressed in *Connel* v. *Mitchell* would today gain acceptance in its entirety. Certainly it would probably still be seen as inappropriate to examine all the details of previous offences, and to examine again all the arguments about, for example, provocation, or the pleas in mitigation. On the other hand, standing the complete absence of detail that is normal in the Scottish system of recording convictions, it may be helpful for a court to know, in for example a case of wife assault, whether or not previous convictions for assault were of a similar character. In practice this sort of information is frequently given to the court either by the prosecutor or by counsel or solicitor for the defence, and it is submitted that it is not improper for this to be done.

Notice of penalties

8–07   Where any complaint includes a statutory charge a notice of penalties, in the form prescribed by statute,[20] must be served on the accused with the complaint, and a copy of the notice should be laid before the judge after the accused has pled or has been found guilty. Although errors in a notice of penalties may be rectified by amendment,[21] there is no power to serve a notice of penalties on an accused after he has been called on to plead; and, if a prosecutor has failed to serve a notice at the proper time, so that he cannot lay one before the court prior to sentence, it is incompetent for the court to impose any penalty.[22] Disqualification for holding or obtaining a driving licence is a penalty in this sense,[23] but endorsement of a driving licence may not be.[24] Forfeiture, on the other hand, is a penalty and, unless is is expressly mentioned in the notice of

[18] *Campbell* v. *MacPherson* (1910) 6 Adam 394.
[19] *Connel* v. *Mitchell* (1908) 5 Adam 641.
[20] 1975 Act, s. 311 (5).
[21] *Ibid.* s. 335 (1).
[22] *Coogans* v. *Macdonald*, 1954 J.C. 98.
[23] *Coogans* v. *Macdonald*, *supra.*
[24] *Pirie* v. *Rivard*, 1976 S.L.T. (Sh. Ct.) 59.

penalties, it cannot competently be ordered.[25] A failure by a prosecutor to sign a notice of penalties is not fatal,[26] but he must take care, when referring to the section or sections in which the penalties are set forth, to state the correct sections.[27]

PLEA IN MITIGATION

8–08 After previous convictions have been admitted or proved, and after a notice of penalties has, where appropriate, been laid before the court, the accused, or his counsel or solicitor, may address the court in mitigation. This is a right which cannot be denied to an accused,[28] and, if an accused is not legally represented the presiding judge must ask him if he has anything to say,[29] though failure to do this may not constitute a good ground of appeal unless the judge has acted oppressively. Mitigating circumstances may not be a matter of dispute, or may already have emerged in the course of the trial.[30] In any other case they should be established by oral evidence on oath.[31] Notwithstanding this rule it is not uncommon in summary cases, and even occasionally in cases on indictment, for the defence to produce a document, such as a letter from an employer, or a minister of religion, to establish an accused person's good character. Although, strictly, such documents should not be considered in place of oral evidence, it is submitted that it is not unreasonable to do so provided that the court can be reasonably satisfied as to the authenticity of the documents, and provided that they are not submitted as evidence of material facts as distinct from being expressions of opinion on the general character of the accused. It is, equally, common for all courts to accept, without oral evidence, statements from counsel and solicitors concerning matters such as an accused person's employment, marital status and family position — all of which are factors that may have some mitigating effect on sentence. If all matters relied on in a plea in mitigation had to be established by oral evidence the work of the courts would probably very quickly grind to a halt and in these circumstances, it is submitted, what a judge must do is to exercise a sensible discretion so as to distinguish between those matters which

---

[25] *Duffy* v. *Lakie*, 1962 S.L.T. 30.
[26] *McCoull & Anor.* v. *Skeen*, 1974 S.L.T. (Notes) 48.
[27] *Cumming* v. *Frame* (1909) 6 Adam 57; *Galt* v. *Ritchie* (1873) 2 Couper 470.
[28] *Falconer* v. *Jessop*, 1975 S.L.T. (Notes) 78.
[29] *Grahams* v. *McLennan* (1911) 6 Adam 315; *Ewart* v. *Strathern*, 1924 J.C. 45.
[30] *Clark* v. *H.M.A.*, 1968 J.C. 53; *H.M.A.* v. *Murray*, 1969 S.L.T. (Notes) 85.
[31] *Forbes* v. *H.M.A.*, 1963 J.C. 68.

can reasonably be taken as established without oral evidence, and those which can not.

-09   Sometimes a judge will be obliged, or will consider it desirable, to obtain reports before deciding on sentence. If this obligation, or desirability, is apparent at an early stage, it may be sensible for him to suggest to the accused, or his counsel or solicitor, that any plea in mitigation should be held over until the reports have been made available. Sometimes, indeed, an accused's counsel or solicitor may suggest this course to the judge.

ADJOURNMENT FOR INQUIRY

-10   The normal power which a court has to adjourn the hearing of a case includes the power, after a person has been convicted or the court has found that he committed the offence and before he has been sentenced or otherwise dealt with, to adjourn the case for the purpose of enabling inquiries to be made or of determining the most suitable method of dealing with his case. Although there may be more than one adjournment for this purpose, no single period of adjournment should exceed three weeks.[32] This power is used on every occasion when reports on an offender are asked for by the court and, although it is sometimes loosely referred to as "deferring sentence", or in summary courts, by clerks of court, as "deferring conviction and sentence", the power is properly described as one of adjournment. Although there can be several adjournments to enable inquiries to be made, it is generally desirable that the actual date of final disposal should not be postponed more than is necessary and, to that end, it is as well, at the stage of first adjournment, that the court should consider and call for all of the reports that appear to be necessary or desirable. This course is particularly to be commended where an offender is being remanded in custody.

Bail or custody

-11   Generally, a person whose case is adjourned for reports should not be remanded in custody in the absence of special circumstances. This is particularly so in the case of first offenders.[33] If a person is not remanded in custody he must either be released on bail, or be

---

[32] 1975 Act, ss. 179, 380, as amended by Bail etc. (Scotland) Act 1980, and Criminal Justice (Scotland) Act 1980, Sched. 7. paras. 36, 59.

[33] *Morrison* v. *Clark*, 1962 S.L.T. 113.

ordained to attend at the adjourned diet. This is the effect of the amendments to sections 179 and 380 of the 1975 Act made by section 5 of the Bail etc. (Scotland) Act 1980 and paras. 36 and 59 of the Seventh Schedule to the 1980 Act. The special circumstances that may justify a remand in custody will vary from case to case but may include the fact that the offender is a foreigner, or of no fixed abode, or, even where he is a first offender, that he has been remanded in custody prior to trial. If, in such a case, the court is obtaining reports in the anticipation that a custodial sentence may be necessary, it would probably not be appropriate to release the offender during the period of adjournment.

Remand of children and young offenders

8–12   Special provisions exist where a court adjourns for inquiry a case involving a child or a young offender.[34] These provisions are not as clear as one might wish, partly because they are the result of a succession of amendments to provisions originally contained in the Criminal Justice (Scotland) Act 1949,[35] partly because the codifying 1975 Act in fact made some alterations to earlier amendments, and partly because the terminology of the provisions is not appropriate to the scheme of the 1975 Act which treats solemn and summary procedure separately, though frequently repeating the same provision in the different parts of the Act. Thus, section 329, which is in the portion of the Act devoted to summary procedure, still speaks of "the period for which he is committed or until he is liberated in due course of law".[36] In these circumstances, it is submitted, one must, in summary cases, substitute the words which are appropriate to that form of procedure. Subject to the foregoing, the following are the rules that must be observed where a person under 21 years of age is refused bail during the period of an adjournment for inquiry:

(a)   If he is under 16 years of age the court must generally commit him to the local authority in whose area the court is situated. It is then the duty of the local authority to place him in a suitable place of safety chosen by them.

---

[34] 1975 Act, ss. 23, 329.
[35] s. 28.
[36] Subs. (2).

(b)   If he is over 16 years of age, or is a child under 16 but over 14 years of age who is certified by the court to be unruly or depraved, he must be committed to a remand centre, if the court has been notified by the Secretary of State that a remand centre is available for the reception from that court of persons of his class or description.[37]

(c)   If no remand centre is available for the court in question, persons falling under para. (b) above will be committed to prison.

(d)   If a person has been committed to a local authority under para. (a) above and is not less than 14 years of age, and it appears to the court that he is unruly or depraved, the court may revoke the commitment and commit the person to a remand centre or to prison in accordance with paras. (b) and (c) above.

(e)   Conversely, where a person under 16 has been committed to a remand centre or to prison, and the sheriff[38] is satisfied that his detention there is no longer necessary, he may revoke that commitment and commit the person to the local authority.

(f)   Where any person is committed to a local authority or to a remand centre, that authority or centre must be specified in the warrant.

–13   Section 70 of the Children Act 1975 amends sections 23 and 329 of the 1975 Act so as to prohibit the court from certifying a child as unruly or depraved unless conditions prescribed by the Secretary of State in a statutory instrument are satisfied. To date, however, no commencement order has been made in relation to section 70 and, consequently, no statutory instrument under it has been made. A statutory instrument under a comparable provision in section 69 of the Children Act has been made for England and Wales,[39] and it is submitted that for the moment it may offer some guidance as to the criteria which should be considered when making a decision on unruliness or depravity. Generally, and applying Scottish termino-

---

[37] At present there is only one remand institution in Scotland, at Longriggend near Glasgow.

[38] It is not clear why s. 23 (4) of the 1975 Act, which contains this provision, should specify "the sheriff" rather than "the court", which is used elsewhere in the section. It would seem to imply that this power may not be exercised by the High Court.

[39] S.I. 1977 No. 1037.

logy, these criteria are (1) that the child has been charged with a crime of violence or some other serious crime, and either there has been insufficient time to obtain a written report from the appropriate local authority as to the availability of suitable accommodation, or the court is satisfied on the basis of such a report that no suitable accommodation is available, or (2) the child has a history of persistently absconding from List D schools or assessment centres, or of seriously disrupting the running of such establishments.

Remand for inquiry into physical or mental condition

8–14   Where a person is charged before a court with an offence punishable with imprisonment, and the court is satisfied that he did the act or made the omission charged but is of opinion that an inquiry ought to be made into his physical or mental condition before the method of dealing with him is determined, the court must remand him in custody or on bail for such period or periods as the court thinks necessary to enable a medical examination and report to be made. No single period of remand should exceed three weeks.[40] Where bail is allowed it must be a condition of the bail that the person should undergo a medical examination by a duly qualified medical practitioner or, where inquiry is into his mental condition and the bail order so specifies, two such practitioners. Furthermore, it must be a condition of bail that he attends at an institution or place, or on any such practitioner specified in the order and, where the inquiry is into his mental condition, that he should comply with any directions which may be given to him for that purpose by any person so specified or by a person of any class so specified.[41]

8–15   From time to time a court may wish medical reports before deciding on the proper method of disposing of a case but may be of opinion that the offender's mental condition is such that he cannot be relied upon to comply with the above conditions of a bail order, but that it would be better that he should reside in a hospital during the period of remand rather than be committed to prison. Provision exists under sections 25 and 330 of the 1975 Act for committing persons to hospital in certain circumstances, but these sections only

---

[40] 1975 Act, ss. 180(1), 381 (1). Unlike ss. 179 and 380 there is no power to ordain an offender to appear at subsequent diets.

[41] *Ibid.* ss. 180 (2), 381 (2), as amended by Bail etc. (Scotland) Act 1980, s. 6 (*a*).

deal with the case where a court *remands or commits for trial*, and therefore provide no authority for such a course after trial and before sentence. In that situation the proper course is provided by sections 180 (2) and 381 (2) which, in addition to the provisions already described, go on to provide that, if arrangements have been made for his reception, it may be a condition of the bail allowed to a person who is to undergo medical examination that he should, for the purpose of the examination, reside in an institution or place specified in the order. In such a case the institution or place will normally be a hospital.

–16 Where a court exercises any of the above powers it must send a statement of the reasons for which it is of opinion that an inquiry ought to be made into the person's physical or mental condition, and of any information before the court about his condition, to the institution or place where he is remanded in custody or, where he is released on bail, to the institution or place at which or the person by whom he is to be examined.[42] Although the above duty is placed on the court, in practice arrangements exist in a number of courts whereby the relevant information is transmitted by procurators fiscal.

WHEN REPORTS MUST BE OBTAINED

(a) In connection with non-custodial disposals

–17 There is no statutory provision which expressly requires a court to obtain a social inquiry report before making a probation order. However, since a court must, before making a probation order, have regard to the character of the offender,[43] and may in certain circumstances have to consider his home surroundings,[44] it is plainly sensible practice to obtain such a report in all cases where such an order is being considered. Indeed, it may safely be said that this course is now a virtually universal practice. In cases where the court is considering the insertion in a probation order of a requirement that the offender should perform unpaid work it must be satisfied that provision can be made for the offender to perform such work.[45] That information too can best be obtained in a social inquiry report. Moreover, where a court is considering the making of a community service order, it must obtain and consider a report by an officer of a local authority about the offender and his circumstances.[46]

---

[42] 1975 Act, ss. 180 (4), 381 (4).
[43] *Ibid.* ss. 183 (1), 384 (1).
[44] *Ibid.* ss. 183 (5), 384 (5).
[45] *Ibid.* ss. 183 (5A), 384 (5A).
[46] Community Service by Offenders (Scotland) Act 1978, s. 1 (2) (c).

(b) In connection with custodial disposals

Children[47]

8–18   There are no statutory provisions which expressly require a court to obtain a social inquiry report when dealing with a child. However, where a child is convicted on indictment and the court proposes to sentence him to detention it must be of opinion that no other method of dealing with him is appropriate.[48] It is submitted that a court could not properly be so satisfied without obtaining and considering at least a social inquiry report. Moreover, where a child who is subject to a supervision requirement is charged with an offence and pleads guilty to, or is found guilty of, that offence the High Court may, and the sheriff court must, request the reporter to arrange a children's hearing for the purpose of obtaining their advice. In practice, since children are seldom prosecuted, at least where they are under the age of 16, unless their offence is a serious one, it is submitted that it is sensible practice to obtain a social inquiry report in all cases, even where a custodial disposal is not in contemplation.

Young offenders

8–19   In the case of a person who is not less than 16 but under 21 years of age a court may not impose detention unless it is of opinion that no other method of dealing with him is appropriate; and to enable the court to form such an opinion it must obtain (from an officer of a local authority or otherwise) such information as it can about the offender's circumstances. It must also take into account any information before it concerning the offender's character and physical and mental condition.[49] It is essential that the foregoing provisions should be complied with.[50] Formerly, when a sentence of borstal training was competent, a duty was imposed on the Secretary of State to cause to be furnished to the court a report on the offender's physical and mental condition and his suitability for the sentence of borstal training: in practice such a report was normally furnished by a governor of the prison in which the offender was remanded, together with a brief medical report by the prison doctor. Although, as noted above, an offender's physical and mental condition is still something of which the court must take

---

[47] For a definition of "child" see para. 5–01.
[48] 1975 Act, s. 206 (1), as amended by 1980 Act, s. 44.
[49] *Ibid.* ss. 207 (3) and (4), and 415 (3) and (4), as substituted by 1980 Act, s. 45.
[50] *Hogg* v. *Heatlie*, 1962 S.L.T. 38; *Deasley* v. *Hogg*, 1976 S.L.T. (Notes) 7.

account — and, indeed, may found on as a reason for sentencing an
offender to detention in a young offenders' institution rather than in
a detention centre[51] — a court is no longer obliged to obtain a report
on these matters. In practice, therefore, unless there are indications
to the contrary, a court need only obtain a social inquiry report as a
basis for forming an opinion that no other method than detention is
appropriate.[52]

Adult offenders

-20   A court must not pass a sentence of imprisonment other than
one fixed by law on a person of or over 21 years of age who has not
been previously sentenced to imprisonment or detention by a court
in any part of the United Kingdom unless the court considers that no
other method of dealing with him is appropriate. Before a court can
so determine it must obtain (from an officer of a local authority or
otherwise) such information as it can about the offender's
circumstances. It must also take into account any information
before it concerning the offender's character and physical and
mental condition.[53] The foregoing provisions replace previous
legislation concerning the imprisonment of first offenders and not
only concentrate on the first sentence of imprisonment rather than
the first offence but also apply equally to courts of solemn and
summary jurisdiction.

-21   For the purpose of determining whether a person has been
previously sentenced to imprisonment or detention by a court in any
part of the United Kingdom the court must (a) disregard a previous
sentence of imprisonment which, having been suspended, has not
taken effect under section 23 of the Powers of Criminal Courts Act
1973 or under section 19 of the Treatment of Offenders Act
(Northern Ireland) 1968, and (b) construe detention as meaning (i)
in relation to Scotland, detention in a young offenders' institution or
detention centre, (ii) in relation to England and Wales, borstal
training or detention in a detention centre, and (iii) in relation to
Northern Ireland, borstal training.[54] It is to be noted that, in
anticipation no doubt of the long-term effects of the 1980 Act, the
foregoing provisions do not construe detention in relation to

---

[51] 1975 Act, ss. 207 (6) and 415 (6), as substituted by 1980 Act, s. 45.

[52] Presumably, where a young offender is remanded in custody, the court will
still find it helpful to seek an assessment by the prison or remand centre governor.

[53] 1980 Act, s. 42 (1).

[54] *Ibid.* s. 41 (2).

Scotland as including borstal training. The rather curious, and perhaps unintended, consequence of this would appear to be that a court would be required to follow the procedures prescribed by section 42 of the Act in a case where an offender had previously served a sentence of borstal training in Scotland, but would not be so required where that sentence had been served in England or Northern Ireland.

Mentally disordered offenders[55]

8–22   Before a court may make a hospital order or a guardianship order it must (a) be satisfied, on the written or oral evidence of two medical practitioners that the offender is suffering from mental disorder of a nature or degree which, in the case of a person under 21 years of age, would warrant his admission to hospital or his reception into guardianship under Part IV of the Mental Health (Scotland) Act 1960, and (b) be of opinion, having regard to all the circumstances of the offence and the character and antecedents of the offender, and to the other available methods of dealing with him, that the most suitable method of disposing of the case is by means of such an order.[56] If the court does not consider it necessary to proceed on the basis of oral evidence for the purpose of (a) above it is customary to refer to the written documents produced by the medical practitioners as medical or psychiatric *reports*: it is to be observed, however, that for the purposes of the section these documents are to be regarded as *evidence*, the absence of which will preclude the making of the order. By contrast, no provision is made as to the means by which the court should reach the opinion referred to in (b) above. It is submitted, however, that a social inquiry report will normally be desirable and appropriate for that purpose, in addition to such other information as the court may have obtained in the course of the proceedings.

WHEN REPORTS MAY BE DESIRABLE

8–23   Apart from the cases where a court is obliged by statute to obtain a report of a particular character before disposing of a case, there are many instances where additional information, either as to the offender's background and home circumstances or as to his physical or mental condition, may be of considerable value. The

---

[55] For a general treatment of the subject see Chap. 4.
[56] 1975 Act, ss. 175 (1), 376 (1).

occasions when the desirability of obtaining such information will suggest itself will depend largely on the circumstances of a particular case or particular offender, and to some extent on the views of individual judges. While in general it may be said that, in the interests of economy, reports (and in particular psychiatric reports) should not be asked for unless there are some positive indications that they are likely to be helpful, it is nonetheless the case that judges increasingly tend to look for additional information to assist them when making any other than the clearest and most obvious sentencing decisions. Although not intended to be either definitive or exhaustive, the following list shows the circumstances in which the obtaining of reports is frequently desirable.

Social inquiry reports:
(a)   cases involving children;
(b)   cases involving young offenders where the offence is of at least moderate gravity;
(c)   cases where the offence is one of violence, and in particular domestic violence, and cases where the offender has a previous record of violence;
(d)   cases where the offence is of at least moderate gravity and the offender either has no previous convictions or has been free of convictions for a substantial period;
(e)   cases where the offence is of at least moderate gravity and the offender is female;
(f)   cases where the offender is presently, or has recently been, the subject of a probation order.

Psychiatric reports:[57]
(a)   cases where the offence is of a sexual nature;
(b)   some, but not all, cases where the offence is related to the misuse of drugs or alcohol;
(c)   cases where the offender has a previous history of mental disorder;
(d)   cases where the offence shows bizarre or unusual behaviour on the part of the offender;

---

[57] If there is reason to suppose that an offender may be suffering from a mental illness so that a hospital order or guardianship order may be appropriate, it is usually sensible to ask for two psychiatric reports at the outset to avoid the necessity of a subsequent adjournment after a single report has been obtained.

(e)   cases where the offender's behaviour in court is bizarre or unusual;

(f)   some, but by no means all, cases where the offenders are female;[58]

(g)   cases where the offence is one of violence, particularly where the offender has a previous record of similar offences.

PROVISION OF REPORTS TO OFFENDER AND OTHERS

8–24   When a social inquiry report has been obtained a copy of it must be given by the clerk of court to the offender, or his solicitor or counsel. In the case of an offender under 16 years of age, who is not represented by counsel or a solicitor, a copy of the report must be given to his parent or guardian if present in court.[59] There is no statutory provision for the situation where a child is unrepresented and has no parent or guardian present in court. In that event it is submitted that the proper course will be for a copy of the report to be given to the offender unless the judge is of opinion that it is more appropriate, having regard to all the circumstances including the age of the offender, that only the substance of the report should be disclosed to him. Where a written report from a medical practitioner is tendered in evidence otherwise than by or on behalf of the accused, a copy of it must be given to his counsel or solicitor. If the accused is unrepresented, the substance of the report must be disclosed to him or, where he is a child under 16 years of age, to his parent or guardian if present in court. Where the court is of opinion that further time is necessary in the interests of the accused for consideration of a report by a medical practitioner, or its substance, the case must be adjourned.[60]

REPORTS IN CASES WHERE THERE ARE SEVERAL ACCUSED

8–25   Where several accused are convicted or found guilty on the same complaint or indictment, it is highly desirable that the same judge should sentence all of the accused. Consequently, where the court asks for reports in respect of some, but not all, of the accused, the proper course, it has been held, is to defer sentence on any in respect of whom reports are not being prepared until the adjourned

---

[58] Theft from shops by middle-aged or elderly females may sometimes be explained by some form of mental disorder, but this is not invariably the case.
[59] 1975 Act, ss. 192, 393.
[60] *Ibid.* ss. 176 (3), 377 (3).

diet when the reports will be available in respect of the others.[61] While this rule can readily be complied with in cases on indictment, and in many summary cases as well, problems may arise in those summary cases where, at the first calling, one of several accused pleads guilty while the others plead not guilty. Even then it may be desirable to defer sentence on the one who has pled guilty so that questions of relative culpability can be considered after the trial. On the other hand — and bearing in mind that in many busy courts the trial may not take place for several months — there may be circumstances which make it desirable that the accused who has pled guilty should be dealt with at once. For example, he may be the subject of a probation order which will have terminated before the trial diet, but of which the offence to which he has pled guilty constitutes a breach. Again, it may be clear that he must be dealt with by a custodial sentence, but there is of course no power to remand him in custody until the trial diet. In such cases, it is submitted, it would be appropriate for the court to consider departing from the general rule outlined above.

REMIT TO HIGH COURT FOR SENTENCE

·26   Where at any diet in proceedings on indictment in the sheriff court, sentence falls to be imposed but the sheriff holds that any competent sentence which he can impose is inadequate so that the question of sentence is appropriate for the High Court, he must:

(a)   endorse upon the record copy of the indictment a certificate of the plea or the verdict (as the case may be);

(b)   by interlocutor written on such record copy remit the convicted person to the High Court for sentence; and

(c)   append to such interlocutor a note of his reasons for such remit. Such a remit is sufficient warrant to bring the accused before the High Court for sentence, and it will remain in force until the convicted person is sentenced.[62]

·27   Prior to the passing of the 1980 Act the necessity of remitting an offender to the High Court for sentence occasionally arose in cases of crimes reserved to the High Court, such as rape. That was because, under the former provisions of section 102 of the 1975 Act,

---

[61] *Thom* v. *Smith*, High Court, 7 December 1978.
[62] 1975 Act, s. 104, as amended by 1980 Act, Sched. 4, para. 15.

where an accused intimated a desire to have his case at once disposed of, it was indicted in the sheriff court regardless of its nature. However, the amendment to section 102 made by section 16 of the 1980 Act now means that such a case may be indicted directly to the High Court, as also may any other case where, had it gone to trial, the trial would have been in the High Court. Consequently, all cases in which a sheriff is now likely to consider it appropriate to remit to the High Court for sentence will arise under section 104 of the 1975 Act, and they will all be cases where the reason for remitting is that the sheriff considers that any competent sentence which he can impose is inadequate.

8–28   Over the years the procedures for remitting offenders to the High Court for sentence have caused some difficulties, and have on occasions been misunderstood by sheriffs. The following points should therefore be borne in mind:

(a)   The statutory provisions relating to the recording of pleas or verdicts, and the recording of the order for remit, must be strictly adhered to, otherwise the remitted diet may be put in peril.[63]

(b)   It is normally desirable, where there has been a trial, that the sheriff who presided at the trial should remit the accused to the High Court for sentence. However, in a case where sentence was originally deferred for a period, it was held that it was permissible for the remit to be made by a sheriff other than the one who had presided at the trial.[64] While there may occasionally be circumstances that make this course necessary, it is submitted that it should be avoided if at all possible if only because difficulties will arise regarding the preparation of the note that is to accompany the interlocutor of remit.

(c)   If a case is of such a character that the sheriff considers that any sentence which he can impose is inadequate, but the case also raises the possibility that the offender may be mentally ill so that a hospital order or guardianship order (which are within the sheriff's competence) may be appropriate, the proper course is

---

[63] *H.M.A.* v. *Galloway* (1894) 1 Adam 375; *H.M.A.* v. *MacDonald* (1896) 3 S.L.T. 317.
[64] *Borland* v. *H.M.A.*, 1976 S.L.T. (Notes) 12.

to remit the accused to the High Court for sentence and to allow that court to consider any evidence relevant to the accused's physical or mental condition.[65] The reason for this is to avoid the necessity of the High Court having to rehear medical evidence which has been considered, but for any reason not acted upon, by the sheriff. It should be added, however, that the case of *H.M.A.* v. *Clark* was a rather special one which dealt only with the problems relating to medical *evidence*. It does not mean that in cases where, for example, a social inquiry report must be obtained before a custodial sentence can be imposed, the sheriff should at once remit the case where he has concluded that, in the event of a custodial sentence being necessary, his own powers will be inadequate. The proper course in such a case, it is submitted, is for the sheriff first to obtain such reports as may be either necessary or desirable, and to consider in the light of such information as they contain, whether a sentence within his own competence is appropriate. If the accused is then remitted for sentence, these reports, together with the sheriff's note, should be available to the High Court.

(d) Where two or more accused appear on the same indictment and the sheriff considers that he could deal with one or more of them within the limits of his own powers, but that the others should be remitted to the High Court, the proper procedure is to remit all of the accused.[66] This is to enable the same court to consider the appropriate sentence for each accused and, where necessary, to adjust a proper balance between these sentences. If the sheriff considers that there are circumstances which would, in the case of one or more of the accused, have justified a sentence within his own competence, he can refer to these circumstances in his note. The foregoing rule may be departed from in exceptional circumstances as, for example, where one accused is convicted of an offence that does not involve any of the others. This exception to the general rule should, however, be used very sparingly.

---

[65] *H.M.A.* v. *Clark*, 1955 J.C. 88.
[66] *H.M.A.* v. *Duffy*, 1974 S.L.T. (Notes) 46.

(e)   Where an accused appears before the court on two
        separate indictments, one of which contains a charge or
        charges the maximum penalty for which is within the
        sheriff's competence, and the other of which contains a
        charge or charges in respect of which the sheriff
        considers that any sentence which he can impose is
        inadequate, the accused must not be remitted for
        sentence on both indictments. The sheriff should
        himself deal with the accused on the former indictment,
        but may refer to that circumstance in his note
        accompanying the remit of the accused on the other
        indictment.[67]

SENTENCE
Form of sentence in cases on indictment

8–29   In any case, whether in the High Court or the sheriff court, the
sentence to be pronounced must be announced by the judge in open
court, and must be entered in the record in the form used in the High
Court. It is not necessary to read the entry of the sentence from the
record.[68] In recording sentences of imprisonment it is sufficient to
minute the term of imprisonment to which the court sentenced the
accused without specifying the prison in which the sentence is to be
carried out. Such entries of sentences, signed by the clerk of court,
are full warrant and authority for all execution to follow thereon,
and for the clerk to issue extracts thereof for carrying the same into
execution or otherwise.[69]

Form of sentence in summary cases

8–30   The finding and sentence and any order of a court of summary
jurisdiction, as regards both offences at common law and offences
under any statute or order, must be entered in the record of the
proceedings in the form, as nearly as may be, of the appropriate
form contained in Part V of Schedule 2 to the Summary Jurisdiction
(Scotland) Act 1954. Such an entry is sufficient warrant for all
execution thereon and for the clerk of court to issue extracts
containing such executive clauses as may be necessary for
implement thereof. When imprisonment forms part of any sentence
or other judgment, warrant for the apprehension and interim

---

[67] *H.M.A.* v. *Anderson & Ors..* 1946 J.C. 81; *H.M.A.* v. *Stern*, 1974 J.C. 10.
[68] 1975 Act, s. 217 (1).
[69] *Ibid.* s. 217 (2).

detention of the accused pending his being committed to prison will, where necessary, be implied.[70]

-31 It is essential that the forms contained in Part V of Schedule 2 to the 1954 Act should be strictly followed.[71] Normally, where an accused is present, the conviction and sentence will be announced orally by the judge, but this intimation is not sufficient to make them effective. Only the signing of the formal judgment in the record of proceedings has that effect.[72]

-32 Every sentence imposed by a court of summary jurisdiction must, except where there is provision to the contrary, be pronounced in open court in the presence of the accused, but it need not be written out or signed in his presence.[73] If the sentence is one which cannot competently be pronounced in the accused's absence it will be set aside.[74] The circumstances where a court may pronounce sentence in the absence of the accused are: (a) where he has tendered a written plea of guilty, or tenders such a plea by a solicitor or any other authorised person:[75] but in such a case the court may not impose a custodial sentence unless it continues the case to another diet when the accused is present;[76] (b) where the trial of a statutory offence for which a sentence of imprisonment cannot be imposed in the first instance has taken place in the absence of the accused;[77] and (c) in cases on indictment against a body corporate.[77a] Where imprisonment is being imposed in respect of default in payment of a fine, that may be done in absence only where the offender is already in prison.[78]

Interruption of proceedings

-33 It is now possible in both solemn and summary proceedings to interrupt these proceedings so as to pass sentence on the accused in respect of a conviction arising from other proceedings. This will not cause the instance to fall nor otherwise affect the validity of the proceedings.[79] This provision gave effect to a recommendation by

---

[70] 1975 Act, s. 430 (1).
[71] *Paterson* v. *McLennan* (1914) 7 Adam 428.
[72] *Cameron* v. *Deans* (1901) 3 Adam 498; *Rintoul* v. *Stewart* (1902) 3 Adam 574.
[73] 1975 Act, s. 433.
[74] *Watson* v. *Argo*, 1936 J.C. 87.
[75] 1975 Act, s. 334 (3).
[76] *Ibid*. s. 334 (4).
[77] *Ibid*. s. 338 (*b*).
[77a] *Ibid*. s. 74 (4).
[78] *Ibid*. s. 398 (1); but see *supra*, n. 58 to para. 2–88.
[79] Act of Adjournal (Sentencing Powers etc.) 1978.

the Thomson Committee[80] following upon the somewhat technical decision in an earlier case[81] where, following a jury trial, the sheriff sentenced the first accused in respect of that indictment, and at the same time sentenced him in respect of an outstanding summary complaint, all before sentencing the second accused on the indictment. It was held that the interruption of the solemn proceedings by consideration of the outstanding summary matter caused the instance to fall so that the conviction of both accused required to be quashed. What took place in that case is now permissible under the act of adjournal, and indeed it will frequently be desirable that sentence in one case should be deferred until the date of a forthcoming trial so that, in the event of the accused then being convicted, both cases can be considered simultaneously for the purpose of determining the appropriate sentence.

Essentials of valid sentence

8–34 According to Macdonald[82] a valid sentence must contain certain features. These are that it must be consistent with the charge and with the law, and must be one that can be passed on the person convicted. Additionally, it must be free from any ambiguity. The last of these essentials has, over the years, given rise to the greatest number of difficulties.[83] Two points in particular should be noted. A sentence of imprisonment which does not clearly indicate the date from which that sentence is to run is a fundamental nullity;[84] and, any order for forfeiture must clearly describe the article concerned.[85]

Cumulo penalties

8–35 A number of problems present themselves where a *cumulo* penalty is imposed: some of these relate to the competency of the sentence itself while some are related to difficulties which may arise in the event of an appeal. Section 430 (3) of the 1975 Act expressly provides that where several charges at common law or under any statute or order are embraced in one complaint, a *cumulo* fine may

---

[80] *Criminal Procedure in Scotland (Second Report)*, Cmnd. 6218.
[81] *Law and Nicol* v. *H.M.A.*, 1973 S.L.T. (Notes) 14.
[82] pp. 350, 351.
[83] *Allan* v. *Lamb* (1900) 3 Adam 248; *Macleman* v. *Middleton* (1901) 3 Adam 353; *Cowans* v. *Sinclair* (1905) 4 Adam 585.
[84] *Grant* v. *Grant* (1855) 2 Irv. 277.
[85] *Rankin* v. *Wright* (1901) 3 Adam 483.

be imposed in respect of all or any of such charges of which the accused is convicted. It has been held that the effect of section 56 (3) of the Summary Jurisdiction (Scotland) Act 1954 (which is now repeated as section 430 (3) of the 1975 Act) is to allow a summary court to impose a *cumulo* fine in respect of several offences which exceeded the maximum provided by the statutes for a single offence.[86] However, it is incompetent, where one of two offences provides only for a penalty of a fine, with imprisonment in default of payment, to impose a *cumulo* sentence of imprisonment, that sentence being competent only in respect of the other offence.[87]

36   A point of some interest falls to be noted in relation to the wording of section 430 (3) of the 1975 Act. As already noted that section permits a court to impose a *cumulo* fine where several charges are contained in the same complaint, and the question may be asked whether there is any power for a summary court to impose a single sentence of *imprisonment* in similar circumstances. That this is regularly done there can be no doubt, and it does not appear ever to have been questioned. It is to be noted, however, that there has been some statutory change on the matter. The Summary Jurisdiction (Scotland) Act 1908, by section 53, gave summary courts a similar power to that now contained in section 430 (3) of the 1975 Act, but with this difference, that the court was empowered to impose a *cumulo penalty*, and in the Full Bench case of *Maguiness* v. *MacDonald*[88] Lord Justice-General Cooper said: "Section 53 certainly authorises any court to impose a single fine or a single sentence of imprisonment on a multiple complaint". When, however, the 1908 Act was replaced by the Summary Jurisdiction (Scotland) Act 1954, the provision, in section 56 (3) was reworded so as to allow for the imposition of a *cumulo fine*, a form of words which, as has been seen, now appears in the 1975 Act. Whether this was deliberate or merely an accident on the part of the draftsman is impossible to say. Certainly, the editor of the 3rd edition of Renton and Brown (published in 1956) appears not to have noticed the change because he quotes section 56 (3) of the 1954 Act as providing for a *cumulo penalty*, an error which is repeated in the current edition of that book.[89]

37   Normally, the rules of statutory interpretation would require

[86] *Wann* v. *Macmillan*, 1957 J.C. 20.
[87] *McLauchlan* v. *Davidson*, 1921 J.C. 45.
[88] 1953 J.C. 31 at 35.
[89] Para. 15–16.

that effect should be given to a change of words such as that noted above, and in that case the result would have been to exclude the power of a summary court to impose a single sentence of imprisonment on a multiple complaint. It is to be noted, however, that the Act of 1954, like the one of 1975, was a consolidating and not an amending statute, and that fact, coupled with the continuing and unquestioned practice of the courts tends to confirm that it was not intended to make any change in 1954, that the power has remained unchanged since 1908, and that it is competent to impose a single sentence of imprisonment where there are several charges on one complaint.

8–38   The use of *cumulo* fines and sentences of imprisonment, even where competent, should be considered carefully since, in the event of a successful appeal in respect of one or more of the charges, it may be difficult for the appeal court to impose an appropriate sentence on the remaining charges.[90] In general it may be said that *cumulo* fines or sentences of imprisonment should be imposed only where the offences are all of a very similar character, and should be avoided where they are in any way disparate. It should be added that, in relation to those road traffic offences which attract endorsement or disqualification, they should be dealt with separately not only on the grounds of disparity but also because separate entries will require to be made on the offender's licence in respect of each conviction.

Sentence on lesser charges

8–39   Where an accused is convicted on a complaint, or particularly an indictment, which contains one very serious charge and a number of lesser charges, it is better to impose shorter, concurrent, sentences on the lesser charges rather than merely to admonish in respect of them. The reason for this was highlighted in a case[91] where an accused was convicted of a charge of murder as well as several lesser, though still quite serious charges. In accordance with what was then Crown practice the advocate-depute moved for sentence on the murder charge alone and, consequently, no sentence was pronounced on the lesser charges. When, subsequently, the accused successfully appealed against his conviction on the charge of murder, the result was that no sentence could be imposed on the lesser charges. By the same token, if a court is considering

---

[90] *Paisley Ice Rink* v. *Hill*, 1944 J.C. 158; *Seaton* v. *Allan*, 1973 J.C. 24.
[91] *H.M.A.* v. *Paterson*, 1974 S.L.T. 53.

sentence and is told that the accused has recently been sentenced to a long term of imprisonment for another offence then, unless the court proposes to impose a consecutive sentence of imprisonment, it is better to impose a concurrent sentence rather than merely to admonish because the earlier sentence may be successfully appealed against.

Dating of sentences of imprisonment or detention

-40   Unless otherwise qualified a sentence of imprisonment will run from the date on which it is pronounced. All courts, both solemn and summary, are directed, when determining a period of imprisonment or detention, to have regard to any period of time spent in custody by the offender on remand awaiting trial or sentence.[92] The effect of that provision may be to persuade a court to reduce the length of sentence that would otherwise have been imposed. Alternatively, the full sentence may be imposed, but it may be back-dated so as to span the period, or part of the period, of the remand. There is no statutory or other authority for that practice, but it appears to be hallowed by long usage. The practical consequences of this practice, however, fall to be noted. On the one hand, to pronounce the full sentence appropriate to the offence, but to back-date it to take account of a period spent in custody, means that, in the event of a subsequent conviction, the offender's record will accurately reflect the gravity of the offence. On the other hand, the effect of remission may significantly alter the period that the offender actually spends in custody. A simple example will illustrate this. Suppose that a sentence of imprisonment falls to be pronounced on 1 January, and the court is informed that the offender has been in custody on remand for three months since 1 October. If the court considers that the appropriate sentence for the offence is one of nine months imprisonment, but wants to take full account of the period spent in custody, it may either impose a six month sentence dated from 1 January, or it may impose a nine month sentence dated from 1 October. Assuming normal remission of one third, the consequence is that in the former case the offender will be released on 1 May, whereas in the latter case he will be released one month earlier on 1 April. While it is improper for a judge to take remission into account in determining the length of a sentence, it is submitted that it is perfectly proper for a judge to be

---

[92] 1975 Act, ss. 218, 431, as amended by 1980 Act, Sched. 7, paras. 40 and 70.

aware of the above considerations, and to take them into account as he thinks proper. In all the circumstances, and bearing in mind that the practice of back-dating appears to be authorised by no more than usage, it is submitted that the better practice, where a person has been remanded in custody, is to pronounce, with effect from the date of sentence, a sentence modified as may be thought necessary to take account of the earlier custody.

Consecutive sentences

8-41   Where an accused person is already serving a previously imposed sentence of imprisonment, his imprisonment may be made to date from the expiry of that sentence.[93] That is so even where the previous sentence of imprisonment was imposed in England.[94] It has, however, been held to be contrary to the spirit and intention of the legislation providing for borstal training to impose a period of imprisonment to take effect at the expiry of a period of such training.[95]

8-42   In summary courts the above general power is given statutory effect by section 430 (4) of the 1975 Act. The words used in that subsection can be construed as giving rise to a problem. They are: "A sentence following on a conviction by a court of summary jurisdiction may be framed so as to take effect on the expiry of any previous sentence which at the date of such conviction the accused is undergoing." If a sentence of imprisonment is being imposed on an offender who is already undergoing the first of two previously imposed consecutive sentences, the question is whether, having regard to the last ten words of the subsection, that sentence can be made to run from the end of the total period of imprisonment, or only from the end of the sentence actually being served, that is to say concurrently with the earlier consecutive sentence. This problem was considered by the Thomson Committee[96] who pointed out that, if what they termed the "narrow interpretation" were to be followed, prisoners could with impunity commit further offences while in prison in the knowledge that they could not be punished summarily for them. The committee accordingly recommended that, if it were thought necessary, the statute should be amended so

---

[93] Macdonald, p. 357; *John Graham* (1842) 1 Brown 445.

[94] *Grey* v. *H.M.A.*, 1958 S.L.T. 147.

[95] *Scott* v. *H.M.A.*, 1964 J.C. 77; but this consideration will soon be of historical interest only.

[96] *Criminal Procedure in Scotland (Second Report)* Cmnd. 6218, paras. 57.06, 57.07.

as to provide clearly for the wider interpretation. To date this recommendation has not been acted on, despite the opportunity provided by the 1980 Act, and it may be thought that the suggested amendment has in fact been regarded as unnecessary. Having regard to the practical considerations referred to by the Thomson Committee it is tentatively submitted that the subsection may properly be read as giving summary courts the power to add to a total existing sentence, even where that already consists of one or more consecutive sentences.[97] In that event, the sentence should be so expressed and recorded as to make the court's intention perfectly clear.

3   Although courts have a general power to impose consecutive sentences in respect of separate charges, or in respect of separate complaints or indictments, that power is subject to a number of limitations. These have emerged in a series of decisions, principally over the last 30 years or so, and still give rise to some difficulty. Although the decided cases still leave some questions unresolved, it may now be stated as a general rule that the sentencing powers of courts other than the High Court are limited, so far as imprisonment is concerned, by the overall maximum sentences permitted by statute. Thus the fact that an accused has been convicted of eight separate charges does not permit a sheriff to exceed, by the imposition of consecutive sentences, his normal maximum sentence of three months imprisonment.[98]

4   It has been held that, where an accused is charged in the same court on the same day with two offences on separate complaints, which could have been put on the same complaint, one sentence should not be made to date from the expiry of the other.[99] That is certainly so when the effect of making the sentences consecutive is thereby to exceed the court's normal maximum in respect of offences appearing on the same complaint.[100] Some comment, however, may be made in regard to the case of *Kesson* v. *Heatly*. In that case an accused was charged in the Burgh Court on two complaints, each of which contained a charge under section 7 of the Prevention of Crime Act 1871, for which the maximum penalty is

---

[97] But see, *infra*, reference to *Kesson* v. *Heatly*, 1964 J.C. 40, in para. 8–45.

[98] *Maguiness* v. *MacDonald, supra*; but there are statutory exceptions to this such as that provided for in the 1980 Act, s. 17 (3).

[99] *Kesson* v. *Heatly, supra*.

[100] *Kesson* v. *Heatly, supra; Wishart* v. *Heatly*, 1953 J.C. 42; *Williamson* v. *Farrell*, 1975 S.L.T. (Notes) 92.

one year's imprisonment. He had previously pled not guilty to one of these charges but in the end pled guilty on both complaints, and both were disposed of together on the same day. He was sentenced to nine months imprisonment on one complaint, and consecutively to six months imprisonment on the other, making a total of 15 months in all. While accepting that a court is always entitled to impose consecutive sentences, either in respect of multiple charges on a single complaint, or in respect of charges in separate complaints dealt with at the same time, the court held that that power is subject to the overriding principle that the total sentence so imposed must not exceed the maximum for a single charge. In the case of *Maguiness* v. *MacDonald*,[1] that maximum had been the one generally appropriate for common law offences; in the present case, the maximum was the higher one provided by this particular statute. Consequently, the appeal was allowed and the sentence reduced.

8–45   In the case of *Kesson* it was argued on behalf of the respondent that the sentences on the two complaints would have been perfectly competent had they been imposed on different days, because of the power conferred by section 56 (4) of the 1954 Act. The Lord Justice-Clerk (Grant), while accepting the competency of consecutive sentences in such circumstances, went on to say this:[2] "It is, however, the general practice in our criminal administration that, except in certain limited and exceptional circumstances, all known outstanding charges against an accused are dealt with at the same time. The situation suggested by the respondent is, accordingly, one which would rarely arise. I should add that, in my opinion, section 56 (4) of the 1954 Act is designed to deal, not with charges which were outstanding when the first sentence was passed, but with offences committed after the first sentence has commenced, *e.g.* offences in prison, prison-breaking and offences committed when the accused is unlawfully at large." Whatever may have been the position in 1964 when these words were written, there is little doubt that they do not accurately represent the position today when, particularly in the busier sheriff courts, it is commonplace for offenders to appear at frequent intervals on complaints containing charges which, upon one view, could all have been contained in the same complaint. Indeed, the number of such charges is often such that, so far from all being put in a single complaint, they might well have merited being put together in an indictment. In practice what

---

[1] *Supra.*
[2] pp. 45, 46.

frequently happens is that they simply all call before the court at the same time, by arrangement between the prosecutor and the defence, or because sentence has been deferred on some so as to enable all to be dealt with simultaneously. On other occasions the complaints may simply call week after week. The problem facing the courts, however, is how these complaints should be dealt with, standing the view expressed in *Kesson* as to the purpose of what is now section 430 (4) of the 1975 Act. The problem is twofold. Firstly, is a court entitled in the contemporary situation which has been described, to disregard the Lord Justice-Clerk's opinion as to the rather restricted purpose of the section? Secondly, if the court is so entitled, is it obliged to ensure that the total sentence created by the imposition of consecutive sentences does not exceed the maximum which could have been imposed had all the outstanding charges been dealt with in a single complaint? So far there is no authoritative answer to these questions, but it may tentatively be ventured that the answer to the first question is in the affirmative, and that possibly the answer to the second is also in the affirmative, for otherwise it would be difficult to support the reasoning in the cases that have been referred to. It is submitted, however, that the contemporary phenomenon of regular repetitive offending creates a situation which was not envisaged in cases such as *Kesson*. In a sense, of course, all charges outstanding at the time a person appears before a court *could* be included in a single complaint but, if a person is reported to a procurator fiscal six times within a period of two months, and again at intervals thereafter during the period before the first complaint calls before a court for sentence, it may be thought to be a little unrealistic that the procurator fiscal should be required to keep on deserting complaints and serving new and even larger ones to encompass all of that person's law-breaking. By the same token, it is perhaps equally unrealistic to expect a judge, or a multiplicity of judges in the larger courts, to keep track of all of these complaints as they appear so as to ensure that the total sentence does not exceed the maximum that would be competent for a single complaint. In practice what tends to happen is that, if a judge is informed that a person has recently been sentenced to imprisonment for other offences committed at about the same time as those in respect of which sentence is to be passed, the judge will normally take cognisance of that earlier sentence, but will not necessarily feel bound to pass a sentence which, taken together with the earlier one, does not exceed the statutory maximum in respect of a single complaint. While it is submitted that this is a proper approach, the matter is not free from doubt.

8-46 Although the principles that have been described in the preceding paragraphs have been expressed as applying in relation to circumstances where the charges could all have been included in a single complaint, it is to be noted that the same principles apply in cases where a charge must appear in a separate complaint for reasons which are of a technical nature. Thus, where a charge under section 99 (*b*) of the Road Traffic Act 1972 was, in accordance with normal practice, libelled in a separate complaint from one containing other, associated charges, it was held that the court could not by consecutive sentences exceed the statutory maximum of six months imprisonment,[3] and doubt was expressed as to a contrary view that appeared inherent in an earlier, unreported, case.[4]

8-47 Two further points may be made in relation to consecutive sentences. The first is that, although all of the decided cases have arisen from decisions in summary courts, there seems no reason why the same principles should not apply to courts of solemn jurisdiction. Thus, a sheriff, dealing with an indictment containing a number of common law charges, could competently impose consecutive sentences in respect of each charge, but they should not in total exceed two years. By the same token, it could be argued that the High Court, if dealing with an indictment containing a number of statutory charges for which a maximum sentence was provided, could impose consecutive sentences but not so as to exceed the maximum for a single charge. That, however, has not yet been the subject of decision by the High Court.

8-48 The second point is that the general principles applicable to consecutive sentences apply equally where one of the sentences of imprisonment is imposed in default of payment of a fine and the result, if that sentence is served, is to exceed the court's maximum powers of imprisonment. Thus, where a court imposed a maximum sentence of three months imprisonment in respect of one charge on a complaint, and a fine on a second charge, it was held to be incompetent to order further imprisonment for non-payment of the fine.[5] It is to be noted, however, that under section 407 (1B) of the

---

[3] *Williamson* v. *Farrell*, 1975 S.L.T. (Notes) 92.

[4] *H.M.A.* v. *Logan*, High Court, 27 January 1972.

[5] *Fraser* v. *Herron*, 1968 J.C. 1; see also *Williamson* v. *Macmillan*, 1962 S.L.T. 63; *Duffy* v. *Lakie*, 1962 S.L.T. 31; *McGunnigal* v. *Copeland*, 1972 S.L.T. (Notes) 70.

1975 Act, as added by the 1980 Act, where an offender is fined on the same day before the same court for offences charged in the same complaint or in separate complaints, the amount of the fine is to be taken to be the total of the fines imposed for the purpose of calculating the maximum period of imprisonment to which the offender may be sentenced in the event of default.

STATEMENT OF REASONS FOR SENTENCE

49   There are several circumstances in which a court is obliged to state its reasons for imposing a particular sentence, and to ensure that these reasons are entered in the record of proceedings. The principal circumstances are: (1) where a young offender is sentenced to detention: the reasons for rejecting any alternative must be stated and, in the case of all courts other than the High Court, must be entered in the record of proceedings;[6] (2) where a sentence of imprisonment is imposed on a person who has not been previously sentenced to imprisonment or detention by a court in any part of the United Kingdom: the reason for deciding that no other method of dealing with the offender is suitable must be stated in the record of proceedings where the sentence is imposed by a summary court;[7] and (3) where time is not allowed for payment of a fine the reasons must be stated and entered in the extract of the finding and sentence as well as in the finding and sentence itself.[8] While the foregoing requirements should be followed at all times, a failure to record the appropriate reasons may not be fatal provided that the court has given the proper consideration to the matter in issue and has stated its reasons orally to the accused.[9]

DEFERRED SENTENCE

50   Normally, where a court has deferred sentence on a person, he may not be dealt with in respect of the offence concerned until the expiry of the period of deferment. There are, however, two exceptions to this. These are:

    (1)   if it appears to the court by which sentence was deferred that the person has been convicted, during the period of

---

[6] 1975 Act, s. 207 (3), as amended by 1980 Act, s. 45.

[7] 1980 Act, s. 42 (2).

[8] 1975 Act, s. 396 (2) and (3); and see *Sullivan* v. *McLeod,* 1980 S.L.T. (Notes) 99.

[9] *Binnie* v. *Farrell,* 1972 J.C. 49, explaining apparently conflicting decisions in *Winslow* v. *Farrell,* 1965 J.C. 49 and *Bruce* v. *Hogg,* 1966 J.C. 33.

deferment, by a court in any part of Great Britain of an offence committed during that period and has been dealt with for that offence, the court which deferred sentence may issue a warrant for the arrest of that person, or may, instead of issuing such a warrant in the first instance, issue a citation requiring his appearance; and on his appearance or on his being brought before the court it may deal with him in any manner in which it would be competent for it to deal with him on the expiry of the period of deferment; and

(2)   where a court which has deferred sentence on a person convicts that person of another offence during the period of deferment, it may deal with him for the original offence in any manner in which it would be competent for it to deal with him on the expiry of the period of deferment, as well as for the offence committed during that period.[10]

8–51   Since there is at present no means for ensuring that courts are, as a matter of course, informed of subsequent convictions of persons on whom sentence has been deferred, the first of the above provisions is perhaps unlikely to be much used. On the other hand, the situation will frequently arise where a person is convicted by the same court that has previously deferred sentence, and in that situation two points should be noted. The first is that, while it is normally desirable that a deferred case should be finally disposed of by the judge who deferred sentence in the first instance, this will rarely be practicable if the subsequent conviction has occurred before a different judge, because only he can properly determine the sentence for that offence. The answer to this problem is probably to be found in the fact that the power to deal with the old and the new offence simultaneously is permissive not mandatory: consequently, if the judge who is dealing with the subsequent conviction considers that there are features in the case which make it desirable that the question of sentence for the original offence should be dealt with by the judge who deferred sentence, he may leave it to be disposed of at the end of the period of deferment. The second point to be noted is that the provision allowing a deferred sentence and a new conviction to be dealt with at the same time contains no provision which would expressly alter, or intrude upon,

---

[10] 1975 Act, ss. 219 (2) and (3), and 432 (2) and (3), as added by 1980 Act, s. 54.

the existing rules relative to the imposition of consecutive sentences of imprisonment.[11] Thus, it may be thought that, in the case of a summary court, for example, the court's powers should be restricted to the maximum term of imprisonment that would have been competent had all the charges been in a single complaint. On the other hand, since the existing rules relative to a court's powers when dealing with more than one complaint on the same day have been formulated on the supposition that all of the charges could have been included in a single complaint, and since, *ex hypothesi*, that could not be so when sentence has already been deferred in respect of one of the complaints, there may, it is submitted, be a basis for the view that in such a case a court could impose consecutive sentences which in total exceeded the court's maximum power to sentence. It may be added that, were this not to be so, the consequence would be that an offender, on whom sentence had been deferred so that he might be of good behaviour, could with impunity commit further offences in the knowledge that he could receive no higher sentence than might have been imposed when sentence was deferred.

ALTERATION AND SIGNATURE OF SENTENCE

Alteration of sentence

52   Without requiring the attendance of the accused, it is competent at any time before imprisonment has followed on a sentence for a summary court to alter or modify it. In that case, however, it is not competent to substitute a higher sentence than that originally pronounced.[12] This power has been held sufficient to enable a court to correct mistakes in executorial detail,[13] but that matter is now largely the subject of express statutory provision.[14] If a court has, in error, imposed a sentence which is beyond its competence, it may reduce the sentence to one that is competent,[15] but, where a magistrate had by mistake imposed, in default of payment of a fine, a sentence of imprisonment in excess of the maximum allowed, it was held to be incompetent for him to seek to correct the error by increasing the amount of the fine.[16] Also, the power to modify a

---

[11] See *supra*, paras 8–41 to 8–48.

[12] 1975 Act, s. 434 (1) and (3), as amended by 1980 Act, Sched. 8.

[13] *Mackenzie* v. *Allan* (1889) 2 White 253; *Stewart* v. *Uppleby* (1899) 3 Adam 6; *Renwick* v. *McDougall* (1913) 7 Adam 91.

[14] See *Infra*. para. 8.55.

[15] *Renwick* v. *McDougall, supra.*

[16] *McRory* v. *Findlay* (1911) 6 Adam 416.

sentence must be exercised before any imprisonment has followed on that sentence.[17] However, it has been held that what is now section 434 (1) of the 1975 Act does not apply where the original sentence is incompetent, and in that case the court may substitute a competent sentence even where it is of greater severity, for the original sentence is void and the second sentence is not an alteration but a *de novo* imposition.[18]

Signature of sentence

8–53   The sentence of a summary court must be signed either by the judge or by the clerk of court,[19] but the signature of either of them is sufficient also to authenticate the findings on which the sentence proceeds.[20] No time limit is stated within which a sentence must be signed, but it has been held that it should be signed as soon as reasonably possible, and in almost every case on the day on which the sentence is pronounced.[21] A court is not *functus officio* until a conviction and sentence have been recorded and signed,[22] but, where an agent for an accused (who was absent) tendered a plea of guilty in error and conviction and sentence followed on that plea, it was held to be incompetent for the sheriff, two days later, to "recall" these orders and to proceed to trial: after conviction and sentence the sheriff was held to be *functus* and without any authority thereafter to alter the finding so far as it related to conviction.[23] In that case the sheriff could, provided no imprisonment had followed thereon, have modified the sentence under section 434 of the 1975 Act, but he could not alter the recorded conviction.

8–54   In the case of *MacNeill* v. *MacGregor* the error which created the problem was that of the accused's agent, but what if the error arises in a different way? Summary complaints which are served by a means other than a warrant to apprehend contain a printed form on which the accused may intimate his plea in writing, and the style of these forms is such that on occasions a written plea may either be ambiguous, or may be construed as a plea of guilty when in fact the

---

[17] *Skeen* v. *Sim*, High Court, 19 March 1975.

[18] *Patrick* v. *Copeland*, 1969 J.C. 42.

[19] 1975 Act, s. 309 (2).

[20] *Ibid.* s. 434 (2).

[21] *Furnheim* v. *Watson*, 1946 J.C. 99; but see *Cameron* v. *Deans* (1901) 3 Adam 498.

[22] *Tudhope* v. *Campbell*, 1979 J.C. 24; but *Cf. Williams and Another* v. *Linton* (1878) 6 R. (J.) 12.

[23] *MacNeill* v. *MacGregor*, 1975 J.C. 55 and 57.

accused intended it to be one of not guilty. In the former case the court will normally continue the case without recording a plea so that the ambiguity can be cleared up, but in the latter case it may proceed to deal with the case in the accused's absence by recording a conviction and passing sentence. The question then is whether, upon receiving the inevitable irate communication from the accused, the court is bound by the decision in *MacNeill* v. *MacGregor*. It is tentatively submitted that the answer to that question is in the negative. Although there is no express statutory authority to deal with the situation above described, it may be thought that, where the error is one of misinterpretation by the court rather than an erroneous statement by an agent, the statutory provisions concerning correction of entries[24] are sufficiently wide to enable the court to correct the error without the necessity of requiring the accused to have the proceedings reviewed in a higher court.

Correction of entries

It is now competent to correct an entry in (a) the record of proceedings in a solemn or summary prosecution, or (b) the extract of a sentence passed or an order of court made in such proceedings, in so far as that entry constitutes an error of recording or is incomplete.[25] Such an entry may be corrected (a) by the clerk of the court at any time before either the sentence or order of the court is executed or, on appeal, the proceedings are transmitted to the Clerk of Justiciary, (b) by the clerk of the court, under the authority of the court which passed the sentence or made the order, at any time after the execution of the sentence or order but before transmission on appeal to the Clerk of Justiciary, or (c) by the clerk of the court under the authority of the High Court, where that court has during the course of an appeal become aware of an erroneous or incomplete entry and has remitted the proceedings for correction.[26] Where a correction is made under the authority of the court which passed the sentence or made the order, that correction must be intimated to the prosecutor and to the former accused or his solicitor.[27] Where, during the course of an appeal, the High Court becomes aware of an erroneous or incomplete entry, it may consid-

---

[24] See *infra*, para 8–55.

[25] 1975 Act, ss. 227A (1) and 439 (1), as added and amended respectively by 1980 Act, s. 20.

[26] *Ibid*. ss. 227A (2) and 439 (4), as added and amended respectively by 1980 Act, s. 20.

[27] *Ibid*. subs. (3).

er and determine the appeal as if that entry were corrected, and may remit the proceedings for correction, as noted above, either before or after the determination of the appeal.[28] Any correction by the clerk of court must be authenticated by his signature and, where it is authorised by a court, it must record the name of the judge or judges concerned and the date of such authority.[29]

8–56   The principal innovations introduced by the 1980 Act in relation to the power to correct entries are, firstly, that this may now be done, with the authority of the court, after sentence has been executed, and, secondly, that the High Court may now consider and determine an appeal as if an erroneous entry had been corrected. As a consequence, some of the older cases on this subject are now of only incidental interest.[30] Other older cases are, however, still relevant, particularly those which stress the importance of properly authenticating any corrections which are made, especially if the correction takes the form of an erasure.[31] Unauthenticated amendments or alterations should be specifically referred to and made the grounds of appeal when an appeal is taken by way of a stated case if the unauthenticated alterations are to be founded on.[32]

---

[28] *Ibid.* subs. (4).
[29] *Ibid.* subs. (5).
[30] See, for example, *Smith* v. *Sempill* (1910) 6 Adam 348; *Anderson* v. *Howman*, 1935 J.C. 17; *Wilson* v. *Brown*, 1947 J.C. 81; *Kelly* v. *MacLeod*, 1960 J.C. 88.
[31] *MacKenzie* v. *Gray* (1898) 2 Adam 625; *Reids* v. *Miller* (1899) 3 Adam 29; *Dunsire* v. *Bell* (1908) 5 Adam 625; *White* v. *Jeans* (1911) 6 Adam 489.
[32] *Sutherland* v. *Shiach*, 1928 J.C. 49.

CHAPTER 9

APPEAL AGAINST SENTENCE

I. Appeals before the passing of the 1980 Act

01   Prior to the passing of the Criminal Appeal (Scotland) Act 1926, all sentences pronounced in the High Court were final and conclusive and could not be made subject to any review.[1] Sentences imposed on indictment in the sheriff court could, in certain circumstances, be brought under review by a suspension, but that procedure was abolished by the 1926 Act which created the Court of Criminal Appeal, and established a uniform right of appeal to that court in all cases on indictment, whether in the High Court or the sheriff court. Subsequent to 1926 the appeals procedure in relation to sentences imposed on indictment remained substantially unchanged until the passing of the 1980 Act.

02   In relation to summary cases review by stated case was first introduced by the Summary Prosecutions Appeals (Scotland) Act 1875, and the procedure provided for in that Act was subsequently adopted in a somewhat amended form as a universal mode of appeal by the Summary Jurisdiction (Scotland) Act 1908. Under the stated case procedure a right of appeal was made available to both the accused and the prosecutor, though in relation to sentence the prosecutor's right of appeal was restricted to points of law only. Like appeals under solemn procedure, review by stated case remained substantially unchanged until the introduction of the extensive amendments contained in the 1980 Act.

03   Since this is a book about sentencing, all of what follows relates principally to appeals against sentence and, notwithstanding that many of the procedures are the same for appeals against conviction, the reader should be alive to the possibility of differences, or of additional procedures, in such cases. One of the consequences of the amendments made by the 1980 Act has been to assimilate to a large extent the rules governing appeals under both solemn and summary procedure. However, to avoid tiresome cross-referencing, the two forms of appeal will be dealt with separately and in full, even though this will involve some repetition of identical provisions.

---

[1] *Mackintosh* v. *Lord Advocate* (1876) 3 R. (H.L.) 34.

II. Appeals under solemn procedure

Right of appeal

9–04   Any person convicted on indictment may appeal against the sentence passed on such conviction, or against both conviction and sentence.[2] By such an appeal a person may bring under review of the High Court any alleged miscarriage of justice in the proceedings in which he was convicted, including any alleged miscarriage of justice on the basis of the existence and significance of additional evidence which was not heard at the trial and which was not available and could not reasonably have been made available at the trial.[3] This latter provision seems unlikely, in so far as it relates to additional evidence, to be of much significance in an appeal against sentence alone, but may well be highly relevant where an appeal is taken against both conviction and sentence.

9–05   There is no right of appeal against any sentence fixed by law.[4] However, where, on sentencing a person convicted of murder, a judge makes a recommendation under section 205A (1) of the 1975 Act as to the minimum period which should elapse before that person is released on licence, it is competent to appeal against that recommendation which, for the purposes of the appeal, is to be deemed part of the sentence passed on conviction.[5]

9–06   It is not competent to appeal to the High Court by bill of suspension against any sentence, judgment or order pronounced in any proceedings on indictment in the sheriff court.[6] It has, however, been held that this rule does not apply in the case of an appeal by a witness who was sentenced for contempt of court in the course of proceedings on indictment in the sheriff court.[7]

Form of appeal

9–07   An important distinction exists between the procedures that must be followed in those cases where a person wishes to appeal against both conviction and sentence, and those where the appeal is

---

[2] 1975 Act, s. 228 (1), as amended by 1980 Act, s. 33 and Sched. 2, para. 1; to avoid constant repetition, all subsequent references in this chapter to the appeal provisions of the 1975 Act are to the relevant sections as amended or as added by the provisions of the 1980 Act.

[3] *Ibid.* s. 228 (2).

[4] *Ibid.* s. 228 (1), proviso.

[5] *Ibid.* s. 205A (3).

[6] *Ibid.* s. 230.

[7] *Butterworth* v. *Herron*, 1975 S.L.T. (Notes) 56.

against sentence alone. In the former case the appellant must, within two weeks of the final determination of the proceedings, lodge with the Clerk of Justiciary written intimation of intention to appeal, and at the same time he must send a copy of that intimation to the Crown Agent.[8] The period of time within which this must be done may be extended at any time by the High Court upon application being made for that purpose.[9] The intimation of intention to appeal must identify the proceedings and must be in as nearly as may be the form prescribed by act of adjournal.[10] Upon such an intimation being lodged by a person in custody, the Clerk of Justiciary must give notice of the fact to the Secretary of State.[11] Proceedings are to be deemed to be finally determined on the day on which sentence is passed in open court.[12]

–08 Within six weeks of lodging intimation of intention to appeal or, in the case of an appeal against sentence alone, within two weeks of the passing of the sentence in open court, the convicted person may lodge a written note of appeal with the Clerk of Justiciary. In this case it is his duty to send a copy to the Crown Agent and also to the judge who presided at the trial. The Clerk of Justiciary has power to extend the above six week period before its expiry,[13] but the two week period may, like the period within which intimation of intention to appeal must be lodged, be extended only upon application to the High Court.[14] On a note of appeal against sentence alone being lodged by an appellant in custody the Clerk of Justiciary must give notice of that fact to the Secretary of State.[15]

–09 A note of appeal must identify the proceedings, must contain a full statement of all the grounds of appeal, and must be in as nearly as may be the form prescribed by Act of Adjournal.[16] Except by leave of the High Court on cause shown it is not competent for an appellant to found any aspect of his appeal on a ground not contained in the note of appeal.[17]

---

[8] 1975 Act, s. 231 (1).
[9] *Ibid.* s. 236B (2).
[10] *Ibid.* s. 231 (2); Act of Adjournal (Procedures under Criminal Justice (Scotland) Act 1980 No. 2) 1981, Form 2.
[11] *Ibid.* s. 231 (3).
[12] *Ibid.* s. 231 (4).
[13] *Ibid.* s. 233 (1).
[14] *Ibid.* s. 236B (2).
[15] *Ibid.* s. 233 (4).
[16] *Ibid.* s. 233 (2); Act of Adjournal, *supra*, Form 3.
[17] *Ibid.* s. 233 (3).

Presentation of appeal in writing

9–10   If an appellant desires to present his case and his argument in writing instead of orally he must intimate this desire to the Clerk of Justiciary at least four days before the diet fixed for the hearing of the appeal. At the same time he must lodge with the Clerk of Justiciary three copies of his case and argument, and send a copy to the Crown Agent. Any case or argument so presented will be considered by the High Court.[18] Unless the High Court otherwise directs, the respondent in such a case does not make a written reply but replies orally at the diet fixed for the hearing of the appeal.[19] Unless the High Court otherwise allows, an appellant who has presented his case and argument in writing will not be entitled to submit in addition an oral argument to the court in support of the appeal.[20]

Proceedings in sheriff court

9–11   In the case of an appeal against a sentence in the sheriff court, the sheriff clerk must furnish to the Clerk of Justiciary a certified copy of the proceedings at the trial, or must forward to him the original record of the proceedings, as may be required by the Clerk of Justiciary.[21]

Judge's report

9–12   As soon as is reasonably practicable after his receipt of the copy note of appeal sent to him by the Clerk of Justiciary, the judge who presided at the trial[22] must furnish the Clerk of Justiciary with a report in writing giving the judge's opinion on the case generally and on the grounds contained in the note of appeal. The Clerk of Justiciary must send a copy of that report to the convicted person or his solicitor, to the Crown Agent, and, in a case referred under section 263 (1) of the 1975 Act (see *infra*, para. 9–41), to the Secretary of State.[23] Subject to the foregoing, the judge's report will be available only to the High Court and the parties.[24]

---

[18] 1975 Act, s. 234 (1).

[19] *Ibid*. s. 234 (2).

[20] *Ibid*. s. 234 (3).

[21] *Ibid*. s. 236.

[22] Although here, and elsewhere, references are made to "the trial", all the provisions concerned apply equally in cases where a person has been sentenced after a plea of guilty.

[23] 1975 Act, s. 236A (1).

[24] *Ibid*. s. 236A (3).

-13   Where the judge's report is not furnished as soon as is
reasonably practicable, the High Court may call for it to be
furnished within such period as it may specify. Alternatively, if it
thinks fit the High Court may hear and determine the appeal
without such report.[25] The High Court may also require the judge
who presided at the trial to produce any notes taken by him of the
proceedings at the trial.[26]

Computation of periods

-14   Where the last day of any period for lodging an intimation of
intention to appeal, or a note of appeal, falls on a day on which the
office of the Clerk of Justiciary is closed, that period is to extend to
and include the next day on which the office is open.[27] As previously
noted, any such period may be extended at any time by the High
Court in respect of any convicted person. Application for such
extension must be in as nearly as may be the form prescribed by act
of adjournal.[28]

Signing of documents

-15   Any intimation of intention to appeal, note of appeal, or
application for extension of time, must be signed by the convicted
person or by his counsel or solicitor.[29]

Disposal of applications to High Court

-16   Generally, any application to the High Court may be made by
the appellant or respondent as the case may be or by counsel on his
behalf, orally or in writing. However, if the appellant is unrepresented and is in custody and is not entitled or has not obtained leave
to be present before the court,[30] he must make any such application
by forwarding it in writing to the Clerk of Justiciary whose
responsibility it then is to take the proper steps to obtain the
decision of the court on that application.[31]

-17   When the High Court has heard and dealt with any application
the Clerk of Justiciary must (unless it appears to him unnecessary to
do so) give to the applicant (if he is in custody and has not been

---

[25] 1975 Act, s. 236A (2).
[26] *Ibid*. s. 237.
[27] *Ibid*. s. 236B (1).
[28] *Ibid*. s. 236B (2); Act of Adjournal, *supra*, Form 4.
[29] *Ibid*. s. 236C.
[30] See *infra*, para. 9–20.
[31] 1975 Act, s. 235.

present at the hearing) notice of the decision of the court in relation to that application.[32]

Admission of appellant to bail

9–18   On the application of a person who has lodged an intimation of intention to appeal or a note of appeal, the High Court may, if it seems fit, admit that person to bail pending the determination of his appeal.[33] An appellant who is admitted to bail must, unless the High Court otherwise directs, appear personally in court on the day or days fixed for the hearing of his appeal. In the event of the appellant failing so to appear the court may decline to consider the appeal and may dismiss it summarily, or may consider and determine it or make such other order as it thinks fit. The foregoing power to determine the appeal is without prejudice to the provisions relating to breach of conditions contained in section 3 of the Bail etc. (Scotland) Act 1980.[34]

Notice of date of hearing

9–19   When the High Court fixes the date for the hearing of an appeal, or of an application for extension of time, the Clerk of Justiciary must give notice to the Crown Agent and to the solicitor of the appellant or applicant, or to the appellant or applicant himself if he has no known solicitor. The appellant or applicant, or his solicitor, must thereupon lodge three copies (typed or printed) of the appeal or application for the use of the court.[35] Where it is proposed that the powers of the court should be exercised by a single judge,[36] one copy only of the application to be disposed of should be lodged for the use of the judge.[37]

Presence of appellant at hearing

9–20   An appellant, notwithstanding that he is in custody, is entitled, if he wishes, to be present at the hearing of his appeal, except where the appeal is on some ground involving a question of law alone. In that case, and on any proceedings preliminary or incidental to an appeal, he is not entitled to be present except where that is provided

---

[32] 1975 Act, s. 260.
[33] *Ibid.* s. 238(1) and (3).
[34] *Ibid.* s. 238 (2).
[35] *Ibid.* s. 239 (1).
[36] See *infra*, para. 9–26.
[37] 1975 Act, s. 239 (2).

for by act of adjournal, or where the High Court gives him leave to be present.[38] There is as yet no provision on this matter in an act of adjournal. Where an appellant has the right to be present but does not wish to do so, the court may hear the appeal in his absence.[39]

Notice of hearing to others than parties

21   Where an appellant or applicant is in custody and has obtained leave or is entitled to be present at the hearing of his appeal or application, the Clerk of Justiciary must notify the appellant or applicant, the governor of the prison in which he then is, and the Secretary of State of the probable day on which the appeal or application will be heard. The Secretary of State must take steps to transfer the appellant or applicant to a prison convenient for his appearance before the High Court, at such reasonable time before the hearing as will enable him to consult his legal adviser, if any.[40]

22   When an appellant or applicant is entitled, or has been granted leave, to be present at any diet before the High Court or any judge thereof, for the taking of additional evidence,[41] or for an examination or investigation by a special commissioner,[42] the Clerk of Justiciary must give timeous notice to the Secretary of State in the form set out in an act of adjournal.[43] That notice is sufficient warrant to the Secretary of State for transmitting the appellant or applicant in custody from prison to the place where that diet or any subsequent diets are to be held, and for reconveying him thereafter to prison. The appellant or applicant is to appear at all such diets in ordinary civilian clothes.[44] The Secretary of State must arrange for a sufficient number of male and female prison officers to attend the sittings of the court.

Abandonment of appeal

23   An appellant may abandon his appeal by lodging with the Clerk of Justiciary a notice of abandonment in as nearly as may be the form prescribed by act of adjournal.[45] On such notice being lodged

---

[38] 1975 Act, s. 240.
[39] *Manuel* v. *H.M.A.*, 1958 J.C. 41.
[40] 1975 Act, s. 241.
[41] See *infra*, para. 9–29.
[42] See *infra*, paras. 9–29 and 9–30.
[43] Act of Adjournal 1926, No. 1373, Sched., Form XI.
[44] 1975 Act, s. 242.
[45] Act of Adjournal (Procedures under Criminal Justice (Scotland) Act 1980 No. 2) 1981, Form 6.

the appeal will be deemed to have been dismissed by the court.[46] A person who has appealed against both conviction and sentence may abandon the appeal in so far as it is against conviction and may proceed with it against sentence alone.[47]

9–24   Once a notice of abandonment has been lodged it cannot be withdrawn.[48] Conversely, where an appeal against sentence has begun to be heard, the court may refuse to allow the appeal to be abandoned where the purpose in doing so is to avoid an increase in sentence.[49]

Powers which may be exercised by a single judge

9–25   The powers of the High Court to extend the time within which intimation of intention to appeal and a note of appeal may be given, to allow the appellant to be present at any proceedings in cases where he is not entitled to be present without leave, and to admit an appellant to bail, may be exercised by any single judge of the High Court. However if the single judge refuses an application, the appellant is entitled to have the application determined by the High Court.[50] In addition to the foregoing, preliminary and interlocutory proceedings incidental to any appeal or application may be disposed of by a single judge.[51] In all proceedings before a single judge the parties may be represented and appear by a solicitor alone.[52]

Appeal against refusal of application

9–26   When an application or applications have been dealt with by a single judge under section 247 of the 1975 Act, the Clerk of Justiciary must notify to the applicant the decision in as nearly as may be the form set out in an act of adjournal.[53] In the event of the single judge refusing all or any of such applications the Clerk of Justiciary on notifying such refusal to the applicant must forward to him the prescribed form[54] to fill up and forthwith return if he desires to have the application or applications determined by the High Court as fully constituted for the hearing of appeals. If the applicant

---

[46] 1975 Act, s. 244(1).
[47] *Ibid*. s. 244 (2).
[48] *Biondi* v. *H.M.A.*, 1967 S.L.T. (Notes) 22.
[49] *West* v. *H.M.A.*, 1955 S.L.T. 425.
[50] 1975 Act, s. 247.
[51] *Ibid*. s. 249.
[52] *Ibid*. s. 250.
[53] *Ibid*. s. 251 (1); Act of Adjournal 1981, *supra*, Form 7.
[54] Act of Adjournal, *supra*, Form 8.

does not so desire, or does not return the form duly filled up within five days, the refusal of the application or applications by the single judge is to be final.[55]

-27   If the applicant desires a determination by the High Court and is not legally represented, he may be present at the hearing and determination of his application. However, an applicant who is legally represented is not entitled to be present without leave of the court.[56] When an applicant duly fills up and returns to the Clerk of Justiciary within the prescribed time the form expressing a desire to be present at the hearing and determination by the court, that form is deemed to be an application for leave to be present, and the Clerk of Justiciary must take the necessary steps for placing that application before the court.[57] If that application is refused by the court, the Clerk of Justiciary must notify the applicant; if the application is granted he must notify the applicant, the governor of the prison where the applicant is in custody, and the Secretary of State.[58]

-28   For the purpose of constituting a court of appeal, the judge who has refused any such application may sit as a member of the court, and take part in determining the application.[59]

Powers of High Court

-29   Without prejudice to any existing power of the High Court, that court may, for the purposes of an appeal against conviction, conviction and sentence, or sentence alone:

(a)   order the production of any document or other thing connected with the proceedings;

(b)   hear any additional evidence relevant to any alleged miscarriage of justice, or order such evidence to be heard by a judge of the High Court or by such other person as it may appoint for that purpose;

(c)   take account of any circumstances relevant to the case which were not before the trial judge;

(d)   remit to any fit person to inquire and report in regard to any matter or circumstance affecting the appeal;

(e)   appoint a person with expert knowledge to act as assessor to the High Court in any case where it appears

---

[55] 1975 Act, s. 251 (2).
[56] *Ibid.* s. 251 (3).
[57] *Ibid.* s. 251 (4).
[58] *Ibid.* s. 251 (5).
[59] *Ibid.* s. 251 (6).

to the court that such expert knowledge is required for the proper determination of the case.[60]

9–30   In connection with the foregoing, an error in the drafting of the 1980 Act falls to be noted. Section 252 of the 1975 Act, prior to its amendment by the 1980 Act, contained in head (d) a provision allowing the reference of certain questions to a special commissioner; and detailed provisions concerning such a reference were to be found in section 253 (2). That subsection, however, was repealed by the 1980 Act, and the former head (d) of section 252, along with the remainder of that section, has been replaced by the provisions set out in paragraph 9–29 above. Notwithstanding that, no amendment has been made to head (c) of section 242 which still contains a reference to "an examination or investigation by a special commissioner in terms of section 252 (d) of this Act."[61] It is submitted that section 242 (c) falls to be construed as if it referred to an inquiry by a fit person in terms of what is now section 252 (d) of the 1975 Act.

Disposal of appeals

9–31   Subject to the provisions noted below[62] for cases where it appears that the appellant was insane at the time of committing the act charged, the High Court may dispose of an appeal against conviction by (a) affirming the verdict of the trial court, or (b) setting aside the verdict of the trial court and either quashing the conviction or substituting therefor an amended verdict of guilty. An amended verdict of guilty must be one which could have been returned on the indictment before the trial court. Further, the High Court may dispose of an appeal by (c) setting aside the verdict of the trial court and granting authority to bring a new prosecution.[63] In setting aside a verdict the High Court may quash any sentence imposed on the appellant as respects the indictment, and (a) in a case where it substituted an amended verdict of guilty, whether or not the sentence related to the verdict set aside, or (b) in any other case, where the sentence did not so relate, may pass another (but not more severe) sentence in substitution for the sentence so quashed.[64]

---

[60] 1975 Act, s. 252.
[61] See *supra*, para. 9–22.
[62] See *infra*, para. 9–33.
[63] 1975 Act, s. 254 (1), and see s. 255 (paras. 9–34 and 9–35).
[64] *Ibid.* s. 254 (2).

–32   Subject again to the provisions for cases where it appears that the appellant was insane at the time of committing the act charged, the High Court may dispose of an appeal against sentence by (a) affirming that sentence, or (b) if the court thinks that, having regard to all the circumstances, including any additional evidence such as is mentioned in section 228 (2) of the Act,[65] a different sentence should have been passed, quashing the sentence and passing another sentence whether more or less severe in substitution therefor.[66] The power to increase a sentence is on occasions used with dramatic effect, as when a sentence of two years in a young offenders' institution was increased to five years on appeal.[67]

Disposal of appeal where appellant insane

–33   Where, in an appeal, it appears to the High Court that the appellant committed the act charged against him but that he was insane when he did so, the court must dispose of the appeal by (a) setting aside the verdict of the trial court and substituting therefor a verdict of acquittal on the ground of insanity, and (b) quashing any sentence imposed on the appellant as respects the indictment and ordering that he be detained in a state hospital or such other hospital as for special reasons the court may specify.[68] The provisions of section 174 (4) of the 1975 Act apply to such an order.[69]

New prosecution

–34   Where authority is granted under section 254 (1) (c) of the 1975 Act, a new prosecution may be brought charging the accused with the same or any similar offence arising out of the same facts; and the proceedings out of which the appeal arose are not to be a bar to such new prosecution. However, no sentence may be passed on conviction under the new prosecution which could not have been passed on conviction under the earlier proceedings.[70] This does not, it is submitted, mean that no higher sentence may be passed on conviction under the new prosecution than was in fact passed originally: that would appear to be competent provided that the higher sentence could have been passed in the earlier proceedings.

---

[65] See *supra*, para 9–04.
[66] 1975 Act, s. 254 (3).
[67] *O'Neil* v. *H.M.A.*, 1976 S.L.T. (Notes) 7.
[68] 1975 Act, s. 254 (4).
[69] See Chap. 4.
[70] 1975 Act, s. 255 (1).

On the other hand, if the earlier proceedings were taken under a statute which prescribed a maximum penalty, and the new prosecution was in respect of a common law crime where the court's powers would normally be without limit, the effect of the above provisions would appear to be to impose a limit at the level of the statutory maximum.

9–35   A new prosecution may be brought notwithstanding that any time limit which would normally prevent its being brought has elapsed.[71] New prosecutions have, however, their own time limit, namely two months after the date on which authority to bring the prosecution was granted.[72]

Failure to appear at hearing

9–36   Where no appearance is made by or on behalf of an appellant at the diet appointed for the hearing of an appeal, and where no case or argument in writing has been timeously lodged, the High Court must dispose of the appeal as if it had been abandoned.[73]

Sentence in absence

9–37   The power of the High Court to pass any sentence when disposing of an appeal may be exercised notwithstanding that the appellant is for any reason not present.[74]

Time spent pending appeal

9–38   The time during which an appellant, after admission to bail, is at large pending the determination of his appeal, is not to be reckoned as part of any term of imprisonment under his sentence.[75] On the other hand, the time during which an appellant is in custody pending the determination of his appeal will be reckoned as part of any such term of imprisonment, unless the High Court gives any direction to the contrary.[76] Subject to any direction which the High Court may give to the contrary, imprisonment of an appellant will be deemed to run, if the appellant is in custody, as from the date on which the sentence was passed and, if the appellant is not in custody, to begin to run or to be resumed as from the date on which he is received into prison under the sentence.[77]

---

[71] 1975 Act, s. 255 (2).
[72] *Ibid.* s. 255 (3).
[73] *Ibid.* s. 257.
[74] *Ibid.* s. 258.
[75] *Ibid.* s. 268 (1).
[76] *Ibid.* s. 268 (2).
[77] *Ibid.* s. 268(3).

Definition of a "sentence"

39 Apart from its normal meaning, the word "sentence", for the purpose of appeals under solemn procedure, includes any order of the High Court made on conviction with reference to the person convicted or his wife or children, and any recommendation of the High Court as to the making of a deportation order in the case of a person convicted; and the power of the High Court to pass a sentence includes a power to make any such order of the court or recommendation. A recommendation so made by the High Court is to have the same effect for the purposes of Articles 20 and 21 of the Aliens Order 1953 as the certificate and recommendation of the convicting court.[78]

Appeals against hospital orders

40 Where a hospital order, guardianship order, or an order restricting discharge has been made by a court in respect of a person charged or brought before it, he may, without prejudice to any other form of appeal under any rule of law, appeal against that order in the same manner as against a sentence.[79]

Prerogative of mercy

41 Nothing in the appeal provisions of the 1975 Act affects the prerogative of mercy, but the Secretary of State on the consideration of any sentence (other than sentence of death) passed on a person who has been convicted, may, if he thinks fit, at any time either refer the whole case to the High Court for hearing and determination as in the case of an appeal, or, if he desires the assistance of the High Court on any point arising in the case, refer that point to the court for their opinion. The above powers of the Secretary of State may be exercised whether or not an appeal against conviction or sentence has previously been heard and determined by the High Court, and whether or not the convicted person has petitioned for the exercise of Her Majesty's mercy.[80] Subject only to the foregoing, all interlocutors and sentences pronounced by the High Court are final and conclusive and not subject to review by any court whatsoever. Further, it is incompetent to stay or suspend any execution or diligence issuing

---

[78] 1975 Act, s. 279; and see *Crolla* v. *Horne*, 1931 J.C. 42.

[79] *Ibid*. s. 280.

[80] *Ibid*. s. 263 (1) and (2).

from the High Court by virtue of the powers conferred by the appeal provisions of the 1975 Act.[81]

Disqualification, forfeiture, etc.

9–42   Where, upon conviction of any person, any disqualification, forfeiture or disability attaches to such person by reason of such conviction, this is not to attach for the period of two weeks from the date of the verdict nor, in the event of appeal proceedings being commenced, until the appeal, if it is proceeded with, is determined.[82] This provision, which was first introduced by the Act of Adjournal 1926, appears to be at odds with the Road Traffic Acts in relation to disqualification for holding or obtaining a driving licence. These Acts contain no provision to suggest that such a disqualification does not have immediate effect and, indeed, the Act of 1972, by section 94 (3) contains express provision allowing a court, if it thinks fit, to suspend a disqualification pending an appeal, a provision which would be unnecessary, at least in solemn cases,[83] if section 264 (1) covered such disqualifications.

9–43   Where, upon a conviction, any property, matters or things which are the subject of the prosecution or connected therewith are to be or may be ordered to be destroyed or forfeited, the destruction or forfeiture or the operation of any order for destruction or forfeiture is to be suspended for the same periods as in the case of disqualifications, forfeitures and disabilities.[84]

Fines and caution

9–44   Where a person has on conviction been sentenced to payment of a fine and in default of payment to imprisonment, the person lawfully authorised to receive that fine must, on receiving it, retain it until the determination of any appeal in relation thereto.[85] If a person sentenced to payment of a fine remains in custody in default of payment he is to be deemed, for the purposes of the appeal provisions of the 1975 Act, to be a person sentenced to imprisonment.[86]

9–45   Where a person has on conviction been sentenced to payment of a fine and in default of payment to imprisonment, and he intimates to the judge who presided at the trial that he is desirous of

---

[81] 1975 Act, s. 262.
[82] Ibid. s. 264(1); cf. supra, para. 6–48.
[83] There is no provision comparable to s.264(1) in relation to summary appeals.
[84] 1975 Act, s. 264 (2).
[85] Ibid. s. 265 (1).
[86] Ibid. s. 265 (2).

appealing against his conviction to the High Court, the judge may, by order entered on the record, appoint that person forthwith to find caution for such sum as the judge may think right to prosecute his appeal. Subject to that the judge may also order that payment of the fine is to be made at the final determination of the appeal, if that is dismissed, to the clerk of the court in which the conviction took place or otherwise as the High Court may then order.[87] If an appellant to whom the foregoing applies does not pay the fine or lodge an intimation of intention to appeal within two weeks from the date of his conviction and sentence, the Clerk of Justiciary must report that omission to the High Court or any judge thereof. The High Court or that judge, after such notice as may be deemed advisable, may find that the caution has been forfeited, and may pronounce against the cautioner decree for such sum as may be thought proper; and may issue a warrant for the apprehension of the appellant, and may commit him to prison in default of payment of his fine, or may make such other order as is thought right.[88]

-46   An appellant who has been sentenced to the payment of a fine, and has paid it in accordance with that sentence, will, in the event of his appeal being successful, be entitled, subject to any order of the High Court, to the return of the sum or any part thereof so paid by him.[89]

Expenses

-47   On the hearing and determination of an appeal, or any proceedings preliminary or incidental thereto, no expenses are to be allowed on either side.

Appeal by Crown

-48   The Crown has no right of appeal against a sentence imposed on a person convicted on indictment. Although certain rights of appeal are given to the Crown by the provisions of the 1980 Act, they do not affect this general rule. The Lord Advocate's reference, under section 263A of the 1975 Act, arises only where a person has been acquitted of a charge, and the right to appeal by bill of advocation (now extended to decisions of the High Court as well as the sheriff court by section 280A of the 1975 Act) is a remedy, not

---

[87] 1975 Act, s. 265 (3).
[88] *Ibid*. s. 265 (5).
[89] *Ibid*. s. 265 (4).

against sentence, but against the dismissal of a prosecution on some preliminary ground.[90]

III. Appeals under summary procedure

Right of appeal

9–49   Any person convicted in summary proceedings may appeal to the High Court against the sentence passed on that conviction, or against both conviction and sentence. The prosecutor may also appeal against a sentence passed in such proceedings, but only on a point of law.[91] Only a party to the original proceedings may pursue an appeal, and executors cannot sist themselves as parties.[92]

9–50   By such an appeal a convicted person may bring under review of the High Court any alleged miscarriage of justice in the proceedings, including any alleged miscarriage on the basis of the existence and significance of additional evidence which was not heard at the trial and which was not available and could not reasonably have been made available at the trial.[93]

Appeals against hospital orders, etc.

9–51   Where a hospital order, guardianship order, or an order restricting discharge, has been made by a court in respect of a person charged or brought before it, he may, without prejudice to any other form of appeal under any rule of law, appeal against that order in the same manner as against a sentence.[94]

Appeal procedures

9–52   Appeals against conviction and sentence, and all appeals by a prosecutor, whether against an acquittal, or against a sentence, are together subject to a detailed procedure set out in sections 444 to 453, 453D and 453E of the 1975 Act.[95] An appeal by a convicted

---

[90] See, for example, *McFadyen* v. *Stewart*, 1951 J.C. 164; *Skeen* v. *Skerret*, 1976 S.L.T. (Notes) 6; *Skeen* v. *McLaren*, 1976 S.L.T. (Notes) 14; *H.M.A.* v. *McCann*, 1977 J.C. 1.
[91] 1975 Act, s. 442 (1).
[92] *Keane* v. *Adair*, 1941 J.C. 77.
[93] 1975 Act, s. 442 (2).
[94] *Ibid*. s. 443.
[95] *Ibid*. s. 442A (1).

person against sentence alone is subject to a different procedure which is set out in sections 453B to 453E of that Act.[96] This latter form of appeal is dealt with *infra*, in paras. 9–83 to 9–88.

Abandonment of appeal against conviction

-53   A person who has appealed against both conviction and sentence may abandon the appeal in so far as it is against conviction and may proceed with it against sentence alone. Procedure for this is prescribed by act of adjournal.[97]

Manner and time of appeal

-54   An appeal against conviction and sentence, or an appeal against sentence by a prosecutor is by application for a stated case. That application must (a) be made within one week of the final determination of the proceedings, (b) contain a full statement of all the matters which the appellant desires to bring under review and, where the appeal is also against sentence, a statement of that fact, and (c) be signed by the appellant or his solicitor and lodged with the clerk of court. A copy of the application must, within the period of one week, be sent by the appellant to the respondent or the respondent's solicitor.[98] In calculating the period of one week the date of the determination of the judge is not counted,[99] and an application posted on the last day of the period has been held to be timeous, although it was not received by the clerk of court until later.[100] An application must be in writing, and may not be submitted orally.[1]

-55   For the purposes of the foregoing, summary proceedings are to be deemed to be finally determined on the day on which sentence is passed in open court. However, where, in relation to an appeal against conviction, or a prosecutor's appeal against an acquittal, sentence is deferred, they are to be deemed finally determined on

---

[96] 1975 Act, s. 442B.
[97] *Ibid*. s. 442A (2); Act of Adjournal (Procedures under Criminal Justice (Scotland) Act 1980 No. 2) 1981, s. 5 and Form 9.
[98] *Ibid*. s. 444 (1); Act of Adjournal, *supra*, Form 10.
[99] *Hutton* v. *Garland*, (1884) 5 Couper 274; *Smith* v. *Gray*, 1925 J.C. 8.
[100] *Smith* v. *Gray*, *supra*.
[1] *Smith* v. *Gray*, *supra*.

the day on which sentence is first so deferred in open court.[2] It is submitted that, in the event of such an appeal being disposed of in a manner which permitted the court subsequently to pass sentence, a further appeal would then be competent against that sentence.

9–56   The clerk of court must enter in the record of the proceedings the date when an application for a stated case was lodged.[3] Thereafter, a limited right is given to an appellant to amend any matter stated in his application, or to add a new matter. He may do so at any time within three weeks after the issue of a draft stated case, or within any further period allowed by the High Court under section 448 (6) of the Act. Any such amendment or addition must be intimated to the respondent or the respondent's solicitor.[4]

9–57   Without prejudice to any other power of relief which the High Court may have, where it appears to that court on application made to it that the applicant has failed to comply with any of the requirements relating to an application for a stated case, the High Court may direct that such further period of time as it may think proper be afforded to the applicant to comply with any of these requirements.[5] An application for such a direction must be made in writing to the Clerk of Justiciary and must state the grounds for the application. Notification of it must be made by the appellant or his solicitor to the clerk of the court from which the appeal is to be taken, and he must thereupon transmit the complaint, documentary productions and any other proceedings in the cause to the Clerk of Justiciary.[6] The High Court will dispose of any such application in the same manner as an application to review the decision of an inferior court on a grant of bail, but has power to dispense with a hearing, and to make such inquiry in relation to the application as it may think fit. When the High Court has disposed of the application the Clerk of Justiciary must inform the clerk of the inferior court of the result.[7]

Caution by appellant

9–58   It is no longer competent to require an appellant to find caution to meet any fine and expenses imposed.[8]

---

[2] 1975 Act, s. 451 (3).
[3] *Ibid.* s. 444 (1A).
[4] *Ibid.* s. 444 (1B).
[5] *Ibid.* s. 444 (3).
[6] *Ibid.* s. 444 (4).
[7] *Ibid.* s. 444 (5).
[8] 1980 Act, Sched. 3, para. 4.

Procedure where appellant in custody

59   If an appellant who has applied for a stated case is in custody, the court may grant bail, grant a sist of execution, and make any other interim order.[9] An application for bail must be disposed of by the court within 24 hours after such application has been made; and the appellant, if dissatisfied with the conditions imposed, or on refusal of bail, may, within 24 hours after the judgment of the court, appeal by a note of appeal written on the complaint and signed by himself or his solicitor. Such an appeal is to the High Court or any judge thereof.[10]

60   If an appellant who has been granted bail does not thereafter proceed with his appeal, the inferior court has power to grant warrant to apprehend and imprison him for such period of his sentence as at the date of his bail remained unexpired. That period will run from the date of his imprisonment under such warrant.[11] Where, however, at the time of abandonment of the appeal the person is serving a term or terms of imprisonment imposed subsequently to the conviction appealed against, the court has power to order that the sentence, or any unexpired portion of it, should run from such date as the court may think fit, not being a date later than the date on which the term or terms of imprisonment subsequently imposed expired.[12]

Preparation of draft stated case

61   Within three weeks of the final determination of proceedings in respect of which an application is made for a stated case, a draft stated case must be prepared. Where the appeal is taken from the district court and the trial was presided over by a justice of the peace or justices of the peace, the draft case is to be prepared by the justice or justices, with such assistance from the clerk of court as may be required. In any other case, the draft stated case is to be prepared by the judge who presided at the trial. As soon as the case is prepared

---

[9] 1975 Act, s. 446 (1).

[10] *Ibid*. s. 446(2); from time to time difficulties arise in relation to the time limits prescribed for the disposal of bail applications (*cf*. 1975 Act, ss. 28 and 298), the problem being whether the 24 hours begins to run from the moment when a bail petition is presented to the clerk of court, or from the moment when it is first presented to the judge. Although the former interpretation has been contended for, it is now clear that the latter one is more consistent with the words of the statute: see *H.M.A.* v. *Keegan*, 1981 S.L.T. (Notes) 35.

[11] *Ibid*. s. 446 (4).

[12] *Ibid*. s. 446 (5).

the clerk of the court concerned must issue the draft to the appellant or his solicitor and a duplicate to the respondent or his solicitor.[13]

9–62   A stated case must be as nearly as may be in the appropriate form contained in an act of adjournal. It must set forth the particulars of any matters competent for review which the appellant desires to bring under the review of the High Court, and of the facts, if any, proved in the case. It must also set forth any point of law decided, and the grounds of decision.[14] Where the appeal is against sentence as well as conviction, care should be taken to ensure that the case sets out any facts relevant to sentence, and the considerations upon which the particular sentence was arrived at.

9–63   A stated case should set out fully the facts proved and not the evidence on which these facts are based;[15] and the facts proved should be set forth in the case itself and not in a separate document.[16] The grounds of a decision should be stated distinctly in a stated case,[17] particularly where evidence has been disallowed.[18] If, for special reasons, a disqualification for holding a driving licence is imposed for less than the statutory period required under the Road Traffic Acts, the grounds of indulgence should be clearly set out in the stated case.[19]

Adjustment and signature of case

9–64   Subject to a power of relief given to the High Court,[20] within three weeks of the issue of the draft stated case each party must cause to be transmitted to the court and to the other parties or their solicitors a note of any adjustments he proposes should be made to the draft case, or must intimate that he has no such proposal. Any proposed adjustments must relate to evidence heard (or purported to have been heard) at the trial and not to additional evidence under section 442 (2) of the Act.[21] Subject to the same power of relief, if the period of three weeks has expired and the appellant has not lodged adjustments and has failed to intimate that he has no

---

[13] 1975 Act, s. 447 (1).

[14] *Ibid.* s. 447 (2); Act of Adjournal 1981, *supra*, Form 11; and see *Mitchell and Others* v. *Smith*, High Court, 21 January 1981.

[15] *Gordon* v. *Hansen* (1914) 7 Adam 441; *Waddell* v. *Kinnaird*, 1922 J.C. 40; *Pert* v. *Robinson*, 1955 S.L.T. 23.

[16] *MacKenna* v. *Dunn*, 1918 2 S.L.T. 66; *Cockburn* v. *Gordon*, 1928 J.C. 87.

[17] *Lyon* v. *Don Brothers, Buist & Co.*, 1944 J.C. 1.

[18] *Falconer* v. *Brown* (1893) 1 Adam 96.

[19] *Campbell* v. *Sinclair*, 1938 J.C. 127.

[20] See *infra*, para. 9–69.

[21] 1975 Act, s. 448 (1); and see *supra*, para. 9–50.

adjustments to propose, he will be deemed to have abandoned his appeal, whereupon the same consequences will follow as in the case of a person granted bail who does not thereafter proceed with his appeal.[22]

5   If adjustments are proposed, or if the judge desires to make any alterations to the draft case, there must be a hearing for the purpose of considering such adjustments or alterations, unless the appellant has, or has been deemed to have, abandoned his appeal. That hearing must take place within one week of the expiry of the three weeks period mentioned above, or of such further period as the High Court may have allowed.[23] The foregoing provision for a hearing in all cases where adjustments are proposed was introduced by the 1980 Act in response to criticisms that, in some cases, proposed adjustments were being ignored by judges. The consequence of the way in which the provision has been drafted would appear to be that a hearing must be held even in a case where the judge and all the parties are perfectly content that a proposed adjustment should be incorporated in the stated case. No doubt from time to time judges and parties may agree to dispense with a formal hearing in such cases, but they will apparently be acting in contravention of the statutory provisions if they do so. The mandatory nature of the provision about hearings is emphasised by the further provision that, where a party neither attends nor secures that he is represented at a hearing, the hearing must nevertheless proceed:[24] consequently, it would seem that, in the admittedly unlikely event of neither party being present or represented, a judge is required to hold a hearing by himself!

6   Where at a hearing any adjustment proposed by a party (and not withdrawn) is rejected by the judge, or any alteration to the draft case proposed by the judge is not accepted by all parties, that fact must be recorded in the minute of the proceedings of the hearing.[25] Within two weeks of the date of the hearing or, where there is no hearing, within two weeks of the expiry of the original three weeks period, the judge must (unless the appellant has been deemed to have abandoned his appeal) state and sign the case. He must append to the case (a) any adjustment which is rejected by him, a note of any evidence rejected by him which is alleged to

---

[22] 1975 Act, s. 448 (2); and see *supra*, para. 9–60.
[23] *Ibid*. s. 448 (2A).
[24] *Ibid*. s. 448 (2B).
[25] *Ibid*. s. 448 (2C).

support that adjustment and the reasons for his rejection of that adjustment and evidence; and (b) a note of the evidence upon which he bases any findings of fact challenged, on the basis that it is unsupported by the evidence, by a party at the hearing.[26]

9–67 Where the judge by whom a person was convicted dies before signing the case, or is precluded by illness or other cause from doing so, it is competent for the convicted person to present a bill of suspension to the High Court and to bring under the review of that court any matter which might have been brought under review by stated case.[27]

9–68 As soon as a stated case is signed the clerk of court must send the case to the appellant or his solicitor and a duplicate thereof to the respondent or his solicitor, and he must transmit the complaint, productions and any other proceedings to the Clerk of Justiciary.[28] Subject again to any power of relief granted by the High Court, within one week of receiving the case the appellant or his solicitor must cause it to be lodged with the Clerk of Justiciary.[29] If the appellant or his solicitor fails to comply with the above requirement the appellant will be deemed to have abandoned his appeal.[30]

Application to High Court for extension of time

9–69 Without prejudice to any other power of relief which the High Court may have, where it appears to that court, on application made to it, that the applicant has failed to comply with any of the time limits relating to the notification of adjustments or the lodging of the case with the Clerk of Justiciary, the High Court may direct that such further period of time as it may think proper be afforded to the applicant to comply with any requirement.[31] Such an application must be made in writing to the Clerk of Justiciary and must state the grounds for the application.[32] The High Court will dispose of the application in the same manner as an application to review the decision of an inferior court on a grant of bail, but has power to dispense with a hearing, and to make such inquiry in relation to the application as it may think fit. When the High Court has disposed of

---

[26] 1975 Act, s. 448 (2D).
[27] *Ibid.* s. 444 (2).
[28] *Ibid.* s. 448 (3).
[29] *Ibid.* s. 448 (4).
[30] *Ibid.* s. 448 (5).
[31] *Ibid.* s. 448 (6).
[32] *Ibid.* s. 448 (7).

the application the Clerk of Justiciary must inform the clerk of the inferior court of the result.[33]

Abandonment of appeal

70 An appellant may at any time prior to lodging the case with the Clerk of Justiciary abandon his appeal by minute signed by himself or his solicitor, written on the complaint or lodged with the clerk of the inferior court, and intimated to the respondent or his solicitor. Such abandonment is without prejudice to any other competent mode of appeal, review, advocation or suspension.[34] Once the case has been lodged with the Clerk of Justiciary the appellant will be held to have abandoned any other mode of appeal which might otherwise have been open to him.[35] Exceptionally, however, in such circumstances a petition to the *nobile officium* may be considered.[36]

Computation of time

71 If any period of time relating to appeals expires on a Saturday, Sunday or court holiday prescribed for the relevant court, the period is to be extended to expire on the next day which is not a Saturday, Sunday or such court holiday.[37] Where a judge against whose judgment an appeal is taken is temporarily absent from duty for any cause, the sheriff principal of the sheriffdom concerned may extend any period specified in sections 447 (1) (preparation of draft case), 448 (2A) (holding of hearing on proposed adjustments and alterations) and 448 (2D) (stating and signing of case). Such extension may be for such period as the sheriff principal considers reasonable.[38]

Hearing of appeal

72 A stated case will be heard by the High Court on such date as it may fix.[39] Where an appellant, in his application for a stated case, refers to an alleged miscarriage of justice, but in stating a case the inferior court is unable to take that allegation into account, the High

---

[33] 1975 Act, s. 448 (8).
[34] *Ibid.* s. 449 (1); Act of Adjournal 1981, *supra*, Form 9; and see *Kay* v. *Local Authority of Kelso* (1876) 3 Couper 305.
[35] *Ibid.* s. 449 (2).
[36] *Patrick McCloy, Petitioner*, 1971 S.L.T. (Notes) 32.
[37] 1975 Act, s. 451 (1).
[38] *Ibid.* s. 451 (2); Act of Adjournal 1981, *supra*, Form 14.
[39] *Ibid.* s. 452 (1).

Court may nevertheless have regard to the allegation at the hearing.[40] Generally, except by leave of the High Court on cause shown, it is not competent for an appellant to found any aspect of his appeal on a matter not contained in his application (or in a duly made amendment or addition to that application).[41]

9–73   Without prejudice to any existing power of the High Court, that court may in hearing a stated case:

(a)   order the production of any document or other thing connected with the proceedings;

(b)   hear any additional evidence relevant to any alleged miscarriage of justice or order such evidence to be heard by a judge of the High Court or by such other person as it may appoint for that purpose;

(c)   take account of any circumstances relevant to the case which were not before the trial judge;[42]

(d)   remit to any fit person to inquire and report in regard to any matter or circumstance affecting the appeal;[42]

(e)   appoint a person with expert knowledge to act as assessor to the High Court in any case where it appears to the court that such expert knowledge is required for the proper determination of the case;

(f)   take account of any matter proposed in any adjustment rejected by the trial judge and of the reasons for such rejection;

(g)   take account of any evidence contained in a note of the evidence upon which a judge bases any finding of fact challenged by a party.[43]

Additionally, the High Court may at the hearing remit the stated case back to the inferior court to be amended and returned.[44]

Disposal of stated case appeal

9–74   Apart from the procedure appropriate in cases where the offender appears to have been insane at the time of the commission of the offence,[45] the High Court may dispose of a case by:

---

[40] 1975 Act, s. 452 (2).

[41] *Ibid.* s. 452 (3).

[42] *cf. Hogg* v. *Heatlie*, 1962 S.L.T. 38, where the High Court obtained a social inquiry report when none had been before the trial judge.

[43] 1975 Act, s. 452 (4).

[44] *Ibid.* s. 452 (5); *Penrose* v. *Bruce*, 1927 J.C. 79; *Cairney* v. *Patterson*, 1945 J.C. 120.

[45] See *infra*, para. 9–90.

(a)   remitting the cause to the inferior court with their opinion and any direction thereon;

(b)   affirming the verdict of the inferior court;

(c)   setting aside the verdict of the inferior court and either quashing the conviction or substituting an amended verdict of guilty. In the latter case the amended verdict must be one which could have been returned on the complaint before the inferior court; or

(d)   setting aside the verdict of the inferior court and granting authority to bring a new prosecution.[46]

In an appeal against both conviction and sentence the High Court will dispose of the appeal against sentence by the exercise of the powers appropriate where the appeal is against sentence alone.[47]

75   In setting aside a verdict the High Court may quash any sentence imposed on the appellant as respects the complaint, and (a) in a case where it substitutes an amended verdict of guilty, whether or not the sentence related to the verdict set aside, or (b) in any other case, where the sentence did not so relate, may pass another (but not more severe) sentence in substitution for the sentence so quashed.[48]

76   Where an appeal against acquittal is sustained, the High Court may (a) convict and sentence the respondent, (b) remit the case to the inferior court with instructions to convict and sentence the respondent, who is bound to attend any diet fixed by the inferior court for such purpose, or (c) remit the case to the inferior court with their opinion thereon. The High Court must not in any case increase the sentence beyond the maximum sentence which could have been passed by the inferior court.[49]

77   The High Court has power in an appeal to award such expenses both in the High Court and in the inferior court as it may think fit.[50]

New prosecution

78   Where authority is granted by the High Court, a new prosecution may be brought charging the accused with the same or any similar offence arising out of the same facts. The proceedings

---

[46] 1975 Act, s. 452A (1); for new prosecution see *infra*, paras. 9–78 and 9–79.
[47] *Ibid*. s. 452A (2); and see *infra*, para. 9–88.
[48] *Ibid*. s. 452A (3).
[49] *Ibid*. s. 452A (4).
[50] *Ibid*. s. 452A (5).

out of which the stated case arose are not a bar to such prosecution. However, no sentence may be passed on conviction under the new prosecution which could not have been passed on conviction under the earlier proceedings.[51] This last provision may be of particular importance in summary courts where different statutes may impose differing maximum penalties. Thus, for example, if a person were convicted in a new prosecution of an offence of police assault under section 41 of the Police (Scotland) Act 1967, the earlier proceedings having been in respect of an assault at common law, the court could not on the latter occasion avail itself of the extended sentencing powers conferred in respect of the statutory offence. It follows that, in all cases of new prosecutions, care should be taken to ascertain the nature of the earlier proceedings before sentence is passed.

9–79   A new prosecution may be brought notwithstanding that any time limit for the commencement of such proceedings, other than the one expressly provided for in relation to new prosecutions, has elapsed.[52] Proceedings in a new prosecution must be commenced within two months of the date on which authority to bring the prosecution was granted. For this purpose proceedings are to be deemed to be commenced on the date on which a warrant to apprehend or to cite the accused is granted, where such warrant is executed without unreasonable delay. In any other case the proceedings are to be deemed to be commenced on the date on which the warrant is executed.[53] Where the two months elapse and no new prosecution has been brought, the order of the High Court setting aside the verdict is to have the effect, for all purposes, of an acquittal.[54]

Consent by prosecutor to set aside conviction

9–80   Where an appeal has been taken by stated case against conviction, or against conviction and sentence, or by suspension or otherwise, and the prosecutor, on the appeal being intimated to him, is not prepared to maintain the judgment appealed against, he may consent to the conviction and sentence being set aside, either in whole or in part. This should be done by a minute signed by him and written on the complaint or lodged with the clerk of court. The minute must set forth the grounds on which the prosecutor is of

---

[51] 1975 Act, s. 452B (1).
[52] *Ibid.* s. 452B (2).
[53] *Ibid.* s. 452B (3).
[54] *Ibid.* s. 452B (4).

opinion that the judgment cannot be maintained.[55] This provision does not authorise a prosecutor to purport to reverse a sheriff on a question of law, that being a matter solely for the High Court.[56]

A copy of a minute by a prosecutor must be sent by him to the appellant or his solicitor, and the clerk of court must thereupon ascertain from the appellant or his solicitor whether he desires to be heard by the High Court before the appeal is disposed of. The clerk must note on the record whether or not the appellant so desires, and must thereafter transmit the complaint and relative proceedings to the Clerk of Justiciary.[57] On receipt of these the Clerk of Justiciary must lay them before any judge of the High Court, either in court or in chambers, and the judge, after hearing parties if they desire to be heard, or without hearing parties, may set aside the conviction either in whole or in part, or may refuse to set aside the conviction. If he sets aside the conviction he may award to the appellant expenses not exceeding £20. If he refuses to set aside the conviction the proceedings must be returned to the clerk of the inferior court when the appellant will be entitled to proceed with his appeal in the same way as if it had been marked on the date when the complaint and proceedings are returned to the clerk of the inferior court.[58] The preparation of a draft stated case is delayed pending the decision of the High Court.[59]

The power to consent to a conviction and sentence being set aside is exercisable, where the appeal is by stated case, at any time within two weeks after the receipt by the prosecutor of the draft stated case, and, where the appeal is by suspension, at any time within two weeks after the service on the prosecutor of the bill of suspension.[60] In so far as it relates to appeals by stated case the foregoing provision is a little puzzling because it appears to imply that a prosecutor may not avail himself of the power to consent to a conviction being set aside until after the draft stated case has been issued. On the other hand the general purpose of these provisions is to save expense and delay,[61] and both subsections (1) and (4) of section 453 (paras. 9–80 and 9–81, *supra*) clearly contemplate the procedure being initiated before a draft case is prepared. Perhaps

---

[55] 1975 Act, s. 453 (1).
[56] *O'Brien* v. *Adair*, 1947 J.C. 180.
[57] 1975 Act, s. 453 (2).
[58] *Ibid.* s. 453 (3); 1980 Act, s. 46 (1) (*f*).
[59] *Ibid.* s. 453 (4).
[60] *Ibid.* s. 453 (5).
[61] *O'Brien* v. *Adair, supra.*

the provisions in subsection (5) do no more than prescribe a point after which the procedure will no longer be competent.

APPEALS AGAINST SENTENCE ALONE

Note of appeal

9–83   An appeal by a convicted person against sentence alone is by note of appeal. The note must state the ground of appeal and must, within one week of the passing of the sentence, be lodged with the clerk of the court from which the appeal is to be taken.[62]

9–84   On receipt of the note of appeal the clerk of court must send a copy of the note to the respondent or his solicitor, and obtain a report from the judge who sentenced the convicted person.[63] No statutory form is prescribed for the judge's report: it should, however, fully narrate any facts pertaining to the offence which are relevant to the sentence, describe the substance of any plea in mitigation submitted by or on behalf of the convicted person, and explain the reasoning behind the sentence that was imposed.

9–85   Within two weeks of the passing of the sentence against which the appeal is taken the clerk of court must send to the Clerk of Justiciary the note of appeal together with the judge's report, a certified copy of the complaint, the minute of proceedings and any other relevant documents. He must also send copies of the report to the appellant and respondent or their solicitors. The above period of two weeks may, however, be extended for such period as is considered reasonable by the sheriff principal of the sheriffdom in which the judgment was pronounced. The sheriff principal may exercise that power in cases where a judge is temporarily absent from duty for any cause.[64] Where the judge's report is not furnished within any of the periods mentioned above, the High Court may extend the period or, if it thinks fit, hear and determine the appeal without such report.[65]

9–86   An appellant proceeding by way of note of appeal may at any time prior to the hearing of the appeal abandon his appeal by minute, signed by himself or his solicitor. That minute must be lodged with the clerk of court in a case where the note has not yet been sent to the Clerk of Justiciary, and in any other case with the

---

[62] 1975 Act, s. 453B (1) and (2); Act of Adjournal 1981, *supra*, Form 15.
[63] *Ibid*. s. 453B (3).
[64] *Ibid*. s. 453B (4); Act of Adjournal 1981, *supra*, Form 14.
[65] *Ibid*. s. 453B (5).

Clerk of Justiciary. In all cases the minute must be intimated to the respondent.[66]

7   Many of the provisions of the 1975 Act relating to stated cases also apply to appeals by note of appeal. These are the provisions of section 444 relating to an allowance by the High Court of further time to lodge an appeal,[67] and the provisions of section 446 (procedure where appellant in custody), section 450 (record of procedure on appeal), and section 452 (4)(*a*) to (*e*) (powers of High Court at hearing of appeal).[68]

Disposal of appeal by note of appeal

8   An appeal against sentence by note of appeal will be heard by the High Court on such date as it may fix, and the High Court may dispose of the appeal by (a) affirming the sentence, or (b) if the court thinks that, having regard to all the circumstances, including any additional evidence, a different sentence should have been passed, quashing the sentence and passing another sentence, whether more or less severe, in substitution therefor. The court may not, however, increase the sentence beyond the maximum sentence which could have been passed by the inferior court.[69] The High Court has power in an appeal by note of appeal to award such expenses both in the High Court and in the inferior court as it may think fit.[70]

PROCEDURE WHERE APPELLANT IS LIABLE TO IMPRISONMENT OR DETENTION

9   Where, following an appeal, other than one at the instance of the prosecutor, the appellant remains liable to imprisonment or detention under the sentence of the inferior court or is so liable under a sentence passed in the appeal proceedings, the High Court has certain powers. Where at the time of disposal of the appeal the appellant was at liberty on bail, it has power to grant warrant to apprehend and imprison (or detain) the appellant for a term, to run from the date of such apprehension, not longer than that part of the

---

[66] 1975 Act, s. 453B (7); Act of Adjournal 1981, *supra*, Form 16.
[67] *Ibid.* s. 453B (6); Act of Adjournal 1981, *supra*, s. 7.
[68] *Ibid.* s. 453B (8).
[69] *Ibid.* s. 453C (1); this provision radically alters the grounds on which the High Court may alter a summary sentence on appeal: for a fuller discussion see *infra*, para. 9–96.
[70] *Ibid.* s. 453C (2).

term or terms of imprisonment (or detention) specified in the sentence brought under review which remained unexpired at the date of liberation. Where at the time of disposal of the appeal the appellant is serving a term or terms of imprisonment (or detention) imposed in relation to a conviction subsequent to the conviction in respect of which the conviction or sentence appealed against was imposed, the High Court may exercise the like powers in relation to him as may be exercised, in relation to an appeal which has been abandoned, by a court of summary jurisdiction in pursuance of section 446 (5) of the 1975 Act (see *supra*, para. 9–60).[71]

DISPOSAL OF APPEAL WHERE APPELLANT INSANE

9–90   In relation to any appeal by a convicted person under summary procedure the High Court, where it appears to it that the appellant committed the act charged against him but that he was insane when he did so, must dispose of the appeal by (a) setting aside the verdict of the inferior court and substituting therefor a verdict of acquittal on the ground of insanity, and (b) quashing any sentence imposed on the appellant as respects the complaint and ordering that he be detained in a state hospital or such other hospital as for special reasons the court may specify.[72] The provisions of section 174 (4) of the 1975 Act are to apply to such an order for detention in hospital; that is to say the order is to have the like effect as a hospital order together with an order restricting the person's discharge, made without limitation of time.[73] The fact that it was found necessary in relation to summary appeals to make reference to section 174 (which is in the part of the 1975 Act dealing with solemn procedure) lends weight to the view expressed elsewhere in this book[74] that the Act contains no provision for a court of summary jurisdiction to deal with the case of a person who is found to have been insane at the time of commission of the offence.

IV. Suspension

9–91   Suspension is a process, which is now effectively confined to summary procedure, whereby an illegal or improper warrant, conviction or judgment issued by an inferior court may be reviewed

---

[71] 1975 Act, ss. 452A (6) and 453C (3).
[72] *Ibid*. s. 453D (1).
[73] *Ibid*. s. 453D (2).
[74] Paras. 4–09 and 4–10.

and set aside by the High Court. It has been held[75] not to be a suitable mode of review in cases where the more appropriate method of appeal is by stated case, and has been said to be truly appropriate "where the relevant circumstances are instantly or almost instantly verifiable and the point sought to be raised is raised promptly, a crisp issue of, say, jurisdiction, competency, oppression, or departure from the canons of natural justice."[76] Suspension is now expressly declared by statute[77] to be available against a conviction in cases where an appeal by stated case would be incompetent or would in the circumstances be inappropriate. As has been seen (para. 9–67, *supra*) it is also competent, in a case where the judge dies before signing a stated case or is precluded by illness or other cause from doing so, to present a bill of suspension so as to bring under review any matter that might have been brought under review by stated case. That, of course, will include an appeal against sentence where there is also an appeal against conviction. It will not, however, include an appeal against sentence alone, since such an appeal now proceeds, not by stated case, but by note of appeal.

92   In general, where an appeal is to be taken against sentence alone, it may be said that a bill of suspension will rarely be appropriate,[78] except where there has been some fundamental incompetence or irregularity of procedure,[79] or clearly oppressive conduct on the part of the judge.[80] Suspension cannot be used as a means of obtaining probation or other reports which were not called for by the judge.[81] On the other hand, matters incidental to sentencing, such as a remand in custody while reports are being prepared, may properly be made the subject of a suspension.[82] It has also been held that, notwithstanding the provisions of section 230 of the 1975 Act, it is competent to proceed by way of suspension in the case of a witness sentenced for contempt of court in the course of proceedings on indictment in the sheriff court.[83] A suspension may also be brought by a person other than the prosecutor or the

---

[75] *O'Hara* v. *Mill*, 1938 J.C. 4; *James Y. Keanie Ltd* v. *Laird*, 1943 J.C. 73.
[76] *Fairley* v. *Muir*, 1951 J.C. 56, *per* Lord Justice-General at p. 60.
[77] 1975 Act, s. 453A.
[78] *Galloway* v. *Smith*, 1974 S.L.T. (Notes) 63.
[79] *Smith* v. *Sempill* (1910) 6 Adam 348; *McRory* v. *Findlay* (1911) 6 Adam 417; *Anderson* v. *Begg* (1907) 5 Adam 387.
[80] *Blair* v. *Hawthorn*, 1945 J.C. 17.
[81] *Farquhar* v. *Burrell*, 1955 J.C. 66.
[82] *Morrison* v. *Clark*, 1962 S.L.T. 113.
[83] *Butterworth* v. *Herron*, 1975 S.L.T. (Notes) 56.

accused where that person has been affected by, for example, an order for forfeiture of his goods.[84]

V. Grounds on which a sentence may be overturned

Solemn jurisdiction

9–93   On an appeal against sentence the High Court may quash the sentence of the inferior court and pass another sentence whether more or less severe in substitution therefor. The court may take that course if it thinks that, having regard to all the circumstances, a different sentence should have been passed.[85] These powers, which are substantially the same as those introduced by the Criminal Appeal (Scotland) Act 1926, have been construed as meaning that a sentence may be reduced if it is clearly excessive, or increased if it is clearly inadequate. The court's power to increase sentences has been used on several occasions.[86]

9–94   A sentence will not be reduced as being excessive merely because it is somewhat higher than that which the High Court would itself have imposed. For a reduction to be justified the sentence must go beyond what is necessary and customary in a case of that kind.[87] Although the test on appeal — and indeed most written grounds of appeal echo this — is whether the sentence appealed against is excessive, some of the cases suggest that it might equally well be expressed as whether the sentence is appropriate having regard to the circumstances of the particular case. However the test is described, the High Court's power to reduce a sentence is clearly a wide one, and, although what is sometimes referred to as "tinkering with a sentence" has been judicially disapproved of, there may sometimes be a fairly fine dividing line between that and a proper exercise of the court's powers.

9–95   It is to be noted that, prior to the passing of the 1980 Act, the High Court had power, where an appeal was against conviction only, to reduce or increase the sentence in like manner as in an appeal against sentence.[88] That power, which was on one occasion

---

[84] *Loch Lomond Sailings Ltd.* v. *Hawthorn*, 1962 J.C. 8; *Semple & Sons* v. *Macdonald*, 1963 J.C. 90.

[85] 1975 Act, s. 254 (3).

[86] *Boyle* v. *H.M.A.*, 1949 S.L.T. (Notes) 41; *Connelly* v. *H.M.A.*, 1954 J.C. 90; *O'Neil* v. *H.M.A.*, 1976 S.L.T. (Notes) 7.

[87] *O'Reilly* v. *H.M.A.*, 1943 J.C. 23; *Dewar* v. *H.M.A.*, 1945 J.C. 5; *Moar* v. *H.M.A.*, 1949 J.C. 31; *Cawthorne* v. *H.M.A.*, 1968 J.C. 32.

[88] Criminal Appeal (Scotland) Act 1926, s. 2 (3).

construed as enabling the court to increase a sentence beyond the maximum which could have been imposed by the sheriff,[89] has been removed by the amended section 254 of the 1975 Act introduced by the 1980 Act. The position now is that, where an appeal is against conviction alone, the High Court may vary the sentence only where it sets aside the verdict of the inferior court; and in that case, while it may quash the sentence originally passed, it may not pass another which is more severe.[90]

Summary jurisdiction

–96   Prior to the passing of the 1980 Act it was well established that the High Court would interfere with a sentence passed by a court of summary jurisdiction only if it could be shown that that sentence was harsh and oppressive.[91] The Thomson Committee,[92] however, took the view that it was undesirable to have different tests for summary and solemn procedure, and their recommendation on that matter was given statutory effect in the new section 453C of the 1975 Act which was introduced by the 1980 Act. That section describes the powers of the High Court, in an appeal against sentence, in the same words as are used in section 254 in relation to solemn appeals, with only this minor difference, that, in section 453C there is a proviso to the effect that the court must not in any (summary) case increase the sentence beyond the maximum sentence which could have been passed by the inferior court. Subject to that, the position now is that summary appeals against sentence fall to be determined by the same criteria that have previously been in use in relation to solemn appeals.

What may be considered excessive or inappropriate

–97   Since so much will depend on the facts and circumstances of each case, it is not possible to make any kind of general statement as to what is or is not an excessive or inappropriate sentence. However, the reported cases, notwithstanding that most of them contain decisions relating to the former summary test of "harsh and oppressive", throw some light on the manner in which the High Court has approached in the past, and may approach in the future, its task of determining appeals against sentence. Since a test of

---

[89] *Connelly* v. *H.M.A., supra.*
[90] 1975 Act, s. 254 (2).
[91] *Stewart* v. *Cormack*, 1941 J.C. 73; *Fleming* v. *Macdonald*, 1958 J.C. 1.
[92] *Criminal Appeals In Scotland (Third Report)*, 1977, Cmnd. 7005, Chap. 16.

"harsh and oppressive" is a more demanding one than a test of "excessive" or "inappropriate" it may be presumed that what has in the past been regarded as harsh and oppressive may readily be regarded as excessive or inappropriate. Conversely, however, as the general approach to sentencing has developed over the years, one cannot say with any confidence that some of the older appeals which were dismissed on the basis that the sentence was not harsh or oppressive would be dismissed today, even simply on the basis that the sentence was excessive or inappropriate.

9–98   In relation to fines it has been held[93] to be oppressive, and would probably now be regarded as excessive, to impose the maximum fine authorised by a statute in the absence of particularly aggravating factors. In the case cited the Lord Justice-Clerk stated:[94] "The heavy penalties so frequently specified in recent statutes, regulations and orders, ought normally to be regarded as the limit set on the powers of the Court when dealing with the gravest type of offence which the Legislature contemplated as likely to arise in practice . . . if in the early stages maximum, or nearly maximum, penalties are imposed in cases where few or no features of aggravation are present, there is a grave risk that, if and when much more serious cases later arise, the Court may find itself powerless to exercise that just discrimination in the award of penalties which is indispensable to the due administration of criminal justice." Although the foregoing principles were expressed in relation to maximum fines, there seems no reason to suppose that they ought not to apply equally to maximum terms of imprisonment or detention.

9–99   On the other hand, it has been held not to be, *per se*, oppressive to impose a maximum penalty,[95] or even imprisonment[96] on a first offender, provided that, in the latter case the appropriate reports are obtained and considered before the sentence is passed. Where a particular sentence has been recommended in such reports, it has been held not to be oppressive to impose a sentence which is more severe.[97] While the foregoing propositions are no doubt still

---

[93] *Edward and Sons* v. *McKinnon*, 1943 J.C. 156.

[94] At p. 168.

[95] *Sinclair* v. *Mackenzie*, 1948 S.L.T. (Notes) 23.

[96] *Stewart* v. *Cormack*, 1941 J.C. 73; *Smith* v. *Adair*, 1945 J.C. 103; *Winslow* v. *Farrell*, 1965 J.C. 49.

[97] *Kyle* v. *Cruickshank*, 1961 J.C. 1; *Scott and Another* v. *MacDonald*, 1961 S.L.T. 257.

perfectly valid, it is probable that, on the facts of some of the cases involved, the court today might well conclude that the sentences were excessive or inappropriate. In *Stewart* v. *Cormack*[98] a young offender, who had no previous convictions, was sentenced to 30 days imprisonment for the theft from a motor vehicle of some mechanical parts of little value. Again, in *Smith* v. *Adair*[99] a motorist was sentenced to 30 days imprisonment for a first offence of driving a motor vehicle while unfit through drink. It is probably most unlikely that sentences of imprisonment would now be imposed in such cases in the first place and, if they were, it is quite probable that they would be reversed on appeal.[100] In the most recent comparable case, *O'Hara* v. *Farrell*,[1] a sentence of imprisonment was quashed as being harsh and oppressive for a second drink/driving offence, in contrast to the view taken nearly 30 years earlier in *Smith* v. *Adair*.

-100 It has been held to be oppressive where a sentence has been imposed on improper considerations,[2] or on the basis of mistaken or misleading information,[3] or on the basis of an approach which fails to distinguish the circumstances of one case from another.[4] It was also held to be oppressive, where a complaint contained two charges, to imprison the offender on one charge and defer sentence on the other.[5] It is possible that the sentences in all these cases might now be held to be, if not excessive, certainly inappropriate.

---

[98] *supra.*

[99] *supra.*

[100] Compare, for example, *O'Hara* v. *Farrell*, 1974 S.L.T. (Notes) 48; *Wheater* v. *Campbell*, 1974 S.L.T. (Notes) 63; *Balloch* v. *Pagan*, 1976 S.L.T. (Notes) 5.

[1] *supra.*

[2] *W. & A.W. Henderson* v. *Forster*, 1944 J.C. 91; *Blair* v. *Hawthorn*, 1945 J.C. 17.

[3] *Galloway* v. *Adair*, 1947 J.C. 7.

[4] *Sopwith and Others* v. *Cruickshank*, 1959 S.L.T. (Notes) 50.

[5] *Lennon* v. *Copeland*, 1972 S.L.T. (Notes) 68.

CHAPTER 10

THE SENTENCING PROCESS

THE JUDGE'S TASK

10–01   When a judge comes to determine the appropriate disposal in a particular case he must consider and weigh in the balance several, and on occasions, many factors. He must (although he may not consciously think of it in every case) decide what his sentencing objectives are, both in general and in relation to the particular case. He must consider the aggravating and mitigating factors bearing both on the particular crime or offence, and on the particular offender. He may have to consider background information relating to the offender. And he will have to consider carefully the advantages and disadvantages of all the different disposals that are available to him. This chapter is an attempt to describe all of these factors, and to say something about how they relate to each other.

10–02   Before attempting this task it must be said that the person who seeks to enunciate established sentencing principles in Scotland will derive little assistance from the reported, or unreported, decisions of the appeal court. This is partly because, in appeals against sentence, it is customary for the judges to say no more than is strictly necessary for disposal of the case. More importantly, it is because the Scottish appeal court has traditionally adopted a pragmatic and individualised approach to questions of sentence, and has always tended to decide cases on their own facts and circumstances rather than on the basis of any declared principles. By contrast, the Court of Appeal in England seems always to have been prepared to lay down principles to be applied in particular types of case with the result that it has proved possible there to describe a comprehensive approach to sentencing based almost entirely on reported appeal cases.[1] While the English approach no doubt has the merit of providing judges with reasonably clear guidelines when dealing with individual cases, it may equally be an approach that would inhibit some of the flexibility which is a feature of the Scottish system. Moreover, Scotland is a much smaller country, and its lawyers, and particularly its judiciary, are relatively few in numbers. As a consequence those involved are perhaps much more aware of each

---

[1] See, for example, Thomas, *Principles of Sentencing*; Cross, *The English Sentencing System*.

other's approach to the problems of sentencing than would be possible in a larger country, and there is not perhaps the same need for the appeal court to set itself the task of establishing general principles. What follows, however, is not an attempt to perform the task that the appeal court has eschewed for nearly 60 years. Rather, it is an attempt merely to describe the factors that are, or may be, present in the sentencing process, and to offer some comment on the way in which these factors may be regarded.

SENTENCING OBJECTIVES

General approach

–03   If one were to ask a random selection of people in the street what objectives they thought judges should have in mind when sentencing convicted offenders, one would probably receive nearly as many answers as there were people. If one were to ask the same question of a random selection of judges, one might receive the same number of answers, but the judges might add that the objectives may vary from case to case, and that sometimes there may be more than a single objective in mind in the one case. That is no doubt true, but the problem is that, faced with the same or similar cases, different judges might consider different objectives to be important, and so might arrive at different results. That of course results in disparity of sentences, for the existence of which there is now some convincing evidence.[2] Equally, there are probably occasions when a false parity is achieved, that is to say when different judges make the same sentencing decision, but with quite different objectives in mind. All of that is no doubt largely inevitable so long as sentencing decisions are made by human beings and not by computers, and one may perhaps be forgiven for supposing that computers might produce at least as many anomalous results as human judges. The fact of the matter is, of course, that many of the aims of sentencing overlap each other, or merge into each other. Moreover, although judges may be, and probably should be, aware of the fine distinctions that have been drawn by philosophers and penologists since at least the days of Kant and Bentham, they will in practice tend, when faced with a sentencing decision, to take a much broader approach to the objectives which they are hoping to achieve, and it is these broader

[2] For a survey of some of that evidence, see Hood and Sparks, *Key Issues in Criminology*, Chap. 5.

considerations which will now be dealt with. The following are probably the main objectives which from time to time, and in varying proportions, figure in sentencing decisions. No special significance is intended by the order in which they are presented.

Punishment

10–04   This has for long been an accepted aim of sentencing though it would now be generally recognised that there must be some restriction on the use of punishment in that it must be fair, and broadly in proportion to the gravity of the offence. Furthermore, there are now several international agreements or conventions prohibiting the use of cruel and unnatural punishments. While punishment may sometimes be seen as an objective on its own it will more often be regarded as going hand in hand with some other objective such as deterrence, or protection of the public. To some extent punishment, as a sentencing aim, is a form of retribution, and the two are sometimes seen as synonymous. Retribution, however, is frequently described by penologists in terms that encompass a wish to make an offender atone, or make amends, to society at large for the harm he has done. Most judges would probably see punishment as distinct from retribution in that sense, and might consider a fine or, in certain circumstances, imprisonment as pure punishment whereas a community service order would be seen more as a form of retribution.

Protection of public

10–05   This is an objective which seeks to secure that for as long as may be necessary the public will be protected from the criminal activity of a particular offender. It is an objective which may be sought in various ways. At one extreme it may involve some form of incapacitation and, since the ultimate incapacitation, the death sentence, is no longer available, will take the form of a very long prison sentence, or a long period of detention in a state hospital. At the other extreme it may be sought by some form of supervision, such as probation, in the expectation that the supervision will inhibit criminal activity in the short term while the probation experience will in the long term result in a beneficial change of behaviour. While this latter means of trying to achieve the aim of public protection is perfectly tenable in theory, research and common experience have shown that in practice it frequently fails to achieve its objective, and consequently, if certain protection of the public is what is wanted, that will only be achieved by a period of incarceration. It is suggested, however, that, unless the incarceration is going to be of at least a reasonably long duration, it cannot be justified on the ground of achieving public protection, whatever other justification it may have. From time to time procurators fiscal have been known to seek a remand in custody for a person awaiting summary trial on the ground that such a course is necessary for the protection of the public. It is submitted that that will rarely be a sound basis for objecting to bail since, even if the person is convicted, he can (allowing for remission, and assuming that he is at least a second offender being tried in the sheriff court) be put out of commission for no more than four months, a period that would normally have little significance in terms of public protection.

Deterrence

-06   This is a common aim of sentencing, and the objective may be to secure individual deterrence, or general deterrence, or both. That is, the purpose may be to deter only the particular individual from further acts of crime, or it may be, more widely to deter others from indulging in the same or similar kinds of criminal activity. It is suggested that, while the aim of individualised deterrence may often be a perfectly valid one since it can be based on extensive and detailed information about the particular offender, the aim of general deterrence is of much more dubious validity. There is unquestionably considerable popular faith in the value and effectiveness of general deterrence as a sentencing objective, but there is little or no evidence to support the view that a particular kind of sentencing policy, or more particularly a well-publicised exemplary sentence, have any significant effect on the kind of criminal behaviour in issue. Indeed, such evidence as there is suggests that likelihood of detection and apprehension are probably much more effective deterrents than the sentence which an offender may thereafter receive.[3] All of this is not to say, however, that a declared intention of seeking general deterrence, expressed at the time when a sentence is imposed, may not have some merit albeit for different reasons (see "Denunciation" below).

---

[3] See, for example, article by Baxter and Nuttal in *New Society*, 2 February 1975.

Denunciation

10–07   When, for example, a murderer is given a life sentence, or a terrorist is given a long, determinate, sentence of imprisonment, it may be as much a part of the judge's intention not only to achieve the protection of the public, and to punish the offender, but also, by the nature of the sentence, to express society's abhorrence of that particular kind of crime. Although most marked in the case of more serious crimes the objective is equally valid in the case of some less serious ones. Strictly, in such cases, the sentence speaks for itself in terms of denunciation, but it is not uncommon for judges, when passing the sentence, to use words which express the public condemnation that is implicit in the sentence. That may be coupled with an expressed desire to achieve the aim of general deterrence and, although the sentence may not achieve that aim, the judge is certainly reinforcing thereby the general tone of denunciation. Although one can readily understand the desire on the part of a judge to show his condemnation of a particularly repellent crime, it may be asked whether that is a proper objective of sentencing. Or, to put the question another way, to whom is the denunciation being addressed? If it is to the offender, it may well be argued that, if his sentence is a substantial one, he is more likely to be aware of the obvious realisation of the aims of punishment or public protection. If it is to the public at large, it may be argued that the denunciation, if it has any value in itself, should be equally effective even if no punishment were to be inflicted on the offender. The answer to these questions is to be found in the duty which, it is submitted, judges have to promote respect for the law, and to maintain public confidence in the way that the law is administered. Just as a law cannot be effective unless it has the assent of a majority of the public, so also a legal system, including its judges and their sentences, must have the confidence of a majority of the public if it is to survive. That does not mean, of course, that judges, in passing sentences, must always pander to public whims or prejudices; nor does it mean that judges must always be looking over their shoulders to make sure that their decisions do not conflict with public opinion. What it does mean, however, is that in appropriate cases judges may, and indeed should, do and say things which reflect and reinforce public concern and condemnation. This may involve, when such a course is otherwise appropriate, the imposition of a severe sentence, but it need not: an expression of condemnation may, in the context that has been described, be equally effective even when a much more lenient sentence is being imposed.

Rehabilitation

08 As an objective of sentencing, rehabilitation has taken some hard knocks in recent years. While reform may be achieved as a reaction to some sentences which are imposed with another objective in mind, such as punishment, the majority of research evidence indicates that those sentences which are intended to secure rehabilitation by some form of treatment are not very successful in doing so. Thus "treatment" by training in a penal establishment is no longer accorded the confidence which it formerly received; and it is perhaps symptomatic of that decline in confidence that the borstal sentence, which had its origins in aspirations about treatment and training, has been abolished in Scotland by the Criminal Justice (Scotland) Act 1980. So too the recidivism rate among those who have been subject to probation orders is high. Consequently, rehabilitation must be regarded as a very uncertain aim of sentencing, and not too much hope should be placed on sentences which are intended to realise that aim. On the other hand, there are those who do respond satisfactorily to, for example, a probation order and it would clearly be unwise to abandon their use simply because they cannot guarantee a high rate of success, particularly since their success rate is at least no worse than that of any other form of sentence.

Restitution

09 This will, perhaps, seldom be an objective on its own but may be linked to some other objective such as punishment; or it may, in cases where sentence is deferred initially so that restitution can be made, be a preliminary objective the realisation or otherwise of which will determine the objectives that are necessary when sentence itself is ultimately passed.

Economy of resources

10 This will always be a subsidiary objective, and in some cases may have to be ignored entirely. However, in cases where there is a reasonable alternative open to the judge, for example between imprisonment and a fine, it is probably reasonable to consider the best use of scarce public resources when deciding which of the two sentences to impose.

Reduction of crime

10–11   This objective — sometimes rather inelegantly called reductiv-
ism — has been left to last because it encompasses most, though not
all, of the objectives that have hitherto been considered. It will be
clear that, although the possible objectives of sentencing can be
named and considered separately, they will rarely stand alone in a
judge's mind when he is deciding on an appropriate sentence. More
often than not he will be seeking simultaneously to give some weight
to several objectives, and what they will have in common is that they
all, to a greater or lesser extent, are intended to reduce crime.
Probably few judges would argue with Professor Walker when he
says: "The reduction of prohibited conduct must be the main aim of
any penal system."[4]

FACTORS WHICH MAY INFLUENCE SENTENCE

The approach to sentencing

10–12   Assuming that a judge has a general awareness of the
objectives that a sentencing policy may be designed to achieve, the
first question that he will have to ask himself in a particular case is:
what type of sentence is appropriate? At the lower end of the
summary scale that question may involve making a choice between
a fine and some other form of non-custodial sentence, whereas, in
more serious cases, the choice may lie between imprisonment or a
non-custodial disposal. In England that distinction is often
expressed as being between a tariff disposal and an individualised
disposal.[5] In Scotland, on the other hand, courts, and particularly
the High Court, have frequently denied the existence of a tariff. It
has, however, been said that in Scotland "the tariff, like that of a
Highland taxi, is invisible, arbitrary and incommunicable, but none
the less operative."[6] While one might question the unqualified use
of the word "arbitrary", the remainder of that statement is probably
true to the extent that all judges — and many criminals — have a
fairly clear idea, based on experience and practice, of the range
within which a custodial sentence for a particular crime will
normally fall. Even more noticeably, the level of fines imposed in
summary courts for what are often referred to as regulatory
offences, such as speeding, will usually display a fairly clear tariff

---

[4] *Sentencing in a Rational Society*, p. 38.
[5] Thomas, *Principles of Sentencing*, p. 8.
[6] Walker, *Crime and Punishment in Britain*, p. 129.

structure. In the end of the day, however, whatever description one applies to the main options that are available to a judge, the manner in which these options are exercised will be influenced to some extent by various factors which the judge will have to take into account. Sometimes, in books of this character, an attempt is made to group these factors under headings such as "aggravating" or "mitigating". This is often less than a wholly satisfactory way of dealing with the subject since many of these factors may assume either of these descriptions depending on the facts of a particular case. What follows, therefore, is an attempt to describe the considerations that may influence a sentencing decision, and to show, where appropriate, how these may tend to be aggravating or mitigating in particular circumstances. It should be added that there is an inevitable amount of overlap between some of the matters that are to be described.

Character of crime or offence

9–13   Some crimes and offences will be more or less grave because of special circumstances peculiar to their commission, or to the victim, or to the offender. These will be dealt with shortly. In general, however, crimes and offences can be classified as more or less grave, or more or less trivial by reason of their own type or character, and this classification may have some bearing on the appropriate kind and level of sentence. In more extreme cases this relativity is easy to see, and probably not open to any dispute. Thus, no doubt, all would agree that an armed robbery is very much more grave than petty shoplifting. The distinction, however, may not be so easy when one moves away from such obvious extremes. Thus, is the theft of some foodstuffs from a supermarket more or less grave than a breach of the peace? The easy answer to that question is that much may depend on the circumstances of the particular breach of the peace. That of course is true, but even once these circumstances are determined the question may still not be an easy one to answer; and for a judge in, say, a busy sheriff court, who may have to determine sentence in several score such cases in a day, the matter of comparability and proportionality of sentences is one of considerable concern. Of course, many other factors will also have a bearing on the decisions, and an apparent disparity, or lack of proportionality, between sentences for different offences may well be explained by, for example, the fact that one offender had a long record whereas the other had an otherwise impeccable character. Even allowing for such distinctions, however, the fact remains that there will be a need for some sort of assessment of the relative gravity of crimes and offences, if only as a base on which to build or from which to subtract the other relevant factors. How one is to arrive at this assessment is not a matter of law, and the answer to the problem will not be found in decided cases. It can, in the end, be no more than a subjective decision based on personal experience and judgment.

Harm done, or harm intended

10–14   Normally, an offence will be regarded as more grave, and therefore more aggravated, the greater the amount of harm done. This approach is reflected in statute where, for example, section 1 of the Road Traffic Act 1972 (causing death by reckless driving) carries a maximum sentence of five years imprisonment, whereas section 2 (reckless driving) carries a maximum of only two years imprisonment. The same approach is also to be found in the common law, and in the practice of prosecutors, where, for example, a distinction is drawn between simple assault and an aggravated assault such as one to severe injury, a distinction which will frequently be reflected by the former type of assault being prosecuted summarily whereas the latter is prosecuted on indictment. This approach can, of course, be justified to a large extent on the retributive principle of sentencing — the greater the harm done, the greater the amount of retribution that must be exacted. Against that, however, it may be asked why an offender should be punished more severely simply because his unlawful act has had serious consequences (which may have been either fortuitous or even unintentional in the strict sense), while another offender who may have intended such harm but in fact failed to achieve it may be punished less severely. Some examples will serve to illustrate this problem.

10–15   Suppose that two offenders each push a glass into the face of a victim. In each case their intention, though perhaps not precisely rationalised, is precisely the same. In one case the victim happily escapes with a few minor scars, whereas in the other case the victim loses the sight of an eye. The retributive approach would no doubt suggest that the offender in the second case should receive a more severe sentence than the other, but is that not to attach undue weight to the, in a sense, fortuitous consequences of the act? Again, suppose that two housebreakers go off about their unlawful business. One breaks into a house at random and is fortunate enough to find — and remove — a large amount of valuable property. The second breaks into a house where he has reason to believe that there is a large amount of valuable property but in fact he is mistaken and leaves with only a few items of little worth. Should any distinction be made in the approach to sentencing these two men? The retributivist would say yes, but to many people it may seem at least as acceptable to have regard to the actual character of the offence (as distinct from its consequences), and to the intention of the offender. This is in effect to distinguish between one aspect of the gravity of the offence and the culpability of the offender. This is a perfectly proper distinction to make, and indeed, in the ultimate example of causing physical harm, namely homicide, it is a distinction which can be taken into account before the stage of sentencing is reached, by reducing a charge of murder to one of culpable homicide. Thus, in all cases save murder, where the sentence is fixed by law, it is possible and appropriate for a court to consider both the amount of harm done, and the actual culpability of the offender, when determining sentence. What effect either of these considerations will have on the actual sentence will, however, be a matter of judgment depending on all the circumstances of a particular case.

Culpability

)-16   Apart from the foregoing, other considerations affecting culpability may arise so as to have some influence on sentence. The age and sex of an offender, or the age and sex of a victim, may be of some significance in determining an offender's culpability. Thus, a middle-aged female shoplifter may be less culpable than a young, adult male who commits a similar crime (though it must be added that the female menopausal delinquent is perhaps less common than pleas in mitigation might tend to suggest). Again, an assault and robbery committed against someone who is elderly and infirm may properly be taken as inferring a greater degree of culpability than if the victim had been young and active. In rather the same way relationship, or lack of it, between an offender and his victim may be an element bearing on culpability. So, an unprovoked attack on a total stranger may be seen as more blameworthy than an attack committed on an acquaintance or relative, at least if, in the latter case, there is evidence to show a previous history of mutual antagonism and conflict. Culpability is also a matter which may be of importance when a court is dealing with a multiplicity of offenders who have all been convicted of the same charge. Very often the amount of blame attaching to each may vary quite substantially, and this may properly be taken into account in determining the appropriate sentence for each offender. A final aspect of culpability which falls to be noted concerns any special status that the offender may have, and in respect of which the offence has been committed. Examples of this are thefts of mail by Post Office employees, or frauds and embezzlements committed by professional men such as accountants or solicitors. In such cases a more severe sentence than would otherwise be appropriate will normally be imposed, and the question must be asked why this should be the case. It cannot be with the aim of individual deterrence since in most of these cases the offender will have been ruined by the conviction, and it will be most unlikely that he will ever again be in a position to commit such a crime. Sometimes, when imposing such a sentence, judges will express it as being with the aim of general deterrence. But, set against the, fortunately, good record that there is in this country of integrity on the part of public officials and professional men and women, it is doubtful whether a more severe sentence than would normally be appropriate is necessary in the interests of general deterrence. Instead, it is submitted, the justification for such a sentence is to be found in the greater culpability which attaches to one who abuses a position of special trust, or who departs from the high standards expected of those in public or professional service.

Prevalence

10–17   The fact that a particular type of crime or offence is especially prevalent, either generally or in a particular area, may be a reason, in the interests of general deterrence, for imposing a more severe sentence than would otherwise be appropriate.[7] Since, however, the deterrent effectiveness of such an approach may be open to some doubt (see *supra*, para. 10–06), it is suggested that this factor should be approached with some caution. Moreover, a judge must take care that he has proper evidence concerning the prevalence of a

---

[7] See, for example, *Blair* v. *Hawthorn*, 1945 J.C. 17, *per* Lord Justice-General at 20.

particular crime before he takes any note of it in his approach to sentencing. In some cases he may be aware that a particular crime is occurring with undesirable frequency simply because of the number of times that it has to be dealt with in his own court. Or again, he may become aware of the increasing incidence of a particular crime from information contained in properly authenticated statistics. On the other hand, he must beware of forming a view that is based on information, such as newspaper reports and articles, which may be biased and unreliable, or of drawing conclusions, even from official statistics, which may not be justified by the figures in question.

General or local concern

0–18   Closely allied to the foregoing is the existence of general or local concern in relation to some particular type of law-breaking. So far as this is concerned it may be stated that, when considering sentence, the normal limitations on judicial knowledge do not apply, and judges are entitled to be aware of, and to take account of, public opinion and public concern where this is generally known to exist. Once again, however, care should be taken that any concern which is to be taken into account should be widespread and general, whether locally or nationally, and not merely a reflection of the views of a possibly small group of people who may be particularly vocal, or have good access to the media. Thus, for example, in recent times public concern about violence at sporting occasions, in particular at football matches, could properly be taken as general and widespread, it not only having been very widely reported in the press and elsewhere, but also having been, on several occasions, the subject of debate in Parliament.

Previous record

0–19   There is no doubt that an offender's previous record is an important factor in sentencing. Having said that, it is necessary to see exactly how the existence of previous convictions, or their absence, may, or should, affect a sentencing decision. It is often assumed that the existence of previous convictions is an aggravating factor, and that their absence is a mitigating factor; but, it is submitted that, put that way, this may be a somewhat misleading view. If, for example, one assumes that the gravity of a particular offence is such as to require a prison sentence within a certain range, one may reasonably say that an offender with a bad record should receive a sentence at the upper end of that range. But if, conversely, one is to say that an offender with no previous convictions thereby has a mitigating factor in his favour and, because of that, should receive a sentence at the lower end of the range, one is by implication saying that somewhere in the middle of the range is a sort of norm to which one may add, or from which one may subtract, depending on the offender's record. In saying that, however, one is inevitably also saying that the norm for any particular offence is the sentence appropriate to an offender with some, but not too many, previous convictions. That is plainly not an acceptable conclusion, but it arises only if one regards a good or bad record as representing opposite ends of the swing of a pendulum. It is submitted that it is more sensible to regard record as a progressive factor, in the way that it is treated in many statutory provisions whereby a certain maximum sentence is prescribed for a first offence, whereas a higher maximum is permitted for a second or subsequent offence. Thus, when dealing with a first offender, a judge may properly limit his attention to the range of disposals at the lower end of the scale of sentencing severity, and progressively move up that scale when dealing with offenders with a previous criminal record. Looked at this way, previous good character is not so much a mitigating factor, but rather an essentially neutral one, whereas previous bad record is certainly an aggravating factor.

10–20   What is the justification for treating the existence of previous convictions as an aggravating factor? An offender must not, in effect, be sentenced twice for past offences but, provided that is kept clearly in mind, there are, it is submitted, two main reasons why previous convictions may properly be regarded as an aggravating factor. In the first place, if one is seeking to achieve the aim of individual deterrence, they may demonstrate that previous attempts have been made to realise that objective, that they have obviously failed, and that a different, though not necessarily a more severe, sentence may now be appropriate. In the second place, if one is seeking to apply the retributivist theory, they may demonstrate simply that the offender is a repeated breaker of the law, and that a more severe punishment is now appropriate. It is important to keep the above distinction clearly in mind because, if one's principal aim is to try to achieve individual deterrence, it would be perfectly reasonable, even where an offender had on previous occasions been fined, or even imprisoned, to consider a disposal such as probation on the occasion of a subsequent offence. On the other hand, if the case were considered to be one that called for retributive measures, then in such circumstances a judge would be obliged to think only in terms of a larger fine or a longer period of imprisonment.

0–21   Formerly it was competent for a prosecutor to libel only those previous convictions which were cognate with the current offence, but now all previous offences may be libelled, though it is common for a prosecutor to exercise a measure of discretion in this and to exclude from a schedule of previous convictions those which are either very old or those which are of a trivial character. The disappearance of the cognate rule regarding previous convictions is consistent with modern thinking which recognises the plural nature of deviancy; and it would be unthinkable now that an offender on, say, an assault charge should be presented as being a first offender if in fact he has several previous convictions for housebreaking. On the other hand, a previous conviction for the same, or a similar offence, will generally be regarded as more serious, or more aggravating, than previous convictions for dissimilar offences.

0–22   Apart from their possible aggravating effect, previous convictions may also indicate a particular line of inquiry that ought to be investigated before sentence is decided upon. Thus, repetitive theft from shops, particularly by the middle-aged or elderly, may suggest the desirability of obtaining a social inquiry report. So, too, the existence of a previous conviction which resulted in some sort of psychiatric disposal may indicate that a psychiatric report should be obtained. Again, it has been suggested by the Scottish Council on Crime[8] that courts should automatically call for social inquiry reports on offenders convicted of a second or subsequent crime of violence. Apart from suggesting a particular form of inquiry, an offender's previous record may also indicate the likely success or failure of particular forms of disposal. Thus, a court may be slow to consider a probation order as being an appropriate disposal where the offender has previously been placed on probation but was subsequently sentenced for a breach of that order.

Provocation

0–23   It is not within the scope of this work to consider what may or may not amount to provocation; the purpose of this section is merely to consider the effect, if any, which the existence of provocation may have upon the sentence to be passed on the person

---

[8] *Crime and the Prevention of Crime*, 1975, para. 112.

thus provoked. The first point to be noted concerns the circumstances in which the judge will come to have the issue of provocation properly before him at the stage of passing sentence. Where there has been a summary trial, and the question of provocation has been put in issue in the course of the trial, the presiding judge will have been able to form his own view as to whether or not provocation has been established and, if so, how great was that provocation. In passing sentence thereafter he may, it is submitted, proceed upon his own assessment of the degree of provocation, and give that such weight in his sentence as he thinks proper. Where the trial has been before a jury, however, the position may be somewhat different. In returning a verdict of guilty it is competent for a jury to say something like "guilty under provocation", and they may indeed be invited to return such a verdict by defence counsel or solicitor. In such a case, it is submitted, the judge would be bound to take that into account when determining sentence, to such extent as he thought proper, notwithstanding that he himself may not agree with the rider attached to the verdict. Conversely, if a jury were invited to add such a rider and did not do so, the judge would be precluded from taking provocation into account, even if he himself was of the view that the act charged had been committed under provocation.

10–24　　Apart from the foregoing fairly clear-cut situations, cases may arise where the defence counsel or solicitor will, for perfectly proper tactical reasons, seek an outright acquittal on the basis of, for example, a special defence of self defence, and will refrain from mentioning to a judge or, particularly, a jury the possibility of a verdict of guilty under provocation. If, in such a case, the jury returns a simple verdict of guilty, and the issue of provocation is thereafter raised in the plea in mitigation, may the judge then take cognisance of it? It is submitted that it would be proper for him to do so, notwithstanding that it was not put in issue during the trial, provided that he is satisfied that the plea is supported by evidence that was led at the trial, and provided that such evidence is of a kind that the jury may be taken not to have rejected in arriving at their verdict.

10–25　　Assuming that an issue of provocation is properly before the court at the stage of passing sentence, what effect should it have upon that sentence? That, of course, will depend entirely on the nature and extent of the provocation, and on the nature of the crime or offence of which the offender has been convicted. It may also depend on other factors such as the offender's previous record. If the crime is a very serious one, or if the provocation is slight, it may have no effect on sentence at all. So too, if the offender has previous convictions for the same type of offence, the mitigating effect of provocation may be substantially diminished. Such cases apart, however, the fact that a crime or offence was committed under provocation will generally be seen as a mitigating factor which will permit the court to take a more lenient course than would otherwise have been appropriate. This may result in a shorter sentence of imprisonment, or a smaller fine, or may permit a sentence of a different type altogether, such as a non-custodial rather than a custodial one.

–26　　If effect is given to the existence of provocation in any of the ways described, the judge may, in passing sentence, indicate to the offender that this has been done by stating expressly the sentence which he would otherwise have imposed. There is not, it is thought, any recognised practice in this and some judges will prefer merely to say, in general terms, that account has been taken of the plea of provocation in arriving at the sentence which is being passed. Whichever course is followed, it is submitted that it is desirable that a judge should, by some means, indicate whether or not some weight is being attached to the plea since, if he does not do so, difficulties may arise in the event of an appeal.

Effect of drink or drugs

–27　　It is frequently submitted, in purported mitigation of sentence, that, at the time of commission of the offence, the offender was under the influence of drugs or, more commonly, alcohol. The question in such cases is whether, in determining sentence, any account should be taken of that. There is no simple answer to that question since much will depend on the whole facts and surrounding circumstances of each case. However, some general observations may be ventured.

–28　　At one extreme there are sometimes cases where the evidence and other information available to the judge may satisfy him that the offender is chronically addicted to alcohol or drugs, and that his law-breaking, often of a repetitive though relatively minor character, is closely related to, if not directly caused by, that addiction. Not infrequently in such cases the judge may feel that a prison sentence would be appropriate, not so much because of the nature or gravity of the immediate offence but simply because it is the latest in a long line of similar offences. He may, however, be invited to explore, by obtaining a psychiatric report, the possibility of adopting a course which would require, or at least permit, the offender to obtain some treatment for his addiction. While it cannot be categorically stated either that this is, or is not, an appropriate course to take in such cases, it may be said that a court will normally consider such an invitation with some care. This is because, although there are now some indications to the contrary, the generally accepted medical view seems to be that any treatment for drug or alcohol addiction is unlikely to be successful unless the addict himself is fully committed to the treatment: and in the sort of case that has been postulated it may well be that the offender is merely seeking to avoid a prison sentence, but without having the necessary, if indeed any, commitment to seeking treatment. If that were the case there would be little point in the court obtaining a psychiatric report since not only might it not recommend any sort of treatment but also, even if it did, there might be little chance of any course of treatment being completed successfully, or even completed at all. The problem for the court, of course, is to distinguish between the offender who is merely clutching at straws in order to avoid being sent to prison, and the one who may have, albeit not very clearly formulated at that stage, a genuine desire to try to do something about his addiction. As with so many other matters this must in the end be a matter of judgment: it may be said, however, that a court will generally be prepared to give the benefit of the doubt to an offender where there is some indication that he has in the past made some voluntary attempt to seek help for his problems.

10–29   At the other extreme is the sort of case where the offence itself is of a grave or very grave character. Although it is by no means unknown for serious crimes to be committed by those who are alcoholics or drug addicts, it is more likely that any intoxication that may be mentioned as having contributed to the commission of such crimes will be represented as having been of a more isolated and occasional character. In such cases it is probable that, whatever the alcohol or drugs background of the offender, the court will take the view that the sentence must be determined by reference to considerations such as the gravity of the offence, the amount of harm done, or the protection of the public, and will take no account, at least by way of mitigation, of the fact that the commission of the crime may have been influenced by an over-consumption of drink or drugs.

-30   Between the two extremes that have been mentioned there will be a range of cases of varying gravity where over-indulgence in drugs or, especially, alcohol may be put forward as an explanation, if not an excuse. Different approaches may be possible here, depending on the circumstances. On the one hand, the information available to the court may show that the offender frequently commits offences when drunk: in such a case the court may well consider that the offender's drunkenness is, so far from being a mitigating factor, if anything an aggravating one, on the basis that, in the light of previous experience, he should have known better than to drink to excess yet again. On the other hand, there may be cases where a person of previously good character commits an uncharacteristic offence while under the influence of drink. If, in such a case, the court can be satisfied that the offence was brought about in large measure because the alcohol had lessened or removed the offender's normal inhibitions, it may be appropriate to impose a more lenient sentence than might otherwise be called for.

Effect of sentence on offender, his family, or associates

-31   From time to time a court may be invited not to impose a particular sentence, especially one of imprisonment, because of the effect that this would have on the offender himself, or on his family, or on his associates. In relation to the offender himself this submission may be put forward, for example, on the ground that his health is such that he could not withstand the rigours of a prison sentence, or that the crime of which he has been convicted is of such a character (*e.g.* sexual molestation of children) that he is likely to receive rough treatment at the hands of fellow prisoners. In relation to the offender's family the submission may be that the offender is the sole support of an elderly relative, or that his wife is unwell and, if he were to be incarcerated, his children might have to be taken into care. In relation to the offender's associates the submission may be that the offender's continuing presence is crucial to some business enterprise and, if he were to be sent to prison, that enterprise might fail with consequent unemployment for innocent third parties.

-32   These are all factors to which the court will give such weight as it thinks proper, having regard to all the other factors which must be taken into account in any particular case. Two points may, however, be made. The first is that, if submissions of the sort exemplified above are made in relation to the likely effect of imprisonment on the offender himself, it is as well to bear in mind, firstly, that all penal establishments have their own medical and, to varying degrees, hospital facilities, and secondly, that provision exists in the Prison Rules to isolate any prisoner who may be at risk if in association with others.[9] The second, and more general, point is that submissions of this sort should be scrutinised with care to ensure that they are adequately supported by facts and are not merely the result of an offender's personal, and unverified, instructions to his counsel or solicitor.

Effect of plea of guilty

10–33   In England there appears to be a well established practice, approved of by the Court of Appeal, of allowing, where there is a plea of guilty, a discount from what would otherwise be an appropriate sentence.[10] This discount, which may apparently be as much as one quarter or one third of the normal sentence,[11] appears to be granted on the basis that the offender, by pleading guilty, has "demonstrated, as plainly as anything could, his remorse and regret for what he had done".[12] With all respect to Lord Justice Bridge, one may be forgiven for supposing that there may be many other reasons why an accused person will plead guilty, and some of them will have nothing whatever to do with regret or remorse. Be that as it may, there is certainly no comparable, approved, practice in Scotland; and, of course, even if there were, it would be much more difficult to operate in the absence of the clearly defined sentencing tariff which exists in England and Wales.

10–34   Having said all that, there may, it is submitted, be occasions when it would be appropriate in Scotland to dispose of a case in a more lenient fashion upon a plea of guilty. The justification for doing so, however, will not be the plea of guilty itself, but other mitigating factors associated with that plea. Thus, if an offender has, from the moment of his apprehension, co-operated fully with the police so that the crime has been cleared up quickly and, for example, stolen property has been recovered, that may properly be taken into account as a mitigating factor in his favour. So too, in the case of certain sexual offences, if an accused person pleads guilty

---

[9] Prison (Scotland) Rules 1952, Rule 36; and see *infra*, para. 11–09.
[10] See, for example, *R.* v. *Hickman*, 20 November 1975 unreported.
[11] See Baldwin and McConville, *Negotiated Justice: pressures to plead guilty*.
[12] *R.* v. *Hickman*, *supra, per* Bridge LJ.

and thereby saves young children or the female victim of a sexual assault from the disagreeable experience of giving evidence, that may be taken as a mitigating factor in his favour. Again, if, upon considerations distinct from the actual plea of guilty itself, a court can be satisfied that an offender is truly remorseful, then some credit should probably be given for that. It is less clear whether any mitigating effect should be allowed when the consequences of a plea of guilty are purely practical as where, in a case of fraud or embezzlement, the consequence of the plea is to remove the necessity for a lengthy and expensive trial. Probably that alone should not be seen as a mitigating factor but, where it is linked to some other factor such as complete co-operation with the police, then that other factor may be thereby made more compelling.

-35   From the foregoing it should be seen that, if any mitigation is to be found in cases where a plea of guilty is tendered, it must be found in factors which are mitigating in themselves, and not in the mere fact of the plea of guilty. The reason for this may be simply stated as being that, in a legal system which presumes innocence and which permits every accused person to go to trial if he wishes, there can be nothing of a mitigating nature in the fact that many people nonetheless plead guilty: and, of course, it would be quite unacceptable that a person who was found guilty after trial should be punished more severely simply because he had not pled guilty. On the other hand, if a person has gone to trial on the basis of a defence which is obviously specious or frivolous, the court, while not being entitled for that reason to impose a more severe sentence than would otherwise be merited, could properly set the nature of that defence against any mitigating factors that there might be in the offender's favour. A more important reason, however, for not accepting a plea of guilty as being a mitigating circumstance in itself is that, if there were a regular practice to that effect, it might easily be seen as the court offering an inducement to accused persons to plead guilty rather than go to trial. It is one thing for a judge to take account — and to be known to be likely to take account — of certain factors which are properly mitigating in themselves. Whether such factors are present or not will depend on the whole circumstances of the case and, although they may influence the accused's plea, they will not be dependent on it. It is quite another thing for a judge to take account — or to be known to be likely to take account — of a plea of guilty simply for its own sake. Such an approach not only smacks of plea bargaining, which is wholly alien to the Scottish system, but is also one which could operate most harshly against those who exercise their entitlement to go to trial.

Background information about the offender

10–36　During the last 30 years or so it has become increasingly clear that the causes of criminal behaviour, in so far as they can be determined at all, are complex, diverse and plural. With that realisation has come a growing awareness that, in determining sentences, attention must be paid in many cases to the whole background of the offender — social, economic, educational, medical, psychiatric, etc. The reason for this, it may be said, is twofold. In the first place, information on these matters may enable a judge, even where he is not considering a custodial sentence, to select one form of non-custodial sentence as being more likely than another to curb or inhibit future criminal behaviour by the offender concerned. In the second place, where a custodial sentence is being contemplated, such information may persuade the judge that a non-custodial measure could be used instead. So far as cases falling into the latter category are concerned there has been a growing statutory insistence in recent years that background information *must* be obtained before a custodial sentence can be imposed.

10–37　Information about an offender will be obtained in reports from various professional people, notably doctors, psychiatrists, and social workers. Less frequently reports may be obtained from others such as teachers, educational psychologists, ministers of religion, and so on. Formerly, when the borstal sentence was available to courts, reports were provided by the governor of the prison or remand establishment in which the offender was remanded prior to sentence. The disappearance of the borstal sentence has removed the necessity for such a report but, where a person is for any reason remanded in custody, it is still open to a judge to ask the governor of the establishment concerned to provide a report on the offender's behaviour in custody, and on his likely response to a custodial sentence. Many of these reports will contain expressions of opinion and, although the judge is not bound to accept these opinions,[13] he must consider them carefully. Certain medical disposals, however, may not be made unless the doctors or psychiatrists concerned express certain opinions.[14]

---

[13] See *Scott and Another* v. *MacDonald*, 1961 S.L.T. 257.
[14] See *supra*, Chap. 4.

8   Social inquiry reports are often, it must be said, called for and used simply as repositories of factual information about the offender; and sometimes, it must equally be said, they amount to little more than that. A good social inquiry report should, however, also contain the considered views of the social worker on a range of matters including the offender's present attitude to his offence, and his likely response to various possible disposals. Social inquiry reports, and their content and purpose, have been considered over the years not only by writers in learned journals, but also by many committees, notably perhaps the Departmental Committee on the Probation Service (the Morison Committee),[15] the Inter-departmental Committee on the Business of the Criminal Courts (the Streatfeild Committee),[16] and the Advisory Council on the Penal System.[17] Formerly, when the term "probation report" was used, the purpose of the report was primarily to express a view as to the offender's suitability for probation. Gradually, however, as the social inquiry report has replaced the probation report, its purpose has become wider and, although there is still no unanimity of view either among social workers or judges, most would now probably agree that a report may properly express opinions not only about an offender's likely response to various types of sentence, but also as to the particular form of sentence which it is thought may be most appropriate. While, as already noted, a judge is not bound to accept any such opinion, in practice a social worker's recommendation is frequently acted upon.

THE SENTENCES THEMSELVES

9   Apart from general sentencing objectives, and the various factors which have been mentioned in the preceding paragraphs, a court must, when determining sentence, also take into account the special characteristics and advantages and disadvantages of the different types of sentence themselves. Sometimes a consideration of different types of sentence will raise issues of a somewhat difficult moral nature. For example, if a judge considers it appropriate in a particular case to seek to achieve the objectives of punishment and/or denunciation, he may consider that this can be done either by the imposition of a moderate term of imprisonment, or by the

---

[15] Report, 1962, HMSO.
[16] Report, 1961, HMSO.
[17] Report, *Young Adult Offenders*, 1974, HMSO.

imposition of a large fine. But a large fine is appropriate only where the offender has the means to pay it and, if he does not have such means, the term of imprisonment may be the only course open to the court, unless it changes its sentencing objectives. If it does not do that, the question must be asked whether it is justifiable in such a case that a rich man should receive a fine whereas a poor man will go to prison. Although this section is primarily concerned with the practical characteristics of certain sentences, some of the moral dilemmas which occasionally face judges when passing sentence will not be overlooked. Not all types of sentence will be mentioned in what follows, but only those which most frequently present specific problems.

Deferred sentence[18]

10–40   Although, of course, not strictly a sentence, the use of the power to defer sentence until a later date merits some consideration. In so far as a generalisation can be made, it may be said that this power is normally used for one or more of three reasons. The first is where the court wishes to allow some time to elapse so that a specific fact relevant to sentence may be established. This might happen, for example, where an offender stated to the court that he expected shortly to ascertain some fact having a bearing on his future, such as the obtaining of a particular job, acceptance into a course of further education, or acceptance into the armed services. It might also arise where, for example, an offender with a history of alcoholism or drug addiction could satisfy the court that he had commenced, or was about to commence, a course of treatment for that addiction, and the court was anxious to discover the outcome of that treatment. Again, it may frequently arise where the court wishes to ascertain the outcome of, for example, a trial which the offender is shortly to undergo in respect of some other charge or charges. Since factors such as this might well influence the appropriate sentence in a particular case, a court will often defer sentence until they have been ascertained. The second common reason for deferring sentence is to allow an offender the opportunity of showing that he can for a period, which may be quite prolonged, keep out of further trouble. The third common reason is to give an offender the opportunity to do something specific such as making

---

[18] See, generally, article by A. D. Smith, "Deferred Sentences in Scotland", 1968 S.L.T. (News) 153.

restitution. The first of the foregoing reasons probably requires no further elaboration, but the other two merit greater consideration.

41   When sentence is deferred to allow an offender the opportunity of showing that he can keep out of further trouble the underlying, and often explicit, understanding will normally be that he will be dealt with less severely than would otherwise be appropriate if he does what is expected of him. Several questions often arise in this context. In what circumstances may such a course be considered appropriate? For how long should sentence be deferred? To what extent, if at all, should a judge indicate the probable outcome of the case in the event of the offender keeping out of trouble for the period involved? Although the precise answers to these questions will depend on the circumstances of each case, some general answers may be ventured.

42   The gravity of the particular offence and the past criminal record of the offender will usually have some bearing on the appropriateness of this form of disposal and, in general, the more grave the offence and the worse the previous record, the less likely it is that this course will commend itself to the court. However, where a court is faced with an offence, even quite a grave one, which seems totally out of character for an otherwise blameless offender, a deferred sentence may be appropriate as a means of establishing that the offence is truly an isolated lapse and not merely the first step in a criminal career. Similarly, where an offender has a long criminal record but pleads with vigour that he now at last intends to "go straight", the court may be disposed to give him a chance to prove his good intentions. Another related situation, where a deferred sentence may be considered appropriate, is where, subsequent to the offence but prior to conviction, an offender has been made the subject of a probation order in respect of a different offence. In such a case the court may wish to see the offender's response to the probation order before determining sentence, and may defer sentence for a period for that purpose. In such a case a court will often ask for a social inquiry report to be available at the end of the deferred period.

43   Two other circumstances fall to be noted where a deferred sentence may be thought to be appropriate. One is where such a disposal may benefit third parties by reason of its deterrent effect. An example of this would be the case of a man convicted of assaulting his wife: the threat of dire consequences might be effective to prevent a repetition during the period of deferment. The second circumstance is one which is sadly being forced upon some courts on occasions at the present time. It arises where a social inquiry report recommends a probation order (a recommendation which the court would wish to follow) but adds that the resources within the particular social work department will not allow such an order, if made, to be allocated to a social worker. Since part of the purpose of a probation order is to give an offender the chance to show that he can be of good behaviour, the court may in such a case consider that the best alternative is to defer sentence for the same purpose, either with a view to imposing some other form of sentence at the end of the period, or in order to review the possibility of a probation order at that stage.[19] Many other circumstances may suggest the desirability of deferring sentence for good behaviour, but the examples that have been given provide some indication of the character which such circumstances are likely to possess.

10–44   The length of the period during which sentence is to be deferred will depend on many factors, not least the precise purpose for which sentence is being deferred in a given case. In general, however, it may be said that there can be disadvantages in deferring sentence for a very long period. Firstly, the offender is more likely to forget the date of the diet for sentence, and so fail to turn up; and secondly, and more importantly, once an offence becomes very old and stale it will often seem to a court to be unreasonable to impose a severe sentence, even where an offender has committed a further offence in the interim. If, for any reason, a lengthy "good behaviour" period is thought to be desirable, it may be preferable to break it up into shorter periods by deferring sentence on more than one occasion. To some extent, however, the force of these comments is reduced by the power which is now available to accelerate a deferred diet where an offender has been convicted of a subsequent offence.[20]

10–45   When a court defers sentence for an offender to be of good behaviour an indication will normally be given that the offender will be dealt with less severely if he complies with the condition of the deferment. On occasions some judges have been known to make this indication quite specific by saying, for example, that, if the

---

[19] Something which is now competent in summary procedure, as well as in solemn procedure, by virtue of the amendments to the 1975 Act contained in s. 53 of the 1980 Act.
[20] 1975 Act, ss. 219 and 432, as amended by 1980 Act, s. 54.

offender is not convicted during the period of deferment, he will be
fined such-and-such an amount but, if he is so convicted, he will go
to prison for such-and-such a period. It is submitted that this is not a
desirable practice for two reasons. Firstly, it may give the impression that the court is striking some sort of bargain with the offender
which, it is thought, would be improper. Secondly, and perhaps
more importantly, such a practice makes no allowance either for the
type or frequency of conviction that may occur during the period of
deferment, or for any changes in the offender's personal circumstances that may have taken place during that same period, all of
which might have a considerable bearing on the type and severity of
sentence that might ultimately prove to be appropriate. It is certainly proper, and may be useful, for a judge to give a general indication
of the type of sentence that he may wish to consider in the event of
the offender acquiring subsequent convictions, especially convictions of a certain character, and to say that a more lenient view will
be taken if such convictions are avoided: but, it is submitted, it is
preferable that a judge should not go further than that.

46   Many of the comments that have just been made in relation to
"good behaviour" cases apply equally to cases where sentence is
deferred for a specific purpose, such as restitution, or repayment,
but these latter cases display certain special features which require
some separate comment.

47   Very often, in cases of embezzlement, fraud and theft, a court
will be asked to defer sentence to allow the offender to repay the
amount wrongfully obtained. The purpose of such a suggestion, of
course, is to seek to mitigate the offence to some extent and thereby
to secure a more lenient sentence: and there is no doubt that
repayment or restitution will often have that effect. However, it is
suggested that in such cases a court may wish to distinguish between
two situations. One is where the primary purpose of the repayment,
in the eyes of the court, is to secure restitution for the victim of the
crime, and the other is where the primary purpose, in the eyes of the
offender, is to demonstrate, or at least to appear to be demonstrat-
ing, remorse for what he has done. Sometimes both of these
features may be present in the same case and, so far as mitigation is
concerned, each may secure the same result. However, the weight
to be attached to each may have some bearing on whether or not the
court considers it appropriate to defer sentence in the first place.
Thus, if the court's primary desire is to secure the payment of

compensation to a victim, it may, in appropriate cases,[21] decide that the best course is simply to make a compensation order, with or without any additional penalty.

10–48   One factor which may influence a court's decision whether or not to defer sentence will be whether or not, prior to that stage, the offender has taken any steps to commence repayment. If the case is one which has gone to trial it will not, of course, be surprising — nor should it subsequently prejudice the accused — if no such steps have been taken. In cases where a plea of guilty is tendered, however, the position may be rather different. In many such cases it is clear that there has never been any intention to do other than plead guilty (indeed, this may even be founded on as a mitigating factor in its own right). Yet, it will often transpire in such cases that the day of sentence is the first occasion when the offender has shown any desire to make repayment. In such circumstances, it is submitted, few judges will have much confidence in the genuineness of the expressed desire, and will see it merely as an attempt to postpone the day of reckoning.

10–49   Closely allied to the foregoing are the means of the offender. While it may be one thing for an offender who is in regular and well paid employment to offer to repay even a large sum of money, it is quite another thing for a person who has, say, fraudulently obtained social security benefits of £1,000, to offer to repay that amount while he is still in receipt of no income other than state benefits. Quite apart from the fact that many judges may feel that it is no part of their function to act as debt collectors for government departments, or large corporations, there would seem to be little advantage in deferring sentence in such a case since the prospects of recovery (and the experience of many judges would tend to confirm this) are very remote.

10–50   This sort of case, however, can pose the kind of moral problem that was mentioned earlier. Is it consistent with justice that the rich or even reasonably rich man should be allowed to mitigate his guilt, and therefore presumably receive a lesser sentence, whereas the poor man may, simply because of his poverty, be denied that opportunity and receive a more severe, and unmitigated sentence? It is possible to answer this question by saying that any restitution which is made by the rich man ought properly to be seen as part of the penalty which he is required to pay, with the result that there

---

[21] See *infra*, paras. 10–75 to 10–78.

may not be any great disparity between the two cases at the end of the day; but the poor man may well retort that it is not much of a penalty to require restitution from a person who, by definition, can well afford it anyway. Moreover, the practical consequence in such cases may well be that the person who makes restitution will receive a non-custodial sentence whereas the person who cannot do so will be sent to prison. A better answer to the question is that in truth it is more hypothetical than real. In practice very few, if any, cases are so identical in all their circumstances (with the exception only of the wealth of the offender) as to pose the kind of dilemma that has been suggested, and often it is possible for a judge to dispose of cases in different ways upon criteria which have nothing to do with the offenders' means. Having said that, however, judges must be mindful to keep a fair and just balance between cases which are similar, even if not identical, and to take care that richer offenders are not permitted, by the use of the deferred sentence, to buy themselves out of the normal consequences of their misdeeds.

Fines

-51   The fine is the most commonly used form of sentence, and is probably used for a much wider range of offences than any other form of disposal. At present it is used for about 80 per cent of all the cases coming before the courts. Thus, at one extreme, a fine may be imposed for a minor regulatory offence related to the parking of a motor vehicle, and, at the other extreme, it may be imposed for a quite serious offence of violence or dishonesty. Two related questions arise regarding the use of fines. The first, and more general, question is: how is the appropriate level of a fine to be determined? The second is: what sort of balance should exist between fines imposed for one kind of offence, and fines imposed for another kind?

-52   In determining the amount of a fine the only statutory provision of consequence is that which requires the court to "take into consideration, amongst other things, the means of the offender so far as known to the court."[22] There is no power to oblige an offender to disclose his means to a court, and consequently there will be some cases where a fine will be imposed without any knowledge as to the offender's ability to pay. Even in cases where some information about an offender's means is given to the court, this may be scanty

---

[22] 1975 Act, s. 395 (1).

and far from comprehensive. It cannot be stressed overmuch, however, that, where information of this kind is provided to a court by an advocate or solicitor, he must take the greatest care to ensure that he does not, by the omission of relevant information, convey a false or misleading impression. A judge will be less than enthusiastic, for example, if he imposes a lower fine than might otherwise have seemed appropriate on the basis of a submission that the offender is earning only a small wage, and then finds the offender offering to pay the fine at the bar out of a wad of notes which he has taken from his pocket!

10–53   The statutory provision gives no indication as to how the court should take an offender's means into consideration. The view has, however, been expressed[23] that, since the fine constitutes a punishment consisting of a deprivation of resources, it must vary in amount so as to penalise the rich and the poor equally: moreover, this variation should be applied in all cases where fines are imposed, including regulatory offences, and should take the form not merely of reducing a fine for those of low means, but also of increasing it for those who are wealthy. The first part of that proposition would no doubt be generally regarded as quite unexceptionable, but the remainder seems not to be so well received.

10–54   In practice a distinction appears to exist in the court's approach to fining by reference to an offender's means between those cases which involve some degree of moral turpitude and those which concern offences of a regulatory character. Thus different levels of fine, to take account of different offenders' means, may be imposed for offences of dishonesty or violence, whereas offences like speeding will be dealt with by what is essentially a tariff structure of fines, regardless of the means of the offender. While the view expressed by the Scottish Council on Crime in relation to dealing with regulatory offences has much to commend it, there are two obstacles in the way of varying the amounts of fines for such offenders according to their means. The first is that the gradually increasing use of fixed penalties would tend to suggest an increasing acceptance, even on the part of the legislature, of a fairly rigid tariff system for minor offences, even where these are not at present subject to the fixed penalty procedure. The second is that, in practice, minor regulatory offences tend to be the ones where courts generally have the least information about an offender's means since many such

---

[23] *Crime and the Prevention of Crime*, Scottish Council on Crime, 1975, para. 178 *et seq.*

offences are disposed of on written pleas of guilty which are tendered without any accompanying information as to means; and, although certain inferences may be drawn if the prosecutor tells the court, in a speeding case, that the offender was driving a new Rolls Royce, such inferences may not always be accurate. In the result, a tariff approach to such offences is probably not unreasonable. Judges should be aware, however, that, in times when the value of money changes rapidly, there is a risk that the level of fines within a tariff system will become ossified, and will quickly cease to have the value which they had when first determined.

-55   In relation to cases not falling within a tariff system, and where the court has reasonably accurate information about an offender's means, the Scottish Council on Crime suggested, as has been seen, that courts should not only (as seems to be common practice) reduce a fine for those of low means, but should increase it for those of above average means. If one accepts that the object of fining is to punish by achieving equivalent deprivation of resources, there is much to be said for this suggestion. It cannot, of course, be operated with complete mathematical accuracy for then, in summary courts in particular it might be found that the rich man's fine would have to exceed the maximum fine available. Operated on a broader basis, however, it seems reasonable to impose a larger than average fine on a rich man. This is to a large extent the principle behind the Swedish day-fine system which, briefly, involves multiplying together a number (from one to 120, or from one to 180 in the case of multiple offences) reflecting the gravity of the offence, and a sum of money calculated on the basis of the offender's means.[24]

-56   One further matter, related to an offender's means, which may have some bearing on the amount of a fine is the court's power to allow time for payment of a fine, and particularly to allow payment by instalments. The effect of this power, it is submitted, is that, in having regard to an offender's means, a court need not feel obliged, especially in the case of poorer offenders, to depart too far from the level of fine that the gravity of the offence is thought to indicate: in such cases the court may simply allow for small instalments payable over a prolonged period of time. Having said that, however, it must be borne in mind that the High Court might, on appeal, consider it oppressive if an offender were ordered to pay a very large fine over

---

[24] A detailed description of this system is to be found in the Report of the Wootton Committee, Advisory Council on the Penal System, *Non-custodial and Semi-custodial Penalties*, 1970, HMSO.

an inordinate period of time. What will amount to an appropriate period for payment of a fine will depend on many factors, including the gravity of the offence and the previous record of the offender, and no hard and fast rule can be laid down for this. Perhaps the most that can be ventured is that, in fixing the amount of a fine which is to be paid by instalments, a court should not set an amount which will require an unreasonably long period for full payment to be made.

10–57   Apart from considerations related to an offender's means, there are other factors which may have a bearing on the amount of a fine. One is the maximum permitted in the particular court, or for the particular offence. It has been said of maximum penalties that they ought "to be regarded as the limit set on the powers of the Court when dealing with the gravest type of offence which the Legislature contemplated as likely to arise in practice . . . if in the early stages maximum, or nearly maximum, penalties are imposed in cases where few or no features of aggravation are present, there is a grave risk that, if and when much more serious cases later arise, the Court may find itself powerless to exercise that just discrimination in the award of penalties which is indispensable to the due administration of criminal justice."[25] This passage which, it is thought, still represents an authoritative statement on the way in which maximum penalties should be regarded, appears in effect to be making two separate, though related, points. The first is that, where a maximum penalty is provided for, it should be seen as being appropriate for the worst possible example of the type of offence in question. Since it is probably impossible to predict with any accuracy what would constitute the worst possible example of any kind of offence, it follows that generally a maximum penalty will rarely in practice be used. The principal exception to that may be in cases — and there are still several — where the maximum penalty was fixed many years ago, and has never been amended to take account of changes in the value of money: in such cases, it is submitted, it may be quite proper for a court to impose the maximum penalty even for cases falling well short of the worst possible example.

10–58   The second point which emerges from the statement that has been quoted is that, in fixing the level of a fine, a court must be mindful of the need to allow a reasonable leeway both above and, generally, below so as to cater for other cases which are either more or less grave. Although in the passage quoted this point was made in

---

[25]*Edward & Sons* v. *McKinnon*, 1943 J.C. 156, *per* L.J.-C. Cooper at 168.

relation to maximum penalties, it is valid as a general proposition regardless of the maximum penalty provided, and equally in cases on indictment where there is no limit to the amount of a fine.

–59 Another matter which may have a bearing on the amount of a fine, at least in cases involving dishonesty, is what may be termed the no-profit principle. By that is meant that, in cases where an offender has gained financially by his criminal activity, any fine imposed should not be less than the amount of that gain. Any other approach would, it is submitted, attract public incredulity, and, if in any case a judge felt that for any reason a fine consistent with that principle ought not to be imposed, then it might be that a different kind of disposal altogether would be more appropriate. Two comments, however, may be made in relation to this. Firstly, although the amount of any gain to an offender can usually be ascertained exactly where, for example, money is stolen, the determination of the amount of an offender's gain may not be so straightforward where property is taken. In such cases a prosecutor will usually say that property to the value of £X or £Y was removed (and if the court is minded to make a compensation order that may be the relevant figure) but the counsel or solicitor for the offender will frequently say that, on selling the goods, the offender in fact realised much less than that figure. While it is probably true that the goods were sold for less than their real value, the court has no means of checking the accuracy of any figure given on behalf of the offender. If, in such cases, a fine is to be imposed, the court can probably do no more than use its best judgment so as to try to ensure that the offender does not end up by making a profit.

–60 The second comment to be made regarding cases where a court may be minded to consider the ultimate profit or loss to an offender is that some victims may take steps to recover their loss and, indeed, may be in a powerful position to do so. An obvious example is the Department of Health and Social Security which, in cases of social security frauds committed by persons who are still in receipt of such benefits, has available the means of recovering its own losses should it wish to do so. In these and similar cases the court may wish to ascertain whether such a course is to be followed before determining the amount of a fine.

–61 One final matter may be mentioned in relation to determining the amount of a fine. That is the situation which arises when an offender is convicted of a number of offences at the same time, particularly where the offences are of a kind that might normally be dealt with by the tariff approach that has been mentioned earlier. A typical example here is the case of the motorist who is convicted of a string of offences under the Motor Vehicles (Construction and Use) Regulations. Few judges would agree with the view that unlawful acts should come "cheaper by the dozen", but in the sort of case mentioned an accumulation of the fines appropriate for each offence may well produce a total which is quite out of proportion to the culpability of the offender. In such a case, it is submitted, it may therefore be proper to regard the individual charges as being essentially the manifestations of a single offence (although it does not appear as such in any statute), namely the driving of a generally unroadworthy vehicle. So viewed, the court can determine a total fine appropriate to the totality of the offence and then, as necessary, apportion that fine to the individual charges. Although the case given as an example is a fairly common one, the same approach may be used in other cases, even of crimes or offences at common law, where the individual charges are truly incidents in a single course of conduct, or parts of a single piece of unlawful behaviour.

10–62 At the beginning of this section on fines two questions were posed, the second being: What sort of balance should exist between fines imposed for one kind of offence, and fines imposed for another? This is a question which frequently exercises judges in summary courts (where the great majority of fines are imposed), particularly if, in the course of the same day, they are required to impose fines for a wide range of offences. The same question, of course, also arises in relation to custodial disposals but, so far as fines are concerned, the question may readily be illustrated by considering, on the one hand, road traffic offences, and, on the other hand, crimes of dishonesty or minor violence. To some extent the problem arises because most traffic offenders do not regard themselves as criminals, and many of them will feel aggrieved if they are fined £50 for, say, careless driving when, in the case called immediately before theirs, a person has been fined the same amount for shoplifting, or for a breach of the peace. A short answer to this sort of problem is that, if a realistic scale of penalties is to be applied in relation to the offence of careless driving, these penalties may inevitably on occasions equal, or even exceed, the fines imposed for minor common law offences, particularly if it is borne in mind that many minor cases of shoplifting involve the taking of goods of little value (all of which are usually recovered), many minor breaches of the peace involve quite trivial disturbances, and in both cases the offenders are often people of very limited means. To answer thus, however, is perhaps to do no more than to say that each case must be judged according to its own facts and circumstances. That, of course, is always necessary, but to say no more than that is to ignore the real danger that a range of penalties for one kind of offence may become unacceptably out of step with the penalties that are imposed for other kinds of offence. For many years it used to be asserted, probably with some justification, that courts dealt very severely with offenders convicted of crimes against property, but not so severely where the crimes were ones of violence against the person. This was plainly not acceptable to the public at large in an age of increasing personal violence, and in more recent years the pattern of sentencing has almost certainly changed. Although a general swing of policy of this character is probably neither possible nor necessary when one is considering the relationship between different specific offences, especially at summary court level, the fact remains that judges must always be aware of the desirability of examining this relationship from time to time to make sure that the level of fines for one class of offence is not out of step with the level for another.

Probation orders

–63   The probation order is probably the disposal by which a judge most clearly expresses the aim of individualised crime reduction, as distinct from aims like punishment, retribution or general deterrence. In saying this, however, it must be stated that there is considerable disagreement among social scientists, social workers, probation officers and others about how a probation order should be operated, about what its objectives should be, and about what a court's expectations might reasonably be when such an order is made. Some of this debate is discussed in more detail in Chapter 11. For the moment it is perhaps sufficient to observe that, along with community service orders, probation orders represent a form of disposal where the court has the least information about, and little or no control over, what will happen to the offender after the disposal has been pronounced. Although a court is required by statute to explain the effect of a probation order to an offender before such an order is made, the statute itself defines a probation order as no more than "an order requiring the offender to be under supervision."[26] What the court often does not know, and therefore cannot explain to the offender, is what form that supervision will take, how intensive it will be , and what view the supervising officer will take of his role in relation to the offender and the probation order.

10–64   For so long as the debate that has been referred to above continues, courts must be content to rely to a very large extent on the professional skills of whichever social worker is appointed as supervisor under the order, and consequently to couch their explanation of the supervision requirement to the offender in the most general terms. In theory, of course, there is nothing to stop a judge from putting to the author of a social inquiry report questions which are designed to discover precisely how he would envisage the probation order being put into effect: in practice this is rarely done, partly because in many courts the social worker who prepared the report is not present in court when the case is being disposed of, and partly because judges in Scotland tend, perhaps unfortunately, not to have the habit of requiring the author of a report to expand on its content. In the result most judges probably tend, both in deciding on a probation order as a suitable means of disposal, and in explaining the order to an offender, to dwell at least as much on the consequences that may follow if the offender fails to comply with the terms of the order, and in particular if he commits further offences. This is, of course, the true sense of the word "probation", and this aspect of a probation order enables a court to use it as a means of imposing a measure of individual deterrence.

10–65   The length of a probation order may be anything from one to three years, and questions may arise as to how long an order should be in any particular case. As with any other form of disposal much will depend on the circumstances in each case, but consideration will have to be given to the extent and duration of any social work intervention that may be indicated as desirable in the social inquiry report, and to the length of time during which the court considers it appropriate to keep the offender subject to the individual deterrence mentioned above. In general, it may be said that it is probably better to make a probation order too long rather than too short, because in the former case it is always open to the supervising officer to apply to the court for an early discharge of the order if it appears to be no longer necessary to keep it in existence.

---

[26] 1975 Act, ss. 183, 384.

Community service orders

0–66   Community service was first introduced in Scotland some two years before the passing of the Community Service by Offenders (Scotland) Act 1978. What happened was that, on an experimental basis, arrangements were made in four areas whereby courts could add to a probation order a condition that the offender should perform a number of hours of unpaid work of service to the community. By the time the Act of 1978 came to be passed it had been found that there were in some cases practical advantages in linking a community service requirement to a probation order. Consequently, the Act not only contains provision for direct community service orders, on the English model, but also expressly authorises the probation linked practice of the experimental period.

0–67   The introduction of community service was first recommended in the United Kingdom in the report of the Wootton Committee,[27] and statutory effect was given to part of that recommendation in respect of England and Wales in the Criminal Justice Act 1972.[28] In general it may be said that the Wootton Committee saw community service as being capable of satisfying three sentencing objectives, namely punishment, reformation, and the constructive use of resources. As to punishment, it would enable the court in appropriate cases to encroach upon what would otherwise be an offender's free time and to oblige him to apply that time to a socially useful purpose. Any element of punishment, however, would be of an entirely constructive character in that it would not only involve work that was of potential benefit to the community at large, but it might also, by its very nature, have some reformative effect on the offender himself. Lastly, if it were used as an alternative to imprisonment, it would assist in relieving the pressures on already over-crowded prisons while not necessarily involving the expenditure of other capital resources.

0–68   Since the Wootton Committee reported, attempts have been made in many quarters, including in Parliament and in some social inquiry reports, to represent community service as a disposal which courts should use only when a custodial sentence is otherwise inevitable, but that does not accurately reflect the view expressed by the Wootton Committee itself (which suggested, for example, that

---

[27] Advisory Council on the Penal System, *Non-custodial and Semi-custodial Penalties*, 1970, HMSO.
[28] Interestingly, the Wootton Committee recommended the introduction of both the direct order and the probation linked order, but only the former of these recommendations has been enacted for England and Wales.

it might be appropriate in respect of certain non-imprisonable offences), it is not stated to be the case in the relevant statutes, and it is not in any event a practice reflected in what judges actually do.[29] In practice most judges would probably agree that community service may often be a suitable alternative to a sentence of imprisonment, but they would probably also say that there may be cases where, were it not available, they might in any event select a non-custodial disposal, such as a probation order; and this is perhaps particularly so when, as in Scotland, community service may be linked to a probation order.

10–69   What, then, are the cases where community service may be appropriate, and what may determine whether a direct order, or a probation linked order, should be made? To some extent the answer to the first part of that question depends on the availability of resources, in that any social work department will be able to accommodate only a certain number of community service cases at a time. Consequently, courts will tend to look for other disposals when dealing with less serious cases, and may for other reasons consider only a prison sentence to be appropriate in more serious cases. In the result, community service will generally tend to be considered in those cases of medium gravity where, it may be said, a custodial sentence would otherwise at least be a possibility, even if not inevitable. Within that range of cases, however, community service may not always be a suitable disposal. It is probably not suitable in the case of sexual offenders, in the case of those suffering from some form of mental disturbance, in the case of many who are elderly, and in the case of many suffering from an addiction to drugs or alcohol. More generally, it is probably not suitable in any case where there is reason to doubt the offender's commitment to undertaking and completing the work given to him. In all cases where community service is being considered as a disposal it is advisable, and in some instances necessary,[30] that the court should obtain a social inquiry report before any order is made. Although practice varies from area to area, that report will often be prepared, at least in part, by a social worker with special responsibility for, and experience of, community service, and should give an indication of the factors pointing towards or against community service.

---

[29] See, for example, Home Office Research Unit Report, *Community Service Orders*, 1975, HMSO.

[30] Community Service by Offenders (Scotland) Act 1978, s. 1 (2) (*c*).

10–70   The social inquiry report will normally also give some indication as to whether the case is one appropriate for a community service order on its own, or for a requirement linked to a probation order. In this matter also opinion and practice may vary among social workers and judges in different parts of the country. Probably, however, there would be some agreement that, in general, a probation linked requirement may be appropriate in cases where there appears to be a need for social work counselling and case work in addition to the community service requirement, whereas the direct order may be appropriate in cases where there is no such obvious need. Following from this, it would seem likely that judges may tend to make more use of community service orders in cases where they would otherwise have imposed custodial sentences, and to use probation linked orders in at least a good many cases where they might otherwise have made probation orders on their own.

10–71   Under either of the options a court may order between 40 and 240 hours of work to be performed. The exact number to be ordered is entirely at the discretion of the judge but it may be submitted that, as with maximum fines,[31] the maximum number of hours should be seen as appropriate for the most serious type of case in which community service is likely to be ordered. Since community service may be imposed both in summary cases and in cases on indictment, it may therefore be reasonable to suggest that the higher numbers of hours are likely to be more appropriate to cases under solemn jurisdiction.

Compensation orders

10–72   The power to make compensation orders was introduced in Scottish criminal courts by the Criminal Justice (Scotland) Act 1980.[32] Under that Act an order may be made against any convicted person requiring him to pay compensation for any personal injury, loss or damage caused (whether directly or indirectly) by the acts which constituted the offence.[33] As with fines, an offender's means must be taken into account when determining the amount of a compensation order,[34] and, if the offender has insufficient means to

---

[31] Compare *supra*, paras. 10-57 and 10-58.
[32] ss. 58 to 67.
[33] *Ibid*. s. 58 (1).
[34] *Ibid*. s. 59 (1).

pay both a fine and a compensation order, the court is directed to give preference to the latter.[35]

10–73   In time the High Court will no doubt give some indication of the way in which courts should approach the use of this power. For the moment, however, some guidance may be found in English authorities (where the power has been in existence since 1972), and in the views expressed by the Dunpark Committee[36] which recommended the introduction of such orders in Scotland.

10–74   One of the main concerns of the Dunpark Committee was that courts should not take up a lot of time in ascertaining the amount of a victim's loss, and the committee concluded that compensation orders should be used only in clear and simple cases. In expressing this view the committee was adopting the approach that has been approved on a number of occasions by the Court of Appeal in England. In a typical case there it was said: "It has been stressed in this court more than once recently that the machinery of a compensation order under the Act of 1972 is intended for clear and simple cases. It must always be remembered that the civil rights of the victim remain. In a great majority of cases the appropriate court to deal with the issues raised by matters of this kind is in the appropriate civil proceedings. A compensation order made by the (criminal) court can be extremely beneficial as long as it is confined to simple, straightforward cases and generally cases where no great amount is at stake."[37] It is submitted that the foregoing is a view which may well commend itself to the courts in Scotland.

10–75   It is probable that compensation orders will most frequently be made in addition to, or instead of, a fine. They may not be made along with an absolute discharge or a probation order, or at the time of deferring sentence.[38] They may be made along with a custodial sentence but, in such cases, no account is to be taken, in assessing the offender's means, of earnings contingent upon his obtaining employment after release.[39] This in effect means — and this was the view of the Dunpark Committee — that, where a custodial sentence is imposed, a compensation order should not be made unless the offender has there and then, probably in the form of capital, the means to satisfy the order.

---

[35] 1980 Act, s. 61.
[36] *Reparation by the Offender to the Victim in Scotland*, 1977, HMSO, Cmnd. 6802.
[37] *R. v. Kneeshaw* [1975] Q.B. 57, *per* Lord Widgery C.J. at 60.
[38] 1980 Act, s. 58 (1).
[39] *Ibid.* s. 59 (1).

Custodial sentences

0–76   In recent years there has been a great deal of discussion in many quarters both about the length of custodial sentences, and about the suitability of custodial sentences at all for certain classes of offenders.[40] While it is generally accepted that long sentences of imprisonment may be necessary in the case of serious crimes, particularly those involving violence, and where the protection of the public is of paramount importance, there is increasing support for the view that, in less serious cases, shorter sentences may be just as consistent with the principles of suitable punishment and public policy. This view has recently been embraced with some enthusiasm by the Court of Appeal in England[41] where it has been pointed out that an excessive and unnecessary use of imprisonment can impose unacceptable strains on the prison system. Moreover, there is now some evidence[42] to show that a reduction in the prison population achieved in this way would not lead to an unacceptable increase in crime.

0–77   The determination by a judge of the length of a prison sentence is in some respects rather arbitrary. It is arbitrary, firstly, in the sense that, as pointed out in the opening paragraphs of this chapter, the appeal court in Scotland has traditionally refrained from setting out sentencing guidelines, far less creating a tariff structure for prison sentences: consequently the choice of the range within which the sentence may fall is dependent on a variety of factors which cannot be precisely quantified — the gravity of the offence, the offender's previous record, any mitigating factors that may be present, and so on. And, because these factors cannot be precisely quantified, the weight to be given to them and the range of sentence selected as a result are in the final analysis entirely dependent on the opinion of the sentencing judge. The determination of sentence length is also in another sense arbitrary because, even when a judge has decided on the range or band within which his sentence will fall, the precise sentence will be determined upon considerations that may be difficult, if not impossible, to describe with any accuracy.

[40] There is a rapidly growing literature on these subjects, but reference may be made, as examples, to: Advisory Council on the Penal System, Interim Report, *The Length of Prison Sentences*, 1977; Final Report, *A Review of Maximum Penalties*, 1978; *Report of Committee of Inquiry into the United Kingdom Prison Services*, 1979; all HMSO. .

[41] See, for example, *R. v. Bibi*, and following cases, [1980] Crim. L.R. 732.

[42] Home Office Research Unit, *Taking Offenders out of Circulation*, 1980, HMSO.

10–78   Other factors than those directly related to a particular case will, of course, play a part in determining the length of a sentence. The extent of a judge's experience, his knowledge and awareness of sentences passed by other judges for similar offences, his own sense of where the particular case stands in relation to other cases he himself has dealt with — all of these will have some influence in persuading a judge that his sentence should, for example, be of between 18 months and two years imprisonment. What may, it is submitted, be more difficult is to pinpoint with any accuracy the reason for selecting 21 months rather than 18 months, or 24 months rather than 21. (For no very good or obvious reason judges appear, when imposing sentences of more than about six months, to proceed by steps of, initially, three months, then six months, and finally 12 months: this may be for the very reason that it would be even more difficult than at present to account fully for the choice of one sentence rather than another if greater discrimination was used in the choice of sentence.) In the circumstances it may be suggested that, if a judge is unable to explain with accuracy the reason for selecting the higher of two possible sentences of imprisonment, then there may be merit in choosing the shorter one.

10–79   Apart from sentence length the other main area of concern in recent times has been the unsuitability of prison for certain types of offender. In the main this concern has concentrated on what are generally referred to as persistent, petty, inadequate offenders. Probably few would argue with the proposition that such people should, where possible, not be sent to prison. Against that it must be said that the alternative range of facilities for such people is very limited, and they themselves sadly sometimes leave the court with no real option but to impose a prison sentence if, despite attempts to deal with them by other means, such as probation or deferred sentences, they still continue to offend.

10–80   Apart from the sort of offenders just mentioned, there may be others for whom prison is not a suitable disposal; and, increasingly, new legislation obliges courts, by requiring them to obtain social inquiry reports, and by other means, to consider alternatives to custody and, where a custodial sentence is chosen, to state the reason for deciding that no alternative is suitable. All of this argues strongly that, in general, imprisonment should be regarded as a sentence of last resort, to be used only where no suitable alternative can be found.[43] Having said that, however, it must be added that

---

[43] See, for example, Ashworth, "Justifying the First Prison Sentence" [1977] Crim. L.R. 661.

courts may generally find it easier to use alternative sentences where the offences are less serious and the offender's record is not very extensive. Conversely, a custodial sentence may be seen as the only reasonable course to take where the offence is grave, where the offender's previous record is substantial, and particularly where the protection of the public is deemed to be of importance.

CONCLUSION

4-81 This chapter has attempted to analyse, describe, and comment on some of the more significant features of the sentencing process. The very fact of doing so, however, tends to obscure the essential feature of sentencing which is that it is a complex, multi-faceted process which often has to be accomplished within a short space of time, and in the course of which a judge will rarely if ever enumerate and evaluate individually the various factors bearing upon his decision. It would perhaps be more accurate to say that, against the background of his experience and his understanding of sentencing problems, he will arrive at a decision which cannot be explained on any scientific basis, but which is based on a subjective, and not perhaps precisely detailed, judgment of a particular case and its particular facts and circumstances.

0-82 One inevitable consequence of this essentially subjective approach to sentencing is that it can very easily lead to disparity between different judges and, as was observed in paragraph 10–03 above, there is now some convincing evidence that such disparity exists. This is not a problem unique to Scotland, and in some parts of the world attempts are now being made to establish a more scientific basis for sentencing decisions in the hope of avoiding, or at least reducing, the risk of disparity.[44] Whether a more structured and controlled approach to sentencing would have that result must remain uncertain for the time being. Whether such an approach can be sure of not creating more injustices than it removes is perhaps even more open to uncertainty. What does seem fairly certain is that the Scottish approach to sentencing is likely to remain substantially unchanged for some time to come, and as long as that is so the matters described in this chapter will be of continuing relevance.

---

[44] See, for example, Wilkins, "Sentencing Guidelines to Reduce Disparity?" [1980] Crim. L. R. 201; Galligan, "Guidelines and Just Deserts: A Critique of Recent Trends in Sentencing Reform" [1981] Crim. L. R. 297.

CHAPTER 11

THE SERVICES RESPONSIBLE
FOR CARRYING SENTENCES
INTO EFFECT

THE PRISON SERVICE

Historical background

11–01   Until well into the 19th century the responsibility for providing prisons in Scotland rested with individual burghs, and in the result there were altogether nearly 200 small prisons around the country. These were often the subject of criticism on account of their poor conditions and low standards of security and discipline. Consequently, in 1839, the financing and administration of prisons were vested in a series of county boards, and a General Board of Directors was appointed to exercise a general oversight, and also to construct and run a new central prison at Perth. The general board continued in existence until 1860 when the central control of prisons was transferred to the Board of Managers of Perth prison. They discharged this function until 1877 when, under the Prisons (Scotland) Act of that year, a Scottish Prison Commission was set up. That body ran the Scottish prison service for much longer than any of its predecessors but eventually, in 1928, the Secretary of State for Scotland became directly responsible for prisons, and that arrangement continues to the present day. By 1928 the scores of small prisons that had existed a hundred years earlier had been reduced to a total of 12 establishments, housing an average daily population of less than 2,000 prisoners.

Present organisation

11–02   While parliamentary responsibility for the Scottish prison service rests with the Secretary of State, the day-to-day administration and running of the service is carried out by the Prisons Division of the Scottish Home and Health Department. It administers the policy for the service as a whole and is responsible for all matters of central organisation — general administration, staffing, personnel and establishment matters, building programmes, certain decisions affecting the categorisation and movement of prisoners, and so on. There is no regional level of organisation in Scotland (unlike England and Wales) and, accordingly, the next tier is formed by the penal institutions themselves. Each of them is headed by a governor of an appropriate grade and, depending on the size of the institution, his staff may consist of a deputy governor, several assistant governors, a chief officer, and prison officers of different ranks.

03   The penal institutions themselves vary considerably in size, and are designed to perform different functions, though some may perform more than one function albeit in different parts of the same institution. The main factors which will have a bearing on the particular institution to which a convicted prisoner will be allocated are age, sex, length of sentence, security classification (see *infra*, para 11–05), previous record and likely response to training, and, to a limited extent, state of health.

04   There is only one penal institution in Scotland for female prisoners, namely Cornton Vale, and consequently arrangements are made there for the reception of all classes of female prisoner, regardless of age, length of sentence, or other considerations. So far as male prisoners are concerned those under the age of 21 must, if their sentence is for 28 days or more but not exceeding four months, go to a detention centre, presently located in part of the establishment at Glenochil. Otherwise their sentence will be in a young offenders' institution and, generally, if that sentence is for less than 18 months it will be served in Polmont, whereas, if it is for more than 18 months, it may be served in Dumfries. Adult male prisoners serving sentences of 18 months or less may generally be allocated to a local prison such as Barlinnie, Edinburgh or Aberdeen, while those serving longer sentences may go to establishments such as the training wings in prisons such as Edinburgh or Perth. Long term, untrainable, recidivists will generally be sent to Peterhead, while those prisoners who can be trusted in semi-open conditions may be located in the prison at Dungavel. Finally, there is in Scotland one open prison, Penninghame, which is used for selected prisoners who by their behaviour and security classification are considered suitable for open conditions.

Security classification

05   One further factor which can affect a prisoner's allocation is his security classification. Following a series of spectacular prison escapes in England in 1964 and 1965 an inquiry into prison security was conducted by the late Lord Mountbatten in 1966. One of his recommendations was that all prisoners should be assigned to one of four categories, namely:

Category A—
    prisoners whose escapes would be highly dangerous to the public or the police or to the security of the State;
Category B—
    those for whom the very highest conditions of security are not necessary but for whom escape must be made very difficult;
Category C—
    those who cannot be trusted in open conditions, but who do not have the ability or resources to make a determined escape attempt;
Category D—
    those who can reasonably be trusted to serve their sentences in open conditions.
That recommendation has, with some minor modification, been given effect to in Scotland and a prisoner's security classification may have some bearing, along with other considerations, on the particular institution in which his sentence is served, or it may simply determine the particular part of an institution in which he is placed. A prisoner's security classification is regularly reviewed and may be changed during the course of a sentence.

Remand prisoners

11–06   Prisoners on remand are dealt with in a somewhat different way from convicted prisoners. They are automatically placed in Category B, unless they justify being placed in Category A, and they will generally be held during the period of remand in the local prison nearest to the court where they are to appear, though there are certain prisons, for example Peterhead and Shotts, which are reserved solely for convicted prisoners. So far as female remand prisoners are concerned, facilities for them exist at Aberdeen, Inverness and Dumfries, as well as at Cornton Vale.

Objectives and regimes

11–07   Rule 5 of the Prison (Scotland) Rules 1952 provides: "The purposes of training and treatment of convicted prisoners shall be to establish in them the will to lead a good and useful life on discharge, and to fit them to do so". Although research into recidivism rates has tended to suggest that these purposes are not very often being achieved, with the consequence that rule 5 has itself been subjected of late to a measure of criticism, the rule remains for the present the only accepted alternative to a sterile concept of mere containment, and forms the ideal which shapes the programmes and regimes which regulate day-to-day life in penal institutions. The details of these programmes and regimes will usually be determined by factors similar to some of those which determine in the first place where a convicted prisoner will serve his sentence, and may to some extent vary from institution to institution depending on the facilities which are available.

Facilities available in penal institutions

8   A wide range of training and other facilities is provided in penal establishments, though many of these are not available to remand prisoners. This is partly because remand prisoners, if untried, must, as presumed innocent persons, be kept separate from sentenced prisoners, partly because remand prisoners are subject to different regimes from sentenced prisoners and, unlike them, cannot be compelled to work while in prison, and partly because, whether they are on remand awaiting trial, or after conviction awaiting reports, they are generally unlikely to be in the institution for long enough to justify any form of training or education. There are, however, certain services which are available to all prisoners regardless of whether they are convicted or not. They, and the different kinds of provision made for sentenced prisoners, are detailed in the following paragraphs.

Medical and psychiatric services

09   General medical services are provided in penal institutions by three full-time Medical Officers who are located at Barlinnie prison and more than 20 part-time Medical Officers all of whom are local general practitioners. In addition there are about 15 consultant psychiatrists who hold joint appointments shared by the National Health Service and the prisons, and who make regular visits to all the larger establishments. Most of the larger institutions have their own hospital staffed by prison officers, all of whom are given training to enrolled nurse standard, and these hospitals are capable of catering for most routine ailments and injuries. Arrangements exist, however, for prisoners to be transferred to National Health Service hospitals in any cases requiring more sophisticated investigation or treatment. Dental care is also available in penal establishments, provided by visiting dental surgeons. In the result, the fact that a person may be suffering from illness or injury, or some form of psychiatric disorder short of a mental illness that would necessitate his admission to a mental hospital, need not militate

against the imposition of a custodial sentence where such a sentence would otherwise be appropriate.

Social work and welfare services

11–10   Most institutions have one or more social workers seconded to them full-time by local social work departments. These social workers offer to prisoners a full range of advice and counselling services, as well as providing a link with their colleagues outside the establishment where that is desirable or necessary. In addition, a range of general and specialised welfare services is supplied by prison governors and officers, and by agencies such as Alcoholics Anonymous, Marriage Guidance Councils, the Scottish Association for the Care and Resettlement of Offenders, the Salvation Army, and others.

Religious ministration

11–11   Part-time chaplains from the Church of Scotland are attached to all penal institutions in Scotland. There are also visiting clergymen from the Roman Catholic Church, and the Episcopalian Church. In addition, visiting ministers of other denominations attend to the religious needs of inmates as required. As well as conducting religious services, bible classes and discussion groups, chaplains also act as advisers and counsellors to many prisoners and, with social workers, are often able to maintain links between prisoners and their families.

Education

11–12   At most penal establishments facilities exist for education at all levels, from basic literacy and remedial teaching through to Open University degree courses. Teaching is provided by a number of education officers and full-time teachers assisted by part-time teachers and a small number of prison officers. In addition, evening classes in a wide range of subjects are available in many institutions. These are usually taken either by local authority teachers or by staff of the prison service. Libraries, run in conjunction with local authority library services, are available in all establishments.

Physical education and recreation

11–13   While the emphasis on physical education varies from institution to institution, and is most marked in those for younger offenders, facilities exist and are widely used, in all institutions for a variety of physical training and recreational purposes. These range from football, athletics and gymnastics to table tennis, snooker and chess. One institution also has a swimming pool. So far as possible attempts are made to involve teams from the local community in some of these activities.

Vocational training

-14 Vocational training is provided at most establishments, including all of those catering for younger offenders. The courses follow the training recommendations of the appropriate City and Guilds and Industrial Training Boards and cover such skills as painting and decorating, general construction, motor vehicle mechanics, radio and television servicing, carpentry and joinery, and catering and horticulture. Training is given either by prison officer or civilian instructors. Inmates who have completed a training course may enter for the appropriate external examinations.

Prison industries

-15 Provision is made in all establishments housing convicted prisoners for them to be given some form of work during the day. While the traditional picture of prisoners being employed on nothing more imaginative than sewing mail bags is largely a thing of the past the quality and variety of work is generally limited, and the type of workshop environment varies quite considerably from institution to institution, and sometimes within a single institution itself. There are several reasons for this. One is that the current policy of providing large well-equipped modern workshops has been given effect to only in newly constructed establishments such as Dungavel, Glenochil and Shotts, or where available finance has permitted effective modernisation, as in Barlinnie. Thus the standard of industrial workshop tends to be determined by the age and form of construction of the establishment itself. However, although some workshops are older and less than wholly convenient, each establishment has some limited range of industries, offering options in the allocation of inmates, including where necessary the option of low grade, repetitive, employment for the alcoholics, social inadequates, and transients who are not suitable for manufacturing employment. Notwithstanding the limitations inherent in the organisation of workshops within the prison system, prison industries are an important feature of prison life, and were responsible in 1979/80 for producing a total sales value of nearly £3 million. The most significant industries in the prison context are textile and wood based, but engineering, farms and gardens, and laundry are also significant. One current problem, affecting some workshops more than others, is that of finding outlets for prison products. During the economic recession of 1980/81 the demand for prison products was not sufficient to maintain the continuity of work activity which ideally should be provided.

Training for freedom

11–16   Under a training for freedom scheme arrangements are made to provide conditions in which an inmate's ability to live in the community can be tested while he is still under sentence, and to ease his transition to normal life in the community on his release. Those selected to take part in the scheme live in hostels attached to penal establishments and go out daily, unescorted, to work with outside employers. The scheme operates in relation to offenders in adult prisons though not at present in relation to those in young offenders' institutions, and is normally available to those serving longer rather than shorter sentences.

Remission of sentence

11–17   Where a sentenced prisoner is serving a sentence, or an accumulation of sentences, he becomes eligible for discharge when one third of his whole sentence has yet to run. In any such case he must serve at least five days before his discharge. Previously he required to serve at least 30 days but that period has very recently been reduced both in England and Wales and in Scotland. Remission is offered to prisoners "with a view to encouraging industry and good conduct". When a prisoner is discharged by virtue of these provisions his sentence there and then expires.[1] All consecutive sentences are aggregated for the purpose of calculating remission regardless of whether or not they were passed by the same or by different courts, or on the same or different days. Formerly where a person was under the age of 21 at the commencement of his sentence it was open to the Secretary of State to direct that, at the time when he would otherwise have been granted remission, such person should be released on licence. That power has now been removed except in relation to children.[2]

---

[1] Prisons (Scotland) Act 1952, s. 20 (1), and Prison (Scotland) Rules 1952, rule 37, as amended by Prison (Scotland) (Amendment) Rules 1981.

[2] Criminal Justice Act 1967, Seventh Schedule, Part II; but see *infra*, paras. 11–24 and 11–32.

Visiting committees[3]

-18   Every penal establishment has a visiting committee whose members are, in the case of adult establishments, appointed by the local authorities around the establishment and, in some cases, also by the local authorities from whose areas the majority of the inmates of that institution come. Visiting committees for establishments housing offenders under the age of 21 are appointed by the Secretary of State. The main functions of the visiting committees are, firstly, to keep under review, and to report to the Secretary of State on, the general management and condition of the establishment for which they are responsible, secondly, to deal with certain breaches of discipline by prisoners which may be referred to them, and, thirdly, to hear any requests or complaints that may be put to them by prisoners.

Discipline in prisons

-19   During a prisoner's stay in an institution he is subject to the normal criminal law in just the same way as he was in the outside community. Additionally, he is also subject to various prison rules and regulations which are designed to promote good order and discipline within the establishments; and the prisoner will be guilty of an offence against prison discipline if he contravenes these rules.[4] Some types of conduct which are forbidden under the prison rules are not in themselves criminal (*e.g.* refusing to work) whereas others are (*e.g.* assault). Breaches of prison discipline may be dealt with in one of two ways. The governor may himself impose a punishment if he considers that his powers are adequate in the particular case. Otherwise, he may, with the permission of the Secretary of State, refer the matter to the visiting committee to deal with. In respect of a breach of discipline a governor may award forfeiture of remission of sentence for a period not exceeding 14 days, and additionally, or alternatively, may order forfeiture or postponement of certain privileges, such as smoking.[5] A visiting committee, on the other hand, may order forfeiture or postponement of privileges for longer periods than are open to a governor, and may order forfeiture of the entire remission of a sentence.[6] Bearing in mind that a prisoner is not legally represented in proceedings before a visiting committee, it may be thought that the

---

[3] Prisons (Scotland) Act 1952, s. 7, and Prison (Scotland) Rules 1952, rules 187 to 205.
[4] Prison (Scotland) Rules 1952, rule 42.
[5] *Ibid.* rule 43 (2).
[6] *Ibid.* rule 45 (1).

unlimited power to order forfeiture of remission is a remarkable power in that, in theory, it could permit a committee to imprison an offender for a longer period than could be ordered by anyone else other than a judge in the High Court. In fact the power is used sparingly and any remission removed by a visiting committee may be restored by the Secretary of State. Moreover, the normal practice, where a prisoner has committed an offence that is also a crime, other than a relatively minor one, is to report the matter to the police and the procurator fiscal with a view to prosecution in the ordinary courts.

Prison population[7]

11–20   The average daily population in Scottish penal establishments has for some years remained fairly constant at around 5,000 persons. That figure includes sentenced and remand prisoners, as well as fine defaulters. The figure corresponds fairly closely with the design capacity of Scottish establishments, but nonetheless there is overcrowding in some institutions. This is mainly because the factors mentioned earlier which determine the institution to which a prisoner will be allocated, and the space available in the institutions concerned, often do not match the numbers of prisoners falling into each category. Thus, at one end of the scale, there is frequently spare capacity at the open prison at Penninghame whereas, at the other end of the scale, the remand wings of the prisons in Glasgow and Edinburgh are often seriously overcrowded.

11–21   The figure for average daily population is to be distinguished from figures for receptions into custody which, in recent years, have fluctuated between about 17,000 and 19,000 per year. The distinction is of particular importance when examining the proportions of prisoners falling into particular groups or categories, because these may differ substantially depending on whether they are related to average daily population or annual receptions. Thus, in recent years, around 40 per cent of all receptions have been fine defaulters, but they have accounted for only some 6 per cent of the average daily population. When sentenced prisoners are categorised according to their crime or offence it is found, not perhaps surprisingly, that by far the largest number were convicted of crimes of dishonesty, in particular theft and housebreaking. When

---

[7] The figures quoted in the following paragraphs are derived from the annual reports of Prisons Division, *Prisons in Scotland*, HMSO.

categorisation is made by age it is found that, at any time, roughly one third of the whole prison population is under the age of 21.

Detention of children

–22   Where a child has been sentenced to detention under section 206, or is committed for residential training under section 413, of the 1975 Act, his place of detention or training is determined by the Secretary of State. The location and type of that place will be determined by many factors, including the age of the child, the nature of his offence, and his character and background. In some cases it may be a List D school, but in other cases the greater security of a young offenders' institution may be required. In the case of longer sentences arrangements are made to move the young person on to different establishments and, if necessary, eventually into an adult prison when he reaches the age of 21.

PAROLE

Introduction

–23   Parole, which is a method by which a person serving a sentence of imprisonment or detention may be released, under specified conditions, to serve part of that sentence under supervision in the community, was introduced simultaneously in England and Wales, and in Scotland, by the Criminal Justice Act 1967.[8] Under that Act there was created a Parole Board for Scotland whose duty it is to advise the Secretary of State on those cases which may be suitable for release on licence. The board must consist of a chairman and not less than four other members: at present there are 14 members.

Release of persons serving determinate sentences

–24   A person serving a determinate sentence of imprisonment or of detention in a young offenders' institution may be released on licence by the Secretary of State after having completed at least one third of his sentence or one year, whichever is the longer period. Because of the normal effect of remission this means in practice that parole is available to persons serving sentences of more than 18 months. A person released on parole is placed on licence requiring him to comply with certain conditions and, to ensure compliance with these conditions, a parolee is supervised by a local authority social worker in the area where he resides after his release. Unless

[8] ss. 59 to 62.

revoked the licence remains in force until the date on which, in the case of an adult, he would have been released upon a grant of full remission; and in the case of a person who was under 21 at the time of sentence, until the date on which his total sentence expires.

Release of children sentenced to detention
11–25   When a child is sentenced to detention under section 206 of the 1975 Act he is not entitled to automatic remission of sentence, but the Secretary of State may release such a person on licence at any time during the sentence. In such a case the licence continues in force until the expiry of the sentence, or until 12 months have elapsed from the date of release, whichever is the later. Where a child has been ordered to be detained for a period exceeding 18 months the Secretary of State may not release him except on the recommendation of the Parole Board.[9]

Release of persons sentenced to imprisonment for life
11–26   A person who has been sentenced to life imprisonment, or its equivalent in the case of young offenders, may be released on licence by the Secretary of State. He must, however, be recommended to do so by the Parole Board, and he must consult the Lord Justice-General and, if he is still available, the judge who presided at the trial. Persons so released are subject to the conditions of their licences for the remainder of their lives.

11–27   Since 1980 there has existed in Scotland a life sentence committee, appointed by the Secretary of State. The principal function of this committee is to consider and advise on when the first formal review by the Parole Board with a view to possible release should take place in the case of each life sentence prisoner. The first formal review of such cases normally starts after a sentence has run for about six and a half years, but the life sentence committee normally begins to examine cases after about four years have elapsed.

Conditions of licence
11–28   Conditions in a release licence normally stipulate that the licensee must report on release to the officer in charge of the social work department in the area where he will be resident and must place himself under the supervision of whichever social worker is

---

[9] 1975 Act, s. 206, as amended by 1980 Act, s. 44.

nominated for this purpose; that he must keep in touch with the supervising social worker in accordance with his instructions; that he must inform his supervising officer if he changes his place of residence, or changes or loses his job; and that he must be of good behaviour and lead an industrious life. Additionally, special conditions may be imposed, such as that the licensee must reside at a particular address.

Revocation of licence and recall to custody

–29   An offender released on licence can have this revoked at any time while it is in force, and be recalled to custody. This can occur because of a failure to comply with the conditions of the licence, or because of the commission of a further offence. Depending on the circumstances such revocation may be ordered by the Secretary of State on the recommendation of, or in emergency without consulting, the Parole Board. In cases where the licensee has committed a further offence it may also be ordered by the High Court or the sheriff court. The circumstances in which this may be done, and the consequences of such an order, are described in paras. 7–18 to 7–20.

Method of working by Parole Board

–30   When a prisoner is eligible for parole, and has not elected to be excluded from consideration, a first review of his case is commenced in advance of the earliest date when he could be released. A dossier of information is prepared which records the inmate's social and criminal history, his conduct and response during any previous periods under supervision in the community, his work record and domestic background, the circumstances of his current offence together with any observations that may have been made by the sentencing judge, his response to treatment and training in prison during his current sentence, and any other information that may be relevant to assist a decision. This dossier is considered by the local review committee appointed by the Secretary of State for the institution concerned, and that committee will make a preliminary recommendation to the Secretary of State. After scrutiny of such recommendations the Secretary of State will refer to the Parole Board for their recommendation those cases where he is prepared to contemplate release, and may seek the board's recommendation on certain cases which have not been recommended for release by the local review committee. Cases in which the Secretary of State is not prepared to authorise release, though recommended to do so by the local review committee, are sent to the Parole Board for information only, but they may ask the Secretary of State to reconsider his decision in any such case.

Extent of use of parole system

11–31   In recent years just over 12 per cent of prisoners serving determinate sentences and eligible for parole have opted not to be considered by the Parole Board. There may be many reasons for this, but one that is commonly suggested is the uncertainty of success and the fear of rejection. Certainly, the number recommended for parole is fairly small and, in 1979, represented less than 30 per cent of those eligible and wishing to be considered. The Parole Board is sometimes criticised not only for this relatively low use of parole but also for the adverse effect which rejection is said to have on the morale and behaviour of those concerned. Against that, the board is also subjected to criticism if a person whose release they have recommended commits a further serious offence while on licence. In the result the board, and the Secretary of State, have to try to maintain a fine balance between the humanitarian and other considerations affecting the prisoner, and the public interest in its own protection and safety. If the board and the Secretary of State sometimes err, it is perhaps better that they should more often do so on the side of caution.

RELEASE OF YOUNG OFFENDERS OTHERWISE THAN BY PAROLE

11–32   Young offenders sentenced to be detained in a detention centre or a young offenders' institution may be granted remission in the same way as adults sentenced to imprisonment.[10] However, a person serving a sentence of detention in a young offenders' institution for 18 months or more may, instead of being allowed remission or parole, be released on licence at any time on or after the day when he could have been discharged on remission. In such a case the licence remains in force until the expiration of his total sentence, and the same recall provisions apply as in the case of those released on parole.[11]

---

[10] Detention Centre (Scotland) (Amendment) Rules 1969; Young Offenders (Scotland) Rules 1965.

[11] Criminal Justice Act 1967, s. 60 (3) (*b*).

–33   Where a person is sentenced to be detained for a period, or periods, totalling six months or more he may be required, by notice of the Secretary of State given to him on his release, to be under supervision and to comply with any conditions that may be specified in the notice. If the person fails to conform to the requirement or to comply with any specified condition, the Secretary of State may recall him to a young offenders' institution for a period not exceeding three months.[12]

–34   In cases where the person is not released on licence under section 60 or section 61 of the 1967 Act the period of supervision which may be required is (a) where the term was less than 18 months, until the expiry of the period of six months from the date of release, or (b) where the term was 18 months or more, until the expiry of the period of 12 months from the date of such release.[13]

PROBATION AND OTHER SOCIAL WORK SERVICES

Historical background

–35   Until the beginning of the 20th century it was to all intents and purposes unheard of for courts to deal with offenders otherwise than by the imposition of some kind of custodial or financial penalty if not by transportation or the use of capital punishment. However, the growing humanitarian trend which during the 19th century turned people away from wholesale hanging and transportation and, towards the end of the century, persuaded prison administrators to concentrate on the concept of treatment within penal establishments, extended beyond these establishments themselves and led, in 1907, to the passing of the Probation of Offenders Act. That Act empowered courts, in appropriate cases, to discharge offenders for a period conditionally on their entering into a bond to be of good behaviour, to comply with specific conditions that might be imposed, and to be under the supervision of such person as might be named in the probation order. Provision was made for the appointment of probation officers and in practice they were the persons named to supervise the probation orders. By section 4 of the Act the duties of a probation officer were stated as being:

(a)   to visit or receive reports from the person under supervision at such reasonable intervals as may be

---

[12] Criminal Justice (Scotland) Act 1963, s. 12, as amended by 1980 Act, Sched. 5.

[13] *Ibid.* s. 11 (1); s. 4 (2).

specified in the probation order or, subject thereto, as the probation officer may think fit;

(b)   to see that he observes the conditions of his bond;

(c)   to report to the court as to his behaviour; and

(d)   to advise, assist and befriend him, and, when necessary, to endeavour to find him suitable employment.

11–36   The arrangements introduced by the 1907 Act continued with minor amendments and modifications until 1949 when the Criminal Justice (Scotland) Act of that year introduced detailed provisions concerning probation orders which have remained substantially unchanged until the present day. The 1949 Act also enlarged on the duties of probation officers by giving them a statutory responsibility for preparing what are now referred to as social inquiry reports, and by making them responsible for the supervision, in certain cases, of persons released from custody. To this was added, by the Criminal Justice (Scotland) Act 1963, the duty, in certain cases, of supervising the payment of fines, and, by the Criminal Justice Act 1967, the duty of supervising persons released from custody on parole licence.

11–37   Until this time the probation service was seen as in some respects complementary to, but in most respects quite separate and distinct from, a local authority's social work services. However, that was entirely changed by the Social Work (Scotland) Act 1968 which transferred the duties and responsibilities of the probation service to a comprehensive, generic, social work service which thereafter became responsible for a range of duties extending from care of the aged to the supervision of offenders. Initially this change provoked much criticism, especially from some judges who were fearful that the skills and experience of former probation officers would be submerged and lost for ever in a service that was suspected of being likely to accord a low priority to work with offenders. At first there was some basis for criticism as some local authorities sought to interpret the task of generic social workers as requiring involvement and skill in all facets of social work activity. In practice this proved to be a virtually impossible task and not infrequently social workers found themselves being assigned to work with offenders when their real interest, and ability, lay elsewhere. Gradually, however, the ways in which local authorities organised their social work services became more varied, complex and flexible, and in some areas provision is now made for a considerable degree of specialisation which, so far as dealing with offenders is concerned, provides a reasonable continuity of skilled and experienced workers with a genuine interest in that sort of work. They are, however, trained in the full range of social work duties and, moreover, have access to all the other services and facilities provided by the department within which they operate.

Duties of local authorities at present time

38   In section 27 (1) of the 1968 Act the duties of local authorities, in respect of the provision of services to the courts, are defined as:

(a)   making available to any court such social background reports and other reports relating to persons appearing before the court which the court may require for the disposal of the case; and

(b)   the supervision of, and the provision of advice, guidance and assistance for:

(i)   persons in their area who are under supervision by order of a court made in the exercise of its criminal jurisdiction by virtue of any enactment, and

(ii)   persons in their area who, following on release from prison or any other form of detention, are required to be under supervision under any enactment or by the terms of an order or licence of the Secretary of State or of a condition or requirement imposed in pursuance of any enactment.

For the purpose of the foregoing every local authority is required, after consultation with the sheriffs having jurisdiction in their area, to prepare a probation scheme which must be approved by the Secretary of State. Probation schemes make provision with regard to such matters as the manner in which social inquiry reports are to be prepared and submitted, and the arrangements for the attendance of social workers in court.

39   While the foregoing still represents the general nature of a local authority's duties within the criminal justice system, the size of the task encompassed by these duties continues to grow, partly as a result of the introduction of new non-custodial disposals such as community service, and partly as a result of the steady increase in crime itself. The specific tasks undertaken by social work departments in pursuance of these duties may be detailed as follows:

(a) *Social inquiry reports.*

As has been seen elsewhere in this volume the obtaining of social inquiry reports is now obligatory in a great many cases before any form of custodial sentence may be imposed. Additionally, many judges are making increasing use of such reports, even in cases where they are not obliged to obtain them, as a means of acquiring detailed information about offenders and in the hope of obtaining thereby fuller information on which to base a sentencing decision. It may be questioned whether this is a proper use of a social worker's report writing duties, and tends to suggest that prosecutors, and in particular defence solicitors and counsel, are not supplying the court in adequate measure with the information which some might think it appropriate for them to provide. A full discussion of the use that is made of social inquiry reports is beyond the scope of this book. For present purposes it may be sufficient to observe that there is now considerable evidence that social inquiry reports, particularly if they contain a strong recommendation, can exert a powerful influence on sentencing decisions.[14]

(b) *Probation.*

This, and the nature of social work intervention generally, are considered below.[15]

(c) *Community service.*

The organisation of community service projects, and the supervision of offenders ordered to perform such work, either under a direct order or as a condition of a probation order, has in recent years imposed considerable extra burdens on social work departments, and will continue to do so as the provision of community service schemes extends further throughout the country.

(d) *Fine supervision.*

Where a fine supervision order is made by a court it is the duty of the appropriate social work department to carry out that supervision until the fine is paid. This will involve advising the offender on the best management of his financial resources and, in the event of him being cited to attend court for an inquiry into why the fine has not been paid, will involve the social worker in submitting a report, which may be either oral or written, setting out the offender's financial circumstances and expressing any views that may be thought helpful as to the further disposal of the case.

---

[14] See, for example, Thorpe, *Social Inquiry Reports: a Survey*, Home Office Research Unit Report, no. 48, 1979, HMSO.

[15] Paras. 11–40 to 11–44.

(e) *Supervision of young offenders released from custody.*

As has been seen[16] many young offenders are required to be under supervision following their release from a custodial sentence, and the carrying out of this supervision is the responsibility of the appropriate social work departments. Although this statutory supervision, or "after-care" as it is sometimes called, is in fact an intrinsic part of the sentences concerned, it is seldom seen as such by the young offenders who have just been released from custody, and consequently they are frequently very resentful of what they then see as an unwarranted and unwelcome intrusion on their new found freedom. Whether this problem would be alleviated if judges were to make a practice of explaining the supervision requirement at the time of sentence is difficult to say: probably any such explanation would in many cases be forgotten by the date of release from custody. More realistically (and not just in statutory after-care cases), offenders can be prepared and helped for the situation which they will have to face on release partly by the assistance given to them by the social workers in the penal establishments themselves, but principally by the maintenance of contact with social workers in their home area who can, throughout the sentence, not only maintain contact with the prisoner concerned but also with his family. This is one aspect of what is now known as "through-care". This concept, which is applied with particular reference to long term prisoners, and to those who may be released on parole licence, proceeds on the basis that the rehabilitative features of after-care are more likely to be achieved if work towards that end begins while the offender is still in custody.

(f) *Supervision of parole licensees.*

This is an important part of a social work department's responsibilities and is one which, in relation to life sentence licensees, is becoming more and more onerous. In the first place, such persons will have a history of some, and on occasions considerable, violent behaviour. In the second place, they will generally have spent a prolonged period in custody[17] and so may require considerable assistance in order to readjust to living in the community. In the third place, and most importantly, their numbers are increasing, because not only are more being released on licence each year,[18] but

---

[16] *Supra,* paras. 11–32 to 11–34.

[17] The largest number of those serving life sentences who are released on licence are released after having served between eight and 11 years.

[18] In 1973, six life sentence prisoners were released on licence; in 1979 that figure had risen to 21 (*Report of the Parole Board for Scotland,* 1979, HMSO).

all who are so released thereafter remain on licence for the rest of their lives.

(g) *Supervision of children.*

Although children placed on supervision by children's hearings do not fall within the scope of this book, it is to be noted that their supervision represents a substantial task for social work departments, and frequently for the same social workers who are also involved in dealing with older offenders.

(h) As already noted earlier in this chapter social work departments are also responsible for seconding social workers to provide social work services within penal establishments.

The nature of probation and of social work intervention

11–40 Although the duties imposed on social work departments by the 1968 Act are not significantly different (at least in general character if not in scope) from those given to probation officers by the Act of 1907, the whole concept of social work intervention with offenders has undergone substantial change and development during the intervening years. It is clear from the opening words of the 1907 Act that, initially at least, probation was seen as a humane and reasonable way of dealing with offenders whose guilt was slight or whose offence was minor, or whose personal or family circumstances were such as to make that disposal more desirable than any other. Probation would not be considered for more serious or more persistent offenders, and no ambitious, reformative purpose was assigned to it. Gradually, however, the hopes and aspirations for probation became greater.

11–41 From the beginning probation has included elements both of control, backed by requirements and sanctions, and of care, backed by the duty to "advise, assist and befriend". As the use of probation expanded it came to be assumed that it was feasible for a probation officer to establish a relationship with the offender which could influence his attitudes and behaviour, and that, through this, help could be given with the offender's personal and social problems, all of which would in time reduce the likelihood of re-offending. Above all, it was assumed that care and control could be combined successfully and without conflict. As these assumptions gained increasing general acceptance, so probation came to be seen not only as a means of dealing with minor offenders but also as a means of bringing about a reformation in those found guilty of more serious crimes. Gradually, too, a further assumption came to be made. This was that offending was a symptom of individual sickness or maladjustment, requiring diagnosis and treatment. This determinist view of deviancy probably never gained the same general acceptance as the other assumptions about probation that have been mentioned. Nonetheless, such acceptance as it had further increased the expectations for probation as a means of dealing successfully with an even wider range of offenders.

–42   In time most of the foregoing assumptions came to be challenged, or at least re-examined. Some researchers found that those probationers with the greatest problems were least likely to achieve the best relationships with their supervising officers, and conversely those with whom the officers had the best relationship tended to be the ones with the fewest problems and the most effective support in their environment.[19] More importantly, there has proved to be little evidence, apart from a few possible exceptions,[20] to suggest that social work intervention with offenders has any significant effect on recidivism rates.[21] Having said that, however, it should be added that there are many who argue, with some justification, that a mere comparison of recidivism rates is by itself too crude a measure of the success or failure of any penal disposal. So too, the assumptions about the combination of care and control have increasingly come under question and many social workers to-day would probably regard the concept of control as being unacceptably at odds with what they see as their primary role, of counselling and caring. This was strikingly illustrated a few years ago when the National Association of Probation Officers argued strongly against the increased supervisory controls recommended by the Advisory Council on the Penal System in the case of young offenders.[22] On the other hand, there is a considerable diversity of views on this matter within the social work profession itself and it would be misleading to convey the impression that all social workers are automatically opposed to exercising any form of control when supervising a probation order. Much will depend on the degree and nature of the control that is expected, and probably few social

---

[19] See, for example, Davies, *Probationers in their Social Environment*, Home Office Research Unit Report, no. 2, 1969, HMSO.

[20] See, for example, Folkard and others, IMPACT, *Intensive matched probation and after-care treatment*, Vol. II, Home Office Research Unit Report, no. 36, 1976, HMSO.

[21] See, generally, Brody, *The Effectiveness of Sentencing*, Home Office Research Unit Report, no. 35, 1976, HMSO.

[22] *Young Adult Offenders*, 1974, HMSO.

workers would consider it inappropriate to set some sort of constraints on an offender's behaviour during the course of a probation order.

11–43   All of the foregoing has considerable implications for judges who may be seeking a non-custodial disposal in a particular case. As has already been observed[23] the probation order is probably unique among the disposals available to the criminal courts in that the judge has very little knowledge of what it is going to involve in practice for the particular offender. He does not know what level of contact the social worker is going to regard as appropriate with the offender; he does not know the extent to which the social worker is going to involve himself with the personal and social problems of the offender; and he does not know the balance, if any, which the social worker will try to achieve between care and control. On the other hand most judges — and probably the public at large as well — are anxious that a probation order should not be seen as a let-off, and that it should be at least as effective as any other disposal not only in preventing future recidivism after the order has terminated, but also in lessening the likelihood of re-offending during the currency of the order itself. Doubts about all of these matters may well have played a part in the considerable reduction in the use of probation that has taken place in recent years,[24] and it may be thought unlikely that this trend will be significantly reversed until there is on all sides a clearer understanding of the nature of probation, and of its attainable aims and objectives.

11–44   In the last few years there seems to have been a considerable increase in discussion and debate on these matters, both inside the social work services themselves, and elsewhere.[25] At least some of these discussions seem to contemplate a change whereby courts would be able to prescribe some sort of control framework for a probation order within which, on a contractual basis, the social worker would be able to offer varying levels of care and intervention. On a more practical note, increased consideration seems to be being given in Scotland to making greater use of volunteer workers in offender cases. Additionally, new statutory provision has been made[26] for the financing of probation and other

---

[23] *Supra*, para. 10–63.

[24] In 1971, in Scotland, 3,053 orders were made in respect of persons aged 16 and over; by 1977 that figure had fallen to 2,255.

[25] See, for example, Bottoms and McWilliams, "A non-treatment paradigm for probation practice", British Journal of Social Work, 1979.

[26] 1980 Act, s. 79.

hostels; and although somewhat similar provision in the Criminal Justice (Scotland) Act 1949 produced no results, a new initiative in this respect may now be under way. All of this suggests that the changes and developments in the role of social workers in relation to offenders that have taken place since 1907 may still have a considerable way to go.

INDEX